THE GOOD
EUROPEAN

THE GOOD EUROPEAN

Nietzsche's Work Sites

in Word and Image

DAVID FARRELL KRELL

+

DONALD L. BATES

THE UNIVERSITY OF CHICAGO PRESS

CHICAGO + LONDON

DAVID FARRELL KRELL is professor of philosophy at DePaul
University. He is the author of *Infectious Nietzsche* (1996) and *Lunar
Voices* (1995). DONALD L. BATES, architect and photographer,
is co-director of LAB Architectural Studios, London.

The University of Chicago Press, Chicago 60637
The University of Chicago Press Ltd., London
© 1997 by The University of Chicago
All rights reserved. Published 1997
Printed in Hong Kong
06 05 04 03 02 01 00 99 98 97   1 2 3 4 5

ISBN 0-226-45278-6 (cloth)

The illustration on the title page is a detail from a photograph of Nietzsche
in Basel, ca. 1876. Photo: Stiftung Weimarer Klassik. GSA 101/17.

Library of Congress Cataloging-in-Publication Data

Krell, David Farrell.
    The good European : Nietzsche's work sites in word and image /
David Farrell Krell and Donald L. Bates.
        p. cm.
    Includes bibliographical references and index.
    ISBN 0-226-45278-6 (alk. paper)
    1. Nietzsche, Friedrich Wilhelm, 1844-1900—Homes and haunts—
Europe. 2. Nietzsche, Friedrich Wilhelm, 1844-1900.
    3. Philosophers—Germany—Biography. I. Bates, Donald L., 1953-.
II. Title.
B3318.H6K74 1997
193—dc21
[B]   96-39541
                                                                 CIP

This book is printed on acid-free paper.

for Marta and Susie

Denn, wenn ich auch ein schlechter Deutscher sein sollte—
jedenfalls bin ich ein sehr guter Europäer.

For, even if I should be a bad German, I am at all events
a *very good European*.

NIETZSCHE TO HIS MOTHER
ON AUGUST 17, 1886
FROM SILS-MARIA

CONTENTS

PREFACE

The subtitle of the book could also have been "Nietzsche's Work *Sights.*" For what we have presented here are the sights of Nietzsche's work sites, views of the locales and climes where Nietzsche jotted down his notes, prepared his book manuscripts, and corrected his proofs. Inevitably, we saw Nietzsche's places as they are now, more than a century after Nietzsche decided to work in them. Although the book does contain much archival material, from Nietzsche's own collection of photographs housed in the Goethe-Schiller Archive in Weimar, the bulk of the photographs were taken by the authors in the summer of 1994 and the winter and spring of 1994–1995.

The text does not constitute a thoroughgoing biography of Nietzsche. That would have taken a great deal more space and would have required a very different orientation. Our overriding desire was to communicate a sense of Nietzsche's *places,* the places where he *worked,* and our overriding question was whether and how the influence of the work sites on the work itself—on the thinking and writing—could be made visible, could be communicated in word and image.

Our principal sources are cited in the body of the text by volume (in italic) and page, according to the following code of abbreviations:

B   Friedrich Nietzsche, *Sämtliche Briefe, Kritische Studienausgabe,* edited by
Giorgio Colli and Mazzino Montinari. 8 vols. Berlin and Munich:
Walter de Gruyter and Deutscher Taschenbuch Verlag, 1986.

J   Friedrich Nietzsche, *Jugendschriften,* edited by Hans Joachim Mette et al.
5 vols. Berlin and Munich: Walter de Gruyter and Deutscher Taschenbuch Verlag, 1994.

N   Curt Paul Janz, *Friedrich Nietzsche Biographie,* 3 vols. Munich: Deutscher
Taschenbuch Verlag, 1981.

W   Friedrich Nietzsche, *Sämtliche Werke, Kritische Studienausgabe,* edited by
Giorgio Colli and Mazzino Montinari. 15 vols. Berlin and Munich:
Walter de Gruyter and Deutscher Taschenbuch Verlag, 1980.

Particular works in the *Sämtliche Werke* are cited according to the following code:

GT   *Geburt der Tragödie [The Birth of Tragedy]*

UB I-IV   *Unzeitgemäße Betrachtungen [Untimely Meditations,* Parts One to Four]

MAM I, II   *Menschliches, Allzumenschliches [Human, All-Too-Human,* Parts One
and Two]

WS   *Der Wanderer und sein Schatten* ["The Wanderer and His Shadow,"
in MAM II]

M   *Morgenröte [Daybreak]*

FW   *Die fröhliche Wissenschaft [The Gay Science]*

ASZ I–IV	*Also sprach Zarathustra [Thus Spoke Zarathustra*, Parts One to Four]
JGB	*Jenseits von Gut und Böse [Beyond Good and Evil]*
ZGM I–III	*Zur Genealogie der Moral [On the Genealogy of Morals*, treatises One to Three]
GD	*Götzen-Dämmerung [Twilight of the Idols]*
A	*Der Antichrist [The Antichrist]*
EH	*Ecce homo [Ecce Homo]*

All translations are our own, and were made especially for this volume.

Even though David Krell was responsible for the first draft of the words, and Don Bates for the majority of the images, each of us became involved in every aspect of the book's development. *The Good European* is therefore coauthored. Indeed, it is the product of an entire team of friends and colleagues and strangers. We would like to thank all who made the researching, writing, photographing, and producing of it an extraordinary adventure, singling out a few of them in what follows.

Everyone who works on Nietzsche's life and thought owes a special debt to Curt Paul Janz, cited above, whose biography provided us with an almost always reliable source of data and much excellent commentary; we are also all indebted to those good Europeans (now deceased) who edited the thousands of pages of Nietzsche's works and letters, Giorgio Colli and Mazzino Montinari. We would also like to thank T. David Brent and Julia Robling Griest, our editor and designer at the University of Chicago Press, along with their colleagues, especially Margaret Mahan; Anthony Polakowski, of Alan Cohen Studios, Chicago, who made the black and white prints with such devotion, skill, and intensity; Alan Cohen, who gave so generously of his time and wisdom; Graham Parkes and Laurence Lampert, whose astute criticisms improved our manuscript; and for their generosity too we thank Artur Zeisse of Umpferstedt bei Weimar, Simone Kant of Röcken, Frau Dr. Roswitha Wollkopf, Frau Küntzel, Frau Gensel, and Frau Wasner of the Nietzsche-Archiv, Weimar; Erika and Bernhard Schopp of St. Ulrich and Rapallo; Michael Walter, Munich; Peter Davidson, London; Dietmar Cray of Steinabad, Paul Kleeb and Anna Fedier-Tresch of the Hotel Maderanertal, and Klaus and Annette Lauer of the Hotel Römerbad, Badenweiler; Attilio and Lisa Terragni of Como and Menaggio, Dominique Janicaud of Nice, Marta and Brigida Cornale of Recoaro, and especially Iris Pozza of the "Tre Garofani." Thanks also to the capable and generous technical experts who developed our films in Freiburg: Dieter Ruf, Harry Schulz, and Peter Trenkle of RST Laboratories; and, for his help with the images, special thanks to Citos of Evanston.

Finally, we would like to thank dozens of people whose names we never learned, people who proved that pride in one's locale and local history has nothing to do with parochialism, among them the owner of a twenty-five-year-old Fiat 500 who put us in touch with the best clutch mechanic in Mestre, the friendly cop in St. Peter's Square who was definitely not of the Swiss Guard, the gas-station owner in Sorrento who sent us to Our Lady of the Sneakers who in turn led us to the Villa Rubinacci, and the solicitous Donna of "Alla Buca di San Francesco" in Turin, who must have been the (great?) granddaughter of the woman who always saved her best grapes for Professor Nietzsche.

The University Research Council and the Liberal Arts & Sciences Faculty Research and Development Committee of DePaul University generously supported our work on this project, and we are most grateful to them.

D. F. K. and D. L. B.
St. Ulrich, London, Chicago

INTRODUCTION

He possessed the most conspicuously
developed talent for discovering
the privileged places on Earth.

Meta von Salis on Nietzsche

Perhaps Nietzsche was a *good European*—a phrase that recurs often in his work during the 1880s—precisely because he sometimes wanted to escape Europe altogether: he dreamed of the highlands of central and western Mexico, perhaps Oaxaca, as a place where no one would interrupt his work or poison his life. He would have been delighted to know that the last great Mayan king of the classical period, Jax Pac, bore the name of one of his books, *Daybreak*. Yet as matters turned out, he never left the continent of Europe. Nor did he ever see many of the places a good European would find "essential" to his or her culture. He never made it to Paris or Barcelona, St. Petersburg or Copenhagen, London or Brussels or Prague. Moreover, Nietzsche was by no means a master of modern European languages: his Italian was execrable and his Russian nonexistent, although Dostoevsky made him want to learn; his English too was poor, and not even Sterne or Twain or Emerson could convince him to make the effort; only his French was passable, his reading French excellent; and some say his German was not bad at all. (He would have admired Twain's confession in *A Tramp Abroad:* "The German language speak I not good, but have numerous connoisseurs me assured that I write her like an angel.")

If it takes "another heading" to think about Europe today, the "new" Europe, we may find Nietzsche too culture-bound, too excessively European, for such thinking.[1] After all, he was a classicist who specialized in Greek literature and philosophy, and an admirer of Rome; he did not open his eyes to Africa or the Orient; Venice is as close to China as he ever got, and German translations are as close as he came to *Huckleberry Finn*. Yet if the requirements and the stakes have been raised much higher for good Europeans nowadays, Nietzsche still seems to have been astonishingly prescient about the new Europe and its old predicaments. His overriding concern was that the "nations and fatherlands" of old Europe not obstruct forever the historic process of European unification. While Nietzsche in so many respects remained the child of a Lutheran country pastor who owed his pastorate to the king, the child who hankered after the nobility and despised the rabble, the child who, as a man, offered little enlightenment concerning the great social questions of modernity, he was nonetheless one of the principal critics of European (and especially German) nationalism, imperialism, and militarism.

---

1. See Jacques Derrida, *The Other Heading: Reflections on Today's Europe,* translated by Pascale-Anne Brault and Michael B. Naas (Bloomington: Indiana University Press, 1992).

Nietzsche's hopes for Europe were almost always bound up with profound despair concerning the German Reich—the Wilhelmine and Bismarckian "miracle" that he feared would create a hell for Europe in the twentieth century. His remarks on Germany and Germans were so consistently acerbic that they would doubtless please current German politicians as little as they pleased Bismarck. Consider the following, from *Beyond Good and Evil: Prelude to a Philosophy of the Future*, published in 1886:

> Thanks to the pathological alienation that the insanity of nationality has injected, and is still injecting, into the peoples of Europe; thanks also to the politicians of myopic vision and overhasty hand who are on top today because of that insanity, politicians who haven't an inkling of the fact that their politics of fragmentation must of necessity be a mere intermezzo;—thanks to all that and to a number of things that are still inexpressible today, the most unmistakable signs are being overlooked or deliberately and mendaciously misinterpreted, signs that clearly point to the fact that *Europe wants to become one.* In all the more profound and more widely talented human beings of this century, such was the general direction and the genuine albeit secret labor of their souls: to prepare the path to a new *synthesis* and to anticipate by way of experiment the European of the future. . . . (JGB, 256; 5, 201–2)

From early on in his life, Nietzsche thought of himself as European rather than "merely" German. At age fifteen he wrote a short story entitled "Capri and Helgoland," in which southern Italian, Swiss, and northern German characters work out their fate. Early in the story, the northern hero, von Adelsberg, proclaims: "We are pilgrims in this world: we have our homeland everywhere and nowhere; the same sun shines over us all. We are citizens of the world—the earth is our realm!" (J *1*, 100). This youthful tendency to a pan-Europeanism, if one can call it that, was further reinforced during his many years in Swiss Basel. However, his traumatic experiences during the Franco-Prussian War, along with an array of complaints concerning Germany's "Gilded Age," the so-called *Gründerjahre,* increasingly disquieted him about the chances for Europe. One of the most personal reasons for his discontent was his sister's marriage to one of Germany's leading imperialists and anti-Semites, Bernhard Förster. In the spring of 1888 he wryly consoled his sister—who was helping her husband to found a German colony in Paraguay: "In every sense the two of you should be content to be *missing* your beloved Europe: the continent today is paralyzed by its porcupine heroics; it has covered itself with weapons and hung all manner of swords of Damocles over its head" (B *8*, 281).

Certainly by the mid–1880s Nietzsche considered himself to be one of those Europeans "who have no homeland" (FW, 377; *3*, 628–31). He sensed that his was a time of transition for Europe, and to that extent, it was a time of hope:

> *How can* those of us who are children of the future be at home in this house of today! We are averse to all the ideals in which anyone today, in this brittle and broken time of transition, might feel at home; but as far as the "realities" of our time are concerned, we do not believe that they will *last.* The ice that barely continues to bear our weight has gotten very thin: winds of thaw are blowing, and we ourselves, we who have no homeland, are something that breaks up ice and all those other "realities" that have gotten too thin. . . . (Ibid.)

Yet the winds of thaw were not simply altruistic. They blew harsh. Nietzsche was far from confident that European humanity would prosper, or even that he wanted it to prosper. The passage continues:

> No, we do not love humanity. Yet for all that we are no longer "German" enough, at least not in the way the word "German" is used nowadays, to put in a good word for nationalism and race hatred; we are not "German" enough to take any joy in the scabrous heart and the venomous blood of the nation; on account of these illnesses now rampant in

Europe, nation is pitted against nation, peoples are set against one another and closed off to one another, as though in quarantine. For all that, we who have no homeland are too disingenuous, too malicious, too spoiled, also too well informed, too well "traveled": we much prefer to live on mountain tops, remote, "untimely," in centuries already past or still to come, if only in order to spare ourselves the mute rage to which we are reduced as witnesses of a politics that is making a wasteland of the German spirit, and doing so by making it vain, a politics that is *petty politics* besides.—Is it not necessary for such a politics to plant itself firmly between two hatreds-to-the-death, inasmuch as its own little creations would otherwise vanish in the wind? Does it not *have* to will the eternal continuation of Europe's fragmentation into tiny nations? . . . We who have no homeland are too multiple and too mixed in race and descent, as "modern human beings"; as a result, we are not very tempted to participate in that mendacious racial self-aggrandizement and ill-breeding that proclaims itself a sign of the German way of life, something that is doubly false and indecent for a nation that has a "sense of history." In a word—and it should be our word of honor!—we are *good Europeans,* Europe's heirs, the rich, superabundant, but also superabundantly obligated heirs of two millennia of the European spirit. . . . (Ibid.)

To be sure, life lived on a mountain top is a luxury no one can afford at the end of the twentieth century. Nietzsche was not a political commentator or political thinker of the first rank, neither a Marx nor a Taine nor a Burckhardt. He needed Europe in order to *write,* and to write what only he could recount: a genealogy of the asceticism that was driving Western culture—its religion, its science, its scholarship, its lust for power—to its end; and an account of the thought that he hoped might bend that asceticism—the thought of the eternal recurrence of the same. For the fate of Europe itself was in his view bound up with the question of writing:

> *Learning to write well.*—The time for speaking well has passed, because the period of city-state civilizations has passed. The ultimate limit that Aristotle set for a great city—a herald would have to be able to make himself heard by the entire assembled community—troubles us as little as the urban communities themselves trouble us: for we want to be understood even beyond our nations. Thus everyone who wants to be properly attuned to what is European must learn how to *write well,* and *become better and better at it.* No excuses, not even if you are born in Germany, where miserable writing is taken to be a national prerogative. However, better writing also means better thinking; it means always inventing something worth communicating, and actually knowing how to communicate it, something translatable into the languages of our neighbors; making oneself accessible to the understanding of those foreigners who are learning our language; working toward the end by which everything good is common good, and by which everything stands free for the free; finally, *preparing* now for that future condition, no matter how remote, in which the great task falls right into the hands of the good Europeans: guiding and overseeing civilization as a whole on our Earth.—Whoever preaches the opposite, whoever does *not* trouble himself about writing well and reading well—both virtues wax and wane hand in hand—in effect will show the nations a path along which they will become ever more *national:* such a one aggravates the sickness of this century—is an enemy of good Europeans, an enemy of free spirits. (MAM II, WS, 87; *2,* 592–93)

No one today can be confident that Europe's task is to guide and oversee world civilization. Yet Nietzsche was thinking not of Europe's prerogatives but of its responsibilities, mainly the responsibilities of its writers. In his view, being a good European required an act of inner obedience: one had to hear what it was one was supposed to be writing, and then hie off to a place that was conducive to the writing of it. If his ill-health served as the barometer that sent him packing from one work site to another, the storm of thinking and writing was all he ever craved. He was clear enough about this in *Ecce Homo: How One Becomes What One Is.* There he both claimed to be a natural good European and demonstrated how difficult it was to be such a thing. "Natural," because he had inherited a pan-European tendency from his father's side, the side he (vainly) hoped was Polish, so that "no great exertion" was required for him "to be a 'good European'" (W *14, 472*). "Difficult," because no one could inherit all the things, the "closest things," that had to be right if one were to be clever and write such good books: diet, climate, terrain, companions, each exacting its measure of influence and control. In the present volume we emphasize climate and terrain, concerning which Nietzsche, also in *Ecce Homo,* wrote:

> The question that is most closely related to that of nourishment is one of *locale* and *climate*. No one is free to live wherever one likes; and whoever has important tasks to carry out, tasks that call upon one's every force, has in this respect a very narrow choice. The influence of climate on *metabolism,* its inhibition or acceleration, extends so far that a mistake in locale and climate may not only alienate one from one's task but also deprive one of it altogether: one never gets to see it face-to-face. One's animal vigor never reaches the point at which it spills over into the coursing freedom of the greatest spirituality, never reaches the point at which one comes to recognize, *"That* is something I alone can do. . . ." Even the slightest lethargy of the bowel, once it becomes a bad habit, is quite enough to turn a genius into something mediocre, something "German." The German climate all by itself is enough to dishearten strong and even heroic innards. The tempo of one's metabolism stands in precise relation to the animation or paralysis of the *feet* of spirit; indeed, "spirit" is itself but a kind of metabolism. Think of all those places where spirited people used to live and still live, places where wit, ingenuity, and a malicious sense of humor were the very meaning of happiness, places where the person of genius almost necessarily had to settle down: they all have exceptionally dry air. Paris, Provence, Florence, Jerusalem, Athens—these names prove something, namely, that genius is *conditioned* by dry air and a clear sky, *conditioned* by a rapid metabolism, by the possibility of supplying continuously abundant and even vast amounts of energy. I know of a case in which a significant and fundamentally autonomous spirit, merely because of a lack of instinctive acuity concerning matters of climate, turned into a spindly, spidery specialist and sourpuss. And in the end I myself could have become such a case, had illness not brought me to my senses, causing me to ponder what is rational about reality. Now, after long practice, I can read off the effects of climatic and meteorological change on myself, as though from a very fine and very dependable instrument. Even on the shortest of journeys, say, from Turin to Milan, I can calculate the physiological effects in me of the change in humidity. And so I now think with terror on the *uncanny* fact that my life prior to the past decade, in which that very life was at threat, was played out upon stages that were always in false places—for me, actually, *prohibitive* places: Naumburg, Schulpforta, Thuringia in general, Leipzig, Basel, Venice—all of them most unfortunate places for my physiology. If I do not have a single happy memory from my entire childhood and youth, it would be a stupid mistake to look for so-called "moral" reasons, such as the undeniable lack of *adequate* companions. For this lack persists today, as it always has, and it does not prevent me from being cheerful and confident. Rather, it was ignorance in matters physiological—that accursed "idealism"—that constituted the genuine fatality in my life, the superfluous and silly aspects of my life, the things from which no good could come, the things for which there could be no compensation, for which restitution was impossible. I declare that all the mistakes, all the grand instinctual follies of my life, all the "modest proposals" that distracted me from the *task* of my life, such as the one that caused me to become a philologist—why did I not become a doctor or something else that could have opened my eyes?—all are consequences of this "idealism." During my Basel period my entire spiritual diet, including the way I scheduled my day, was an entirely senseless misuse of extraordinary powers, without a recharging of energies to make up for what I was expending, without a single thought given to matters of exhaustion and replenishment. I was bereft of that finer form of selfishness, that *guardianship* of a commanding instinct; I identified myself with sim-

ply anyone at all, it was a kind of "selflessness," <u>a forgetting of one's own distance</u>—something for which I will never forgive myself. When I was almost at an end, and precisely *because* I was almost at an end, I began to think about the rock-bottom irrationality of my life—I began to ponder "idealism." *Illness* alone made me rational.— (EH, "Why I Am So Clever," section 2; *6, 281–83*)

Some might be tempted to reduce Nietzsche's style of life in the 1880s to the desire to be footloose and fancy-free, to avoid job and family, to escape obligations and claims upon one's loyalties. Yet Nietzsche did hanker after job and family during the greater part of his life. In a letter to his friend Franz Overbeck in 1886 he complained:

> The *antinomy* of my current situation, of the form of my existence, consists in this: everything that I *need* in order to be *philosophus radicalis*—freedom from profession, wife, child, society, fatherland, faith, etc. etc.—I equally suffer as *deprivations*, inasmuch as I have the good fortune to be a living creature and not merely an analyzing machine or objectivizing apparatus. I have to add that this juxtaposition of necessities and deprivations is driven to extremes by the lack of an even moderately durable health. For in my moments of health I feel the deprivations *less* keenly. Further, I absolutely do not know how to bring together the five conditions that would *restore* my delicate health to a bearable modicum. Finally, the worst possible situation would prevail if in order to attain those five conditions of health I had to *deprive myself of* the eight freedoms of the *philosophus radicalis.*—This strikes me as the **most objective** account of my rather complicated situation. . . . Excuse me! Or, rather, you may have a good laugh at all this!—(B *7, 282–83*)

Footloose and fancy-free? Nietzsche's fancy remained captive to his task, and his foot was certainly never as free as the vaunted dancer's. Indeed, travel for him was always agony: one day's train journey would cost him at least three days' recuperation in bed. Nietzsche undertook his journeys against all the odds, and he seldom won for losing. He was clearly driven by the need to find the places that would be propitious for his *work,* even if the search and the discovery of new sites should menace his *life.*

Had we wished to focus in this book on Nietzsche's (nonworking) vacations or his (rare) romances, we would have visited different—and fewer—sites. We wanted instead to probe the relationship between work and work site, and to do so as much by images as by words. Each of the four chapters, themselves illustrated by photographs contemporary to Nietzsche or to us, is followed by a portfolio of photographs and texts. Of course, we had to choose some places over others, had to make judgments of selection, of inclusion and exclusion. The need to exclude gave us our worst headaches, although the inclusions too, and the very concept of the book, were not easy for us.

True, many of the passages cited in the portfolios are obvious ones, passages to which Nietzsche himself attached the titles "Genoa," or "At the waterfall," or "In high mountains." "The Wanderer and His Shadow" is probably the most famous of these titles. Yet what are we to make of it when Nietzsche tells us that he conceived the "Old and New Tablets" episode of *Thus Spoke Zarathustra* while climbing the path at Èzé, near Nice, or that the thought of eternal return overwhelmed him near a pyramidal boulder at Surlej? "Of Old and New Tablets" is a long and carefully composed text: it was not written on a hike. Eternal recurrence of the same is a thought that took shape quite gradually in Nietzsche's mind and under his pen: we find incipient expressions of it in his early Basel lectures on ancient Greek philosophy and even in some of his secondary school essays. Although there is an explosion of notes on eternal return during the summer and autumn of 1881 at Sils-Maria and Surlej, Nietzsche did not fall off that boulder as Paul fell—at least according to Mannerist painters—from his horse.

The influence of work site on the work cannot be reduced to the site's serving as a reservoir of available metaphors—snowcaps for purity and rigor of thought, the sea for rhythm and fecundity in the writing. The metaphors are rich enough, no doubt; yet their function is highly complex. And the sites themselves—their odors, colors, sounds, silences, virtually everything that goes into the *feel* of them—are inexhaustibly rich. High above the Mediterranean coast or on the shores of Lake Silvaplana it is hard to distinguish the vehicle from the tenor of metaphor. In Nietzsche's texts it is impossible. For the ways in which larch and pine, grass and wildflower, sea air and cityscape *feed* Nietzsche's thinking and writing resist easy depiction. The images in this book are there for reasons the words do not know.

Nietzsche's relation to nature was not that of the collector. He would have loved to discuss with Charles Darwin the teleological underpinnings of the theory of natural selection, but he would have turned down even the most importunate invitation to board *The Beagle*. Whereas Goethe's house in Weimar was lavishly furnished with overfilled specimen cupboards, Nietzsche's cupboard was always bare. One might say that Nietzsche's relation to nature was that of the cosmologist rather than the naturalist, his relation to the city that of the culture critic rather than the architect. Yet the breadth of detail and depth of reflection in his relations to both countryside and cityscape are truly impressive, the psychological refinement of his associations in both cases always surprising and sometimes disconcerting. Vast historical learning, a highly developed literary sensibility, and an intimate relation to the world of ancient myth and culture—all enriched Nietzsche's ties to nature and to the city.

To push the question a bit harder: Can one calculate the influence of Nietzsche's work sites on his principal ideas—will to power, eternal recurrence of the same, overman, transvaluation of all values, the innocence of becoming, perspectivism, genealogical critique, tragic affirmation, and love of fate—assuming that one can calculate the list of principal ideas? Is eternal return a thought of Alpine lakes, will to power an effulgence of the northern Italian city-states, overman a dream of the mountains near Nice, genealogy a strategy for defeating the tourists at Sils-Maria? Such judgments could only be quirky, and this book has no desire to make them.

Other judgments seem easier to live with: that the few days Nietzsche spent deep in the Maderan Valley immediately before his engagement in the Franco-Prussian War brought him closer to Parnassus, the mountain of both Dionysos and Apollo, than he would ever be in his life—even if he did journey to Paestum; that the long summer in Steinabad near Bonndorf in the Black Forest gave him ample time and seclusion to think about his relation to Richard Wagner in Bayreuth—the chance to gain some distance on the hubbub that had captivated him five or six years earlier; that the maritime Alps near Nice and the slopes of Mount Corvatsch above Silvaplana in the Swiss Engadine gave Nietzsche's Zarathustra the craggy terrains of his mountain solitude; that the tiny church and parsonage at Röcken gave the boy sheltered corners for his nostalgia and gaping crypts for his nightmares; that the seaport cities of Nice, Genoa, and Venice put him in touch with the larger world, including the vanished world of the ancients; and that Turin put him in touch with the post-Renaissance princes and potentates of modernity—the perfect cityscape for his final obsessions concerning the "grand politics" of Europe. If it is as much a cliché to say that a text speaks for itself as to say that a picture is worth a thousand words, we hope that in the present book the conjunction of these two clichés yields unforeseen fruit—the unexpected insight, the unanticipated connection, the waxing suspicion, the stolen glimpse, the secret pleasure, happy science.

Nietzsche's hopes for the good Europeans, for whom he wrote his books, were perhaps best expressed in the preface he added to the second edition of *Human, All-Too-Human,* Part Two. There he reflected on his travels, his illness, and the convalescence that was his work. The preface is signed *"Sils-Maria,* Oberengadin, September 1886," and it concludes—as we shall conclude this Introduction—with the following:

> Will my experience—the story of an illness and a convalescence, inasmuch as it did come to a convalescence—have been merely my personal experience? And nothing more than precisely *my kind* of "human, all-too-human"? Today I am inclined to believe the contrary. I find a kind of confidence coming to me again and again, assuring me that my wander-books were not jotted down for me alone, though that is the way it seemed for quite some time—. After six years of waxing confidence, may I now send these sketches off anew, on another journey, another adventure? May I ask some to take them to heart and to ear, namely, those who are still fettered to some sort of "past," and who are still sufficiently spirited to suffer on account of the *spirit* of their past? Most of all I commend them to you who find everything difficult, you rare ones, endangered ones, most spirited ones, most courageous ones, you who have to be the *conscience* of the modern soul and who therefore have to possess your own kind of *knowing,* in which everything today that inflicts illness, poison, and danger comes together—those of you whose lot it is to be sicker than any individual can be, inasmuch as you are not *"mere* individuals," you whose consolation is that you know—and, yes, that you travel—the path to a *new* health, a health of tomorrow and the day after tomorrow, you who are preordained, you victorious ones, you strongest ones, you *good Europeans!* — — (W *2,* 376)

Die Liebe höret nimmer auf. "Charity never faileth"; or, "Love never ceases." The grave-stone of Nietzsche's father, Pastor Karl Ludwig Nietzsche, in Röcken (B 7, 138).

ONE

BEGINNINGS
AND ENDS

. . . without a father,
without a homeland.
Nietzsche at age 14

Anarrow corridor stretching southwest from Leipzig to the towns of Weimar and Jena encompasses Nietzsche's beginnings and ends. Except for his first year of university study, the "wasted year" at Bonn in 1864, Nietzsche spent his youth here and lived out the years of his madness and paralysis here. Here Nietzsche was born, went to elementary and secondary school, and attended university. After ten years of research and teaching at the University of Basel, and ten more years as a writer and thinker who spent his winters on the Riviera and his summers in Switzerland, he sank ever deeper into insanity and physical paralysis here. Here he died and was interred, leaving behind him a corpus of writings that are among the most remarkable in European letters—a corpus whose handwritten originals are still housed within that narrow corridor.

Friedrich Wilhelm Nietzsche was born on October 15, 1844, in the tiny village of Röcken in Saxony, the first son of the Lutheran pastor Karl Ludwig Nietzsche and his young wife Franziska Oehler. Röcken lay on the fertile but almost treeless plain that seemed anxious to get to the hills, forests, and splendid towns of Thuringia to the south. Yet it was the village of Röcken that Nietzsche loved all his life, the village that surrounded his beloved *Vaterhaus,* that is, the parsonage, the cemetery, and the church in which his father served.

It was a simple country house of two stories, with a lofty tile roof, a plastered exterior, and a dark-stained pine interior. Built between 1820 and 1825, it was only twenty years old when Nietzsche began to occupy it. Both the parsonage and the church were spacious when compared to other buildings in the village, but tiny and cramped when compared to anything else. A heavy schist stone threshold at the right of the entrance led to Pastor Nietzsche's study, with its heavy door and lever handle.[1]

A wide staircase led from the main entrance and the parsonage's public rooms up to the living quarters. The front door, a double door, was battered at the bottom of one of the panels, and had a tale of it own to tell. When Franziska and Karl Ludwig were married, the good pastor wanted to deliver a heartfelt speech from the portal of the parsonage to the congregation gathered about the

1. Nietzsche speaks of his father's study as having been on the second floor, whereas today the study is the first room off to the right when one enters the building. Perhaps the pastor, who was a man of learning, had both a private and a public study—the upstairs study for his own reading and writing, the downstairs study for consultations and other parish business.

Karl Ludwig Nietzsche, 1813-1849. "His image stands before my soul as though he were alive: a tall, delicate figure, a fine-featured face, amiable and beneficent. Everywhere welcomed and beloved as much for his witty conversation as for his warm sympathy, esteemed and loved by the farmers, extending blessings by word and deed in his capacity as a spiritual guide, for his family the most gentle husband and most loving father, he was the perfect embodiment of a country pastor" (*My Life,* version C, from May 1861, written at age sixteen; J *1,* 281-82). Photo: Stiftung Weimarer Klassik. GSA 101/323.

Franziska Oehler Nietzsche, 1826-1897. "My dear Mother, I think of you quite a lot and always want to know how you are doing; come back to us soon. I am healthy and happy love you lots and want to be . . . Your . . . obedient Fritz" (B *1,* 1; written at age five). Photo: Stiftung Weimarer Klassik. GSA 101/315.

Röcken. Rear view of Nietzsche's *Vaterhaus,* constructed in 1825. Photo: Stiftung Weimarer Klassik. GSA 101/583.

porch. And he wanted to have his new helpmate at his side. Yet because only one panel of the door was commonly used, the closed half was stuck. He tried to kick it open, and put his foot through it; it was difficult to make the speech after that. The repair to the lower boards on the left half of the front door is still visible.

The bedrooms at the back of the house today look out onto a green lawn that used to contain the village's ancient cemetery. Each time the young Nietzsche turned the butterfly-wing latch of the tiny framed windows to their vertical position, opened the window, and leaned out, he had that cemetery in view—God's acre, the Germans sometimes call it—with the stone wall of the church and its bell-tower off to his left. During his early years he would play in the gardens and farm buildings in front of the house; if he ventured around the back to the cemetery, three unrelenting eyes on the roof—the three gabled windows called *Gaupen,* a common feature in Thuringian and Saxon architecture—would glare down at him.

Front entrance of the Röcken parsonage. (Photograph presumably taken early in the twentieth century.) Photo: Stiftung Weimarer Klassik. GSA 101/583.

Door to Pastor Karl Ludwig Nietzsche's ground-floor study

The repaired front door.

"I have yet to mention something that secretly filled me with terror: in the gloomy sacristy of the church, over on one side, stood an over-life-size image of St. George, carved in stone by a skillful hand. The impressive figure, his terrible weapons, and the mysterious twilight of the place caused me always to shrink back when I looked at it. They say that once upon a time the eyes of the relief flashed so terribly that everyone who gazed on it was filled with terror" (*From My Life,* written at age thirteen; J *1,* 3).

The boy would have been able to enter the church at the tower-end of the nave whenever he liked, looking down at the threshold to see the word *ewig,* "eternal," still visible on the worn stone, the familiar musty smell rising to meet him. He might have heard the white walls still echoing his father's florid speech at his own baptism: "O thou blessed month of October, which throughout the years hath encompassed the most important events of my variegated life, today I am experiencing the grandest, the most splendid event: today I am to baptize my little child! O blessed moment, O savory feast, O unspeakably holy deed, I bless you in the name of the Lord! With all my heart, and most profoundly moved, I command: *Bring me now this child, that I may dedicate him to the Lord!* My son, Friedrich Wilhelm, thus shall be your name on Earth, in memory of my king and benefactor, on whose birthday you were born" (N *1,* 42). The boy might have made his way down the rows of gray pews and over the red carpet to the two doors that led to the tiny sacristy behind the altar, where his father had access to the pulpit high over the stone altar. There in the sacristy a bas-relief of St. George would have waited in ambush. Or he could have mounted the old wooden stairway near the entrance that led to the choir loft and its tiny organ, where he often sat with his father.

It was his father's house and the village of Röcken that Nietzsche loved, not the town of Naumburg, to which he moved in April 1850 with his mother Franziska, his sister Elisabeth (born to the couple on July 10, 1846), three maiden aunts, and a widowed grandmother—the stern and stolid Erdmuthe. The move took place after the deaths of Nietzsche's father, on July 30, 1848, and younger brother, in early March 1850. Both father and brother were buried outside the southern wall of the church at Röcken.

In dozens of poems and autobiographical sketches written during his youth, Nietzsche portrayed the drastic impact these two deaths had on his life. Here is an extended passage from one of the earliest sketches, "From My Life," written between August 18 and September 1, 1858, when Nietzsche was not yet fourteen years old. It begins with a rather grown-up, albeit thoroughly pious preface, then tells of Nietzsche's birthplace, which is always called his "father house," and of the shadow that soon loomed over that house:

> *I. The Years of My Youth: 1844–1858.* By the time one has grown up, one usually remembers only the truly salient points concerning one's earliest childhood. True, I am not yet a grown-up, and have scarcely left the years of my infancy and youth behind me, yet so much has already disappeared from my memory, and the little that I know of these things has probably been handed down to me by tradition. The sequence of years flits past my gaze like a confused dream. It is therefore impossible for me to tie myself to dates for the events of the first ten years of my life. Nevertheless, several things remain vivid and vital in my soul, and of these things, combined with what is obscure and gloomy, I shall paint my picture. For it is always instructive to observe the gradual formation of one's understanding and one's heart, and thereby to see the omnipotent guidance of God! —
>
> I was born in Röcken, near Lützen, on October 15, 1844; I received in holy baptism the name *Friedrich* Wilhelm. My father was the preacher in this village and also in the neighboring villages, Michlitz and Bothfeld. The perfect picture of a country parson! Gifted in spirit and heart, adorned with all the virtues of a Christian, he lived a tranquil, simple, yet happy life. All who knew him respected and loved him. His refined manner and cheerful demeanor illuminated the many gatherings to which he was invited, and he was beloved of all from the very first moment he appeared among them. His leisure hours were filled by pursuit of science and music. He played the piano with great skill, and was particularly adept at free variation. . . . (J *1*, 1–2)

Nietzsche's father improvised both on the piano at home and on the church organ. The boy would sit for hours on his father's lap, rapt to the music. His own later talent for improvisation on

Left: Röcken. The south wall and the apse of the church, looking toward the parsonage.

Right: The church organ at Röcken. "Words will never exhaust the cosmic symbolism of music . . ." (GT, 6; *1*, 51).

the piano, his musical compositions, his fascination with Richard Wagner and friendship with Heinrich Köselitz (*alias* Peter Gast), his ideas concerning the crucial role of music in the chorus of Greek tragedy—these things and more were borne upon, if not born from, that paternal lap. Indeed, quite late in his life, not long after his forty-third birthday, he wrote to a conductor of Wagner's music, "Perhaps at bottom there never was a philosopher who was also a musician, at least not to the degree that I am one" (B *8,* 172). But to continue with "From My Life":

> During this fateful time [i.e., the 1848 revolution in Paris and throughout the great cities of Germany] I had a baby brother, named in holy baptism Karl Ludwig *Joseph,* a most lovely child. Up to now happiness and joy had shone upon us all; our life flowed on unperturbed, like a bright summer's day. But now heavy storm clouds towered over us, lightning flashed, and fatal blows from heaven struck us. In September 1848 my beloved father suddenly became mentally ill. However, we consoled ourselves and him with the hope that he would soon recover. Whenever a better day did come he would preach and hold his Confirmation lessons, for his active spirit could not be slothful. Several physicians endeavored to discover the cause of the illness, but in vain. Then we sent for the famous Dr. Opolzer, who was in Leipzig, and he came to Röcken. This excellent man immediately recognized where the seat of the illness was to be found. To our consternation, he took the illness to be a liquefaction of the brain, not yet hopelessly advanced, but already extremely dangerous. My father had to suffer terribly, and the illness would not diminish but grew worse from day to day. Finally, he went blind, and had to endure his sufferings in eternal darkness. He was bedridden until July 1849; then the day of his redemption drew nigh. On July 26 he sank into a deep slumber, from which he awoke only fitfully. His last words were: "Fränzchen—Fränzchen—come—mother—listen—listen—O God!" Then he died, quietly and blessedly. † † † † on July 27, 1849. When I woke up in the morning I heard all around me loud weeping and sobbing. My dear mother came to me with tears in her eyes and cried out: "O God! My good Ludwig is dead!" Although I was very young and inexperienced, I still had some idea of death; the thought that I would be separated forever from my dear father seized me, and I wept bitterly.
>
> The next few days passed amid tears and preparations for the funeral. O God! I had become a fatherless orphan, my dear mother a widow! — — — — On August 2 the earthly remains of my beloved father were committed to the womb of the earth. The parish had prepared a crypt of stone for him. At one o'clock in the afternoon the ceremonies began, with the bells pealing their loud knell. Oh, never will the deep-throated sound of those bells quit my ear; never will I forget the gloomily surging melody of the hymn "Jesus, My Consolation"! Through the empty spaces of the church the sounds of the organ roared. (J *1,* 4–5).

"Fatal blows from heaven struck us." Emblem on the exterior apse of the Röcken church.

Röcken. The grave of Nietzsche's father. Photo: Stiftung Weimarer Klassik. GSA 101/585.

The altar of the church at Röcken, with fallen lupine petals on the altar cloth. "We all bleed on secret sacrificial altars; we burn; we are roasted in order to honor the ancient idols" (ASZ III, "Of Old and New Tablets," section 6; *4, 251*).

Nietzsche's strong ties to his father—and the severing of those ties—marked him for life. When he was awarded seven thousand Swiss francs in a court settlement against a publisher, Ernst Schmeitzner, the very first thing he bought after paying off his debts to bookstores was an engraved tombstone for his father. The purchase occurred some thirty-six years after his father's death! As far as we know, it was also the son, the budding Antichrist, who designed the stone—including the verse from Paul that concluded the inscription on it:

✝

Here
reposeth in God
Carl Ludwig
Nietzsche
Pastor of Röcken
Michlitz and Bothfeld
born 11 October 1813
died 30 July 1849
Whereupon followed him into Eternity
his younger son
Ludwig Joseph
born 27 February 1848
died 4 January 1850
C h a r i t y   n e v e r   f a i l e t h
1 Cor. 13, 8.

"Die Liebe höret nimmer auf." Love never stops. Not even in an abandoned *Vaterhaus*.

Nietzsche's ancestors on both sides had been either preachers or butchers. Nietzsche himself wanted very much to claim Polish rather than German ancestry, especially toward the end of his active life when he was thoroughly disenchanted with his erstwhile homeland. He despaired of finding an ennobling ancestry on his mother's side (the Oehler side), and so invested all his hopes for nobility in his father's family, which he took to be descended from the aristocratic Polish *Nietzky.* Yet *Nietzsche* was a common German name, especially in the northern and eastern parts of the country. It presumably derived either from *Nicholas,* connoting the gift-giving of Christmas time, or from *Neid, nît,* meaning envy and wrath, connoting the German *Gift,* which means poison. Nietzsche doubtless relished the ambivalence of the name, and seems to have been delighted by the "excessively flattering etymology" of *Nietzky,* which, he said, the Poles took to mean *the nihilist* (B 8, 346). However, in spite of his conviction that remote ancestry had a greater impact on an individual than parentage, that is, that one's forebears passed on more qualities than could be embodied in the mother and father alone, Nietzsche never really investigated his family tree.

Only his paternal grandfather, Friedrich August Ludwig Nietzsche, seems to have shown interest and skill in writing, although distant blood relatives of Nietzsche's included Goethe and the Schlegel brothers. Nietzsche himself was raised, not to be a writer or thinker, but to take his father's place, to assume the duties of an evangelical pastorate. Not until the beginning of his university career was he able to escape from the prisonhouse of so much past. Perhaps he only partly escaped it, for his scrupulous training in classical philology reflected a Protestant fervor and rigor, and was itself rooted in reverence to scriptures and devotion to the past.

The move from Röcken to Naumburg in April 1850, although minuscule in terms of kilometers, meant a radical change for the boy, a change from the country to the city, from a peasant to a bourgeois existence. Indeed, when one compares the grand residences of his Naumburg chums, Wilhelm Pinder and Gustav Krug, to the modest country house in which Nietzsche was born, or even to the three successive sets of modest lodgings that the family occupied in Naumburg, one sees how far the boy who dreamed of nobility had to climb in order to reach even the middle class. He described the move in "From My Life," but only after reflecting once again on the dire consequences of his father's death, compounded by the death of his little brother, Joseph:

> When a tree is deprived of its crown, it withers and wilts, and the tiny birds abandon its branches. Our family had been deprived of its head. All joy vanished from our hearts and profound sadness held sway in us. Yet scarcely were our wounds somewhat healed when a new event painfully tore them open.—At that time I once dreamt that I heard organ music in the church, the music I had heard during my father's funeral. When I perceived what lay behind these sounds, a gravemound suddenly opened and my father, wrapped in a linen shroud, emerged from it. He hurried into the church and returned a moment later with a child in his arms. The tomb yawned again, he entered it, and the cover closed over the opening. The stertorous sounds of the organ ceased instantly, and I woke. On the day that followed this night, Little Joseph suddenly fell ill, seized by severe cramps, and after a few hours he died. Our grief knew no bounds. My dream had been fulfilled completely. The tiny corpse was laid to rest in his father's arms.—In this double misfortune, God in Heaven was our sole consolation and protection. This happened at the end of the year 1850.— — —[2]
>
> The time approached when we were to leave our beloved Röcken. I can still remember the last day and the last night we spent there. That evening I played with several local children, thinking that it would be for the last time. The vesper bell tolled its melancholy

2. This happened, in fact, during March of 1850. The date of Little Joseph's death inscribed on the tombstone, January 4, 1850, is also apparently incorrect. Janz (N *1,* 47) informs us that, according to the parish registry, Nietzsche's younger brother actually died several days *after* his second birthday. With regard to the premonitory dream, we should note that there is a second account of it in a later autobiographical sketch (J *1,* 282). The text of this second account appears in the

The view from the second floor of the parsonage—and from what well may have been the boy's bedroom—of the church and former cemetery.

peal across the meadow, dull darkness settled over the earth, and in the night sky the moon and the shimmering stars shone. I could not sleep for long. At one-thirty in the morning I went down to the courtyard again. Several wagons stood there; they were being loaded. The dull glimmer of their lanterns cast a gloomy light across the courtyard. I took it to be entirely impossible that I would ever feel at home in another place. How painful it was to abandon a village where one had experienced joy and pain, where the graves of my father and younger brother lay, where the village folk always surrounded me with love and friendship! Scarcely had the dawning day shed its light on the meadows, when our wagon rolled out onto the country road that took us to Naumburg, where a new home awaited.—Adieu, adieu, dear house of my father!! (J *1, 6–7*)

---

portfolio of "Beginnings and Ends," below. A number of details in the second account differ from those of the first. Moreover, as far as the parish records and the photographic record in the Nietzsche Archive show, the father's grave was always alongside the south wall of the church, not in the cemetery that bordered the north wall. *Nietzsche therefore could not have seen his father's grave from any window of the parsonage.* Thus he either transposed his deceased father and brother to someone else's grave, somewhere in the cemetery that was in full view below his window, or he displaced the entire matter to the imaginative realm of the world of dreams. The first option seems to apply in Nietzsche's first account, which uses the indefinite pronoun, ". . . a gravemound suddenly opened," leaving open the possibility that the father is occupying someone else's crypt—at least for the length of his first son's dream; by contrast, the later account refers specifically to "my father's grave," suggesting the more radical and total displacement effected by oneiric imagination. For a discussion of the double recounting of the dream, especially in terms of the interpretation of Pierre Klossowski, see Krell, *Infectious Nietzsche* (Bloomington: Indiana University Press, 1996), chap. 11, "Consultations with the Paternal Shadow." See also Pierre Klossowski, *Nietzsche et le cercle vicieux,* second edition (Paris: Mercure de France, 1969), pp. 251-84. Finally, for a fictional account, see Krell, *Nietzsche: A Novel* (Albany: State University Press of New York, 1996), Part IV.

Nietzsche now describes his new home, the beautiful walled city of Naumburg, sometimes with loving attention to detail, at other times in the derogatory terms he would later use when referring to his mother's and sister's meddling in his affairs—what he called their "Naumburg morality," which he despised.[3]

> It was terrible for us to live in the city, after we had been living in the country for so long. For that reason, we avoided the gloomy streets and looked for the open spaces, like birds trying to escape from a cage. For the city-dwellers seemed much like that to us. When I first saw the city park, they say I cried out with childlike glee, "Oh, look! Christmas trees all over!" In general, everything seemed new and strange to me during those early days. The huge churches and buildings of the market place, with its *Rathaus* and fountain, the throngs of people, to which I was unaccustomed—all this aroused my great admiration. Then too I was astonished by the fact that often these people did not know one another; whereas in the peaceful village everyone knew everyone else. Among the most disturbing things to me were the long paved streets. The way to my aunts seemed to me at least an hour long. . . . (J *1, 7*)

Of Nietzsche's infancy in Röcken and his early childhood in Naumburg we know very little. Family tradition relates that the pregnancy and birth went well, that the child was quiet but generally content. Nevertheless, Nietzsche as a toddler apparently threw temper tantrums, which his mother was helpless to control, but which his father energetically undertook to discipline. After that, whenever the boy's desires were frustrated he betook himself to a corner of the room or to the bathroom, sharing his solitude only with his anger. Apparently he did not talk until he was several years old: the local doctor advised Franziska not to baby her son so much, otherwise he would never have to speak up and declare his wants! The boy's favorite toy was a porcelain squirrel that an aunt had brought back from Dresden for his father. By the time Nietzsche was nine, living in Naumburg,

---

3. Much later in his life, in a letter from Nice written on March 14, 1885, Nietzsche expressed the hope that he would soon be able to visit with his mother and sister. Yet he emphasized that it would *not* be in Naumburg: "You know that Naumburg isn't good for me, and there is nothing in my heart that speaks for the place. I was not 'born' there, and I was never 'at home' there" (B *7, 23*).

The Naumburg market square, then and now. First photo: Stiftung Weimarer Klassik. GSA 101/555.

he was writing plays for *König Eichhorn,* Oak Crescent, the squirrel king (J *1,* 310–11). In later years, when he signed a letter to his sister with the name "Prinz Eichhorn," both sister and mother readily understood the reference (B *7,* 108).

His mother never remarried, but devoted her life to her two remaining children, Friedrich Wilhelm, and Elisabeth, eighteen months younger than her brother. Franziska learned enough piano to give Nietzsche his first lessons, then arranged for more advanced lessons when she could no longer keep up with him. The boy always associated music with his father, however, an association that the friendships with the Krug family and, later, Richard Wagner further reinforced. By the time Nietzsche was eleven years old he was composing his own oratorios and other religious pieces. His mother also arranged for the boy's schooling, first in a public school (hoping that he would mix with a larger cross-section of humanity), then in a small private institute, and eventually in the local Cathedral School. Young Nietzsche was a diligent scholar, so diligent that it worried the women of the presbytery. True, they wanted him to become the pastor who would take the place of the father who had died at age thirty-six, but the boy seemed to be bent on skipping youth altogether.

Of his early school days Nietzsche reports little, but that little is very revealing:

> By the time we went to Naumburg, my character began to show itself. I had already experienced considerable sadness and grief in my young life, and was therefore not as carefree and wild as children usually are. My schoolmates were accustomed to teasing me on account of my seriousness. This happened not only in the public school but also later at the institute and in my secondary school. From childhood on, I sought solitude, and I felt best whenever I could give myself over to myself undisturbed. And this was usually in the open-air temple of nature, which was my true joy. Thunder storms always made the most powerful impression on me: the thunder rolling in from afar and the lightning bolts flashing only increased my fear of the Lord. (J *1,* 8)

A later account, written at age sixteen, tells much the same story: "Various qualities developed in me quite early: a certain capacity for tranquil observation and taciturnity, which enabled me to keep my distance from the other children, although from time to time my passionate nature erupted" (J *1,* 279).

Nietzsche found the greatest relief from the town life of Naumburg in Pobles, the village in which his maternal grandfather, David Ernst Oehler, served as pastor. The large number of aunts, uncles, and cousins in the parsonage at Pobles, and the playmates who joined the family children in the surrounding fields and orchards, made Pobles the goal of summer vacations throughout Nietzsche's youth. In that earliest autobiographical sketch from which we have been quoting at length, the boy reports: "My dear, terribly earnest, but also cheerful Grandpa, my O so friendly Grandma, the uncles and aunts—everywhere in this house genuine German conviviality prevailed, drawing us there again and again, evoking in us a deep love for this place. My favorite spot was Grandpa's study; my greatest pleasure was to browse through the old tomes and notebooks" (J *1*, 24). In honor of a birthday celebration for Grandfather Oehler in the summer of 1859, the fourteen-year old wrote the following poem:

> In the parsonage at Pobles
> Life is full of fun:
> Sometimes it's my close family,
> Sometimes my friends have come.
> From near and far they gather,
> And all by joy are won;
> With happiness and deep delight,
> Like dazzling stars shining bright,
> They are this house's sun. — (J *1*, 108–9)

Yet however much the boy, and later the man, may have despised the bourgeois town of Naumburg, the scholarship he won to the boarding school at Pforta in 1858 brought him tears as well as pride. It was Schulpforta that gave Nietzsche the education that needed only four years of

The parsonage of Franziska Nietzsche's father, Pastor David Ernst Oehler, in Pobles . . .

Field and orchard between Grandfather Oehler's church and parsonage at Pobles.

. . . today an abandoned storage building. Parsonage photo: Stiftung Weimarer Klassik. GSA 101/576.

Schul-Pforta.

Schulpforta as it was in Nietzsche's youth. The road on the left wends its way, via "Almrich," to Naumburg. Photo: Stiftung Weimarer Klassik. GSA 101/597.

The main entrance at Schulpforta. "I shall now try to provide a picture of an altogether normal day at Pforta. . . . The dormitory is opened at 4:00 A.M., and from then on everyone is free to get up. But at 5:00 anyone who is still asleep is roused by the familiar school bell, after which the dormitory proctors yell: "Get up! Get up! Move it out here!" And they punish whoever has a hard time getting out from under his covers. Then everyone throws something on as fast as he can and hurries to the washroom, to find a free spot before it gets too crowded. . . . At 5:25 the first call to prayer is rung; by the second bell we have to be in the chapel. Here, before the teacher enters, the proctors enforce order, forbid us to speak, and hurry the senior students to their places, for they often come quite late. . . . Then the organ starts up and, after a brief prelude, intones a matins hymn. Then the teacher reads a section from the New Testament, with now and then another hymn, says the Lord's Prayer, and concludes the convocation with a final verse" (Journal entry, Pforta, August 9, 1859; J *1,* 119-20).

university training in order to produce a brilliant philologist. The secondary school student excelled in all subjects but mathematics, which he found "boring," and which almost prevented him from graduating. It was at Pforta, founded in 1543 on the grounds of a splendid twelfth-century Cistercian monastery, still quite monastic in its appearance, that Nietzsche learned enough Hebrew, Greek, Latin, German, and French to enable him to read the primary sources of an entire tradition. Such tears as he shed flowed from homesickness, from which the boy suffered for many years, although he could see his mother, sister, and other relatives every Sunday—usually in the town of Altenburg, known by the Pforta pupils as "Almrich," which lay halfway between Pforta and Naumburg. In mid-November 1858, during his first term at Schulpforta, Nietzsche wrote his mother:

> I wait every day now for a letter from the family, yet none turns up. So I am writing again. I can't come to Naumburg on Sunday; I've got only two hours and your lodgings are too far away. Come instead to Almrich; we'll meet there. Also, I'm thinking, because no letter from you has come, that you yourselves may be planning to come all the way out to Pforta to visit me. Can Uncle Oscar come out again? I need several things, he could bring them along: my philology textbook by Süpfle, Hahn's *History of Prussia,* cocoa, a mirror, scarves, and above all spectacles. Don't keep me waiting long, okay? I need all these things desperately.— — Incidentally, I am almost convinced that homesickness is creeping up on me; every now and then traces of it show themselves.—How is Wilhelm [Pinder]? Is he all better? Give him lots of greetings, Gustav [Krug] too, and Aunt Rosalie, and Auntie Riecke, and Aunt Lina. Surely Lisbeht [*sic*] too will come to Almrich with you and Uncle! (B *1,* 29)

Naumburg. Weingarten 18, the house to which Franziska Nietzsche and her children moved in the summer of 1858, and in which she died in April 1897. Photograph from 1895. Photo: Stiftung Weimarer Klassik. GSA 101/554.

In the summer of 1858 his mother set up a separate household in Naumburg, since by that time Grandmother Erdmuthe and Aunt Auguste had died, while Aunt Rosalie's nerves required her to live alone. Ironically, the new home that Franziska Nietzsche was to occupy until her death in 1897, number 18 Weingarten, was a home that her son knew only on holidays from Pforta. And, as a more terrible irony would have it, number 18 Weingarten was to be his home for seven long years after his release from the Jena asylum into his mother's custody in the spring of 1890.

Something of the spirit of Pforta, and of Nietzsche's feeling of separation from his mother, of yet another abandonment, is reflected in the following letter to his Naumburg friend Wilhelm Pinder. In April 1859, after an enjoyable Easter holiday, the fourteen-year-old wrote:

> When I returned to Pforta at nightfall, I was quite depressed. The sky was covered with clouds, with only a few bright spots showing, including the traces of the sun that had just set. The wind blew fitfully through the high trees; their branches groaned and swayed. My heart was in a similar condition.—It too was darkened by clouds of sadness, and only the happy memory of my vacation gave me some joy, although it was that joyous/painful feeling of melancholy. Of course, you won't believe it—but it makes a huge difference whether one has one's home and school in the same place or in different locations! When your vacation is over, you merely abandon your sweet recreations and your pleasant Muse; but I leave my home and family, and all the joys they represent, for a not insignificant amount of time, heading off into foreign territory. (B *1*, 59)

Pforta nevertheless became a second *Vaterhaus* to Nietzsche, albeit a far more rigorous and regulated one than Röcken had been. The boy did establish close relations with some of his teachers and a few of his classmates; yet the years of secondary school only intensified young Nietzsche's sense of estrangement, of being "otherwise." Further, the school took particular pride in its exacting discipline. Although humanistic in its curriculum, and more liberal-parliamentarian than monarchist in its political sympathies, the handling of its pupils was strictly martial. A Pforta rector from the period of Nietzsche's matriculation defined the principles of the institution in this way:

> What is peculiar about Pforta is that it constitutes a self-enclosed school-state, into which the life of the individual in all its sundry relations is completely absorbed. . . . You will find here in the totality of your education something very much like a second paternal home [*Vaterhaus*]. . . . The fruits of the discipline and training that you will receive here are these: the school looks upon its pupils as whole human beings who are to become accustomed to obedience to the law and to the will of their superiors, to rigorous and punctual fulfillment of their obligations, to self-control, to serious work, to energetic initiative out of love for their work, to thoroughness and method in their studies, to regularity in the allotment of their time, and to flawless tact, self-awareness, and fortitude in their dealings with their fellows. (N *1*, 65–66)

The Saale River, near Schulpforta. "The swimming trip finally took place yesterday. It was terrific, we were lined up in rows and they played cheering music as we marched through the gates. We all wore our red swim caps, which made a very pretty sight. But we young swimmers were very surprised when we were taken a long stretch down the Saale in order to begin our swim, and all of us were afraid. However, when we saw the big swimmers approaching from a distance, and heard the music, we all jumped into the river. We swam in the very same order in which we had marched from school. In general, things went quite well; I tried my very best; but I was always in over my head. I also swam a lot on my back. When we finally got there, we were given our clothes, which had been brought along in a boat. We dressed in a hurry and marched in the same order back to Pforta. It was really terrific!" (Journal entry, Pforta, August 18, 1859; J 1, 130).

One of the early terrors at Pforta, soon to become one of the great joys of Nietzsche's life, was swimming: each pupil had to pass a rigorous swimming test in the Saale River. Nietzsche, although robust and still quite healthy, was not the most agile and daring of athletes, and he approached the test with trepidation. Long before he had to take the test, the boy found it easy to be rapturous about swimming, and even to pontificate about it, as long as he was writing rather than swimming. In "From My Life" he wrote: "Oh, it is delightful to surrender oneself to the warm waters of summer! I especially felt this once I had learned to swim. To give oneself over to the current, and to float effortlessly on the surface of the tide—can one imagine anything more lovely? In this regard I also esteem swimming not only as pleasant but also as very salubrious and refreshing. One cannot recommend it too strongly to our youth" (J 1, 24). Yet in a journal entry from about the same time, dated Pforta, August 6, 1859, this youth to whom swimming has so strongly commended itself confesses: "We went swimming outside again today. The water was unusually calm; we swam all over the Saale, wherever we wanted. It was also unusually warm. . . . I haven't taken my swimming test yet. I'm always afraid I'm going to embarrass myself" (J 1, 116).

When he did pass the test he was jubilant and relieved. Swimming now became one of the profound pleasures of his life: as an adult he would swim in the Mediterranean Sea near Nice, Genoa, and Sorrento, even during the months of November and December, and—as we shall see in

Confirmation portraits of Friedrich and Elisabeth Nietzsche, ca. 1861.
Photos: Stiftung Weimarer Klassik. GSA 101/1 and 101/158.

greater detail in chapter 4—he would always crave to live by the sea. In a letter to his mother and sister written twenty-four years after his swimming exam, Nietzsche virtually cried out: *"Only one thing is certain: I have to live on the **sea**! I cannot describe it in words—the sea is the very salvation of my brain and my eyes"* (B *6,* 447). And for Nietzsche the sea was never a place for mere gazing, but always for plunging.

Although our focus in this book is on Nietzsche's *work* and *work sites,* we should not ignore his adolescent struggles. They began with homesickness, and perhaps ended there as well. For most of the situations that caused problems for the boy at Pforta were exacerbated by the guilt he felt when the eye of Naumburg fell upon him. When the eighteen-year-old senior made a few witty remarks about the school proctors, he had to endure several weeks' worth of letters from his mother upbraiding him for his flippancy and disrespect. When he drank too much beer with the boys, perhaps for the only time in his life, and of course got caught, here is the letter (B *1,* 236–37) he felt compelled to write home:

> Pforta, Thursday morning, April 16, 1863
>
> Dear Mother.
>
> If I am writing you today it is nonetheless one of the most unpleasant and saddest things I have ever had to do. For I have committed something terrible, and I don't know whether you will or can forgive me. With a heavy heart and against all my own natural inclinations I take up the pen, especially when I call to mind the splendid conviviality we enjoyed during the Easter holidays, a conviviality no discord was able to darken. Well, last Sunday I got drunk, and I have no other excuse than the fact that I don't know how much I can hold, and besides I was rather excited that afternoon. As I was on my way back to school, Professor Kern caught me. He had me called before the Synod on Tuesday and they demoted me to third place in my class and gave me an hour's detention for the following Sunday. You can imagine how depressed and upset I am, one of the worst things about it being the fact that my little adventure will cause you worry, and it is all so unworthy of me, it is worse than anything that's ever happened to me in all my life. . . . I'm so angry with

myself that I can't make any progress on my assignments; I can't calm down and get a hold of myself. Write me soon and be strict with me, for I deserve it; no one knows more than I how much I deserve it. . . .

—Incidentally, please don't let the affair get out, if it hasn't already been bruited all over the place. . . .

Farewell for now, write me soon, and don't be too angry with me, dear Mother.

Disconsolately,

Fritz.

The reference to Easter and its "splendid conviviality," which no discord could darken, reminds us of one of the first cracks in Nietzsche's piety, and one of the first strains in his relation to Naumburg. During the Easter vacation of 1861, two years before the drinking episode, Nietzsche refused to participate in religious services; instead, he sought to enlighten his sister and mother concerning the impact of critical hermeneutics on all received religious dogma. The sixteen-year-old meditated on the incident in the following pained letter, written from Pforta at the end of April 1861 (B *1,* 154–55):

> Dear Mama!
>
> . . . And now a word with you alone, dear Mama, if I may. To me as well that otherwise lovely Easter holiday seems to have been overcast and darkened by those ugly events; it strikes me as a most painful thing each time I think of it, that I could have saddened you so much, I beg your forgiveness with all my heart dear Mama! For it would be sad indeed if this discord were to disturb our beautiful relationship of reciprocity. But forgive me dear Mama, and, I beg you, never again dwell on these events, regard them rather as having never happened. Furthermore, I shall try as hard as I can through my conduct and my love for you to repair the rift I have opened. Write me about this once again sometime, dear Mama!—Greet Lisbeth a lot for me. I really hope to see you soon, hopefully on Sunday between four and six in Almrich!
>
> From your Fritz, who loves you dearly.

Would Nietzsche's mother have been placated by the knowledge that by the age of twelve her son was thinking thoughts that made Easter duty a less pressing matter for him than it was for her? Nietzsche recorded several times his earliest theological speculations, inspired perhaps by similar reflections of Goethe's. In 1884 Nietzsche jotted down the following recollection: "When I was twelve years old I conjured up for myself a marvelous trinity: God the Father, God the Son, and God the Devil. My deduction was that God, thinking himself, created the second person of the godhead, but that to be able to think himself he had to think his opposite, and thus had to create it.—That is how I began to philosophize" (W *11,* 253; cf. *11,* 616, *5,* 249, and *8,* 505). No, she would not have been placated. The high school pupil who was her son found himself in the position of constantly having to beg his mother's pardon. When the university student returned from Bonn for Easter in 1865, the same refusal to participate in religious services occurred, but the style was mocking and unrepentant, and there was no subsequent letter of apology.

Perhaps the most revealing text from Nietzsche's adolescence is the scurrilous short story the seventeen-year-old began to write but then abandoned. The fragment "Euphorion" is preserved only because Nietzsche sent a copy of it to his Pforta chum, Raimund Granier; either Nietzsche himself or his mother and/or sister destroyed all other copies. Concerning the story, Nietzsche wrote Granier from Gorenzen on July 28, 1862: "You remember my plan for a repulsive novelette—O my God! Don't tell me! You've forgotten that, too! Never mind!—well, after I'd written

EUPHORION

"Chapter One"

A flood of soft and tranquil harmonies washes over my soul—I do not know what has made me feel so melancholy, I would like to weep and then die. It's no good any more! I am played out, my hand trembles....

The crimson dawn plays in multichrome upon the sky, fizzling fireworks, how boring. How differently my own eyes scintillate. I fear they will burn holes in the sky. I feel that I have fully emerged from myself. I know me through and through, and would only like to find now the head of my Doppelgänger in order to vivisect his brain, or perhaps my own little boy's head all goldilocks . . . oh . . . twenty years ago . . . child . . . child . . . how strange the word sounds. Was I too a child, turned by the Organ-grinder's crank on the lathe of the old cosmic mechanism? and do I now tug slowly unhurriedly on the cable called fate—I, a bell-clapper on a treadmill—until at last I wither; does the Slave-driver bury me hastily, do only the flies swarming about the carrion of me guarantee me a token of immortality?

With this thought I almost sense a disposition to laughter—meanwhile, I'm embarrassed by another idea—perhaps tiny blossoms will burst from my bones, maybe a "Violet of the Heart" or even—if only the Torturer will aim his micturition upon my grave—a Forget-me-not. Then the dearly beloved gather around.... Revulsion! Revulsion! That is corruption! Meanwhile, as I revel in such thoughts of the future—for methinks it is more pleasant to decompose in the moist earth than to vegetate under the blue sky, to scrabble as a fat worm is far sweeter than to be a human being—a walking question mark—,

it always calms me to see human beings wandering the streets, colorful, cleaned up and made up, adorned, these comic humans! What are they? They are whited sepulchers, as, once upon a time, a nice little Jewish boy said.

In my chamber it is still as death—only my quill scratches the paper—because I love to think by writing and because the machine has not yet been invented that can impress our thoughts on some sort of material without our speaking or writing them. Before me an inkwell in which to drown my black heart; a pair of scissors, that I may grow accustomed to cutting my own throat; manuscripts for to wipe myself, and a chamber pot.

Across from me dwells a nun, whom I visit now and then, in order to take joy in her excellent behavior. I know her with exactitude, from head to toe, more intimately than I know myself. Earlier, she was all nun, thin and fragile; I was her doctor and I saw to it that she soon put on some weight. With her dwells her brother in common-law marriage; to me he seemed too fat and flourishing, I thinned him down—to a corpse. He will die in the next day or so—which pleases me no end—for I wish to dissect him. But first I want to write my autobiography. Apart from the fact that it is scintillating, it is also full of excellent instruction; it will turn youths into dotards.... For in this I am the master. Who is to read it? My Doppelgänger, and there are many of them, the vagabonds of this Vale of Tears."

At this point Euphorion leaned back a bit and moaned, for he suffered from a condition that affected the marrow of his spine......

(J 2, 70–71; N 1, 110–112)

Schulpforta. Main classroom building.

the first chapter I threw up and then threw it away. I shall send you the monster manuscript for use on the . . . . . . well, use it as you like. When I wrote it, a burst of diabolical laughter exploded from me—it isn't likely you'll have any appetite for its continuation." He signed the letter "FWvNietzky (*alias* Muck), *homme étudié en lettres (votre ami sans lettres)."* We reproduce "Euphorion" here because it portrays better than any other early writing the sardonic side of the adolescent Nietzsche.

A detailed picture of the schoolboy's interests—especially his interest in inventories and classifications of his own interests—comes from the following long entry in the Pforta journal, dated late summer 1859, when Nietzsche was still fourteen:

> From my earliest childhood there was always something I was crazy about. The first thing was flowers and plants on the Earth's crust. That at least is what they tell me. Then came my love of architecture (naturally, based chiefly on my building blocks), which I developed in all its forms. I was very small, I remember, it was at the time of the church in Röcken, I built a little chapel. Later it was a splendid temple with several rows of columns and high towers with winding staircases; then it was mine shafts with underground lakes and an interior lighting system; and finally, fortresses, which I built as a result of my third love, the military, spurred strongly by the Crimean War. I first dreamed up machines designed for laying siege (I wrote a little book on military strategy); then I got books on military and sea battles, made huge plans for outfitting ships, played out a large number of battles and sieges in which balls of flaming tar were catapulted; these were all means to the end of a great battle of nations, but I only got as far as equipping the armies. My love of the soldier's life showed itself in my completion of a huge military lexicon; but the decline of my interest occurred when Sebastopol fell. Thereupon a so-called *Theater des arts [sic]* led me to the stage; we ourselves tried to compose and produce plays, the first one being *The Gods on Olympus.* At the same time, already in my ninth year, came my inclination to poetry, and

my modest attempts were repeated year after year. Only in my eleventh year did I turn to church music and finally to my own compositions. . . . My love of painting too stems from this period, prodded by the annual art exhibits.—These inclinations do not follow one another directly but are interwoven, so that it is impossible to define the beginning and the end of each one. Then come my later preoccupations with literature, geology, astronomy, mythology, the German language (Old High German), and so on, in such a way that the following groups can be identified:

1. Enjoyment of nature: a) geology
                          b) botany
                          c) astronomy

2. Enjoyment of art: a) music
                          b) poetry
                          c) painting
                          d) theater

3. Imitations of actions and pursuits:
                          a) military projects
                          b) architecture
                          c) maritime projects

4. My favorite inclinations among the scholarly disciplines:
                          a) a good Latin style
                          b) mythology
                          c) literature
                          d) German language.

5. My inner drive to universal education, which embraces all the above and adds quite a few new things:

Languages	*Arts*
1. Hebrew	1. Mathematics
2. Greek	2. Music
3. Latin	3. Poetry
4. German	4. Painting
5. English	5. Sculpture
6. French	6. Chemistry
etc.	7. Architecture
	etc.

Imitations	*Disciplines*
1. Military science	1. Geography
2. Maritime science	2. History
3. Knowledge of the sundry trades	3. Literature
4. etc.	4. Geology
	5. Natural history
	6. Antiquity
	etc.

and above all, religion, the solid basis of all knowledge!

Great is the realm of knowledge, *infinite* our investigation of the truth!
(J *1*, 152–53)

Schulpforta did not satisfy Nietzsche's cravings in all these fields. Indeed, he seems to have worked harder for the literary club that he formed in 1860 with his Naumburg friends, Krug and Pinder, which they called "Germania," than for his school. Each of the three members committed

Naumburg friends and members of "Germania," Gustav Krug and Wilhelm
Pinder. Photos: Stiftung Weimarer Klassik. GSA 101/275 and 101/376.

himself to composing one musical or literary work each month, submitting it to the other two
members for constructive, candid criticism. It is no surprise that Nietzsche was far more ambitious
in his creative labors and far more drastic in his criticism than his two beleaguered and increasingly
sheepish friends. Even before the club was founded, Nietzsche and Pinder would exchange writing
assignments. In the spring of 1859 Nietzsche wrote to his Naumburg chum (B *1*, 56):

> Please send me some sort of theme for a paper in German, preferably a speech or an essay.
> I think I'll have some free time during the days following the exams and I have to keep in
> practice, otherwise I'll lose the knack.—Here is a theme for you:

> *On Divine and Human Freedom.*

> Maybe you can find an hour or two to reflect on the matter and write about it. Freedom
> is one of the most important points, you know. Just pose the questions What is freedom?
> Who is free? What is freedom of will? etc. Farewell for now, my dear Wilhelm, and often
> think of and write to

> > Your

> > Fr. W. Nietzsche

> *Nostra semper manet amicitia!* — — — [May our friendship last forever!]

Nietzsche concluded one review of a sheaf of poems by Pinder (whom he never confused
with Pindar!) as follows: "What W. Pinder cannot shake off, and what prevents him from coming up
with scarcely a single purely lyrical product, is a certain aridity of feeling, a certain sclerosis of the
imagination, and insufficient consistency in the development of artistic form" (J *2*, 219). As the
official chronicler of "Germania," Nietzsche urged his fellow members not to "inflict damage on
the sacred statutes" of their literary club, which threatened to dissolve "in inner dispersion, disinte-
gration, and apathy" (J *2*, 90). After two years Nietzsche was the only one submitting work, and by

Schulpforta. An early photograph of the road approaching the chapel from the main entrance. Photograph taken from the chapel roof. Photo: Stiftung Weimarer Klassik. GSA 101/597.

August 1863 "Germania" was officially—and no doubt officiously—disbanded.[4] Perhaps the lasting fruit of it for Nietzsche, apart from the opportunity it gave him to hone his skills as a writer and critic, was infection with Gustav Krug's passion for the "new music," that of Wagner in particular, a passion of which Nietzsche at first haughtily disapproved. Music could work for the church or for sin, and Nietzsche still preferred that it work for the church. Yet Krug forced his young friend to *listen* to Wagner's music, and the conversion, realized finally by Wagner's *Tristan und Isolde* (1865), became inevitable.

Among Nietzsche's many literary productions during these years, whether for Schulpforta or "Germania," one may single out a few for comment. In April 1859, at age fourteen, he composed a one-act play entitled *Prometheus*. If the gods on Olympus long fascinated him, Nietzsche proved to be even more intrigued by the philanthropic Titan who according to Aeschylus (whom Nietzsche had read by then) both helped to establish Zeus's rule and predicted its imminent end. The theme of the death of gods would never lose its fascination for Nietzsche. A later play, *The Conspiracy of Philotas,* actually featured Alexander the Great, who was himself viewed as a nascent god. When in later years Nietzsche drew up plans for a drama on the pre-Socratic philosopher, physician, statesman, and magus, Empedocles of Acragas, it was Empedocles' self-understanding vis-à-vis the gods that intrigued him: Empedocles mourned the disappearance of "his" gods, those of the sky, but now declared himself a loyal son of the Earth.

An alert, merciless critic's eye always scrutinized Nietzsche's own dramas and tragedies. His early *Prometheus* was followed by his own sardonic critique of the play, which spoofed the Romantic writers of the past, the philistine public of the present, and the neophyte tragedian himself. The critique served as a kind of satyr-play to cap the tragedy, but it also betrayed something of a split in Nietzsche between creative artist and scathing critic. Finally, one cannot but acknowledge the quality of the writing itself, even in this very early piece: the style of the appended critique blast-

---

4. Nietzsche certainly never lost his penchant for acerbic criticism—one thinks of his later remarks on Wagner and Brahms, or his remarks to Erwin Rohde in 1868 on their friend Hermann Mushacke: "The poetic spark in our friend is not strong enough to kill an ox, but it is sufficient to anesthetize a human being, so that I have ardently begged him to stop playing with his hazardous fireworks" (B *2,* 306).

ed the miasma of piety and sanctimony that suffocated so much of the young Nietzsche's writing; as for the tragedy itself, composed in verse, there were lines in Nietzsche's *Prometheus* that echoed Hölderlin's *Death of Empedocles*.[5]

Indeed, Hölderlin himself soon became an object of Nietzsche's fervor. One of the most remarkable of his school essays is entitled "Letter to my friend, in which I recommend to him my favorite poet" (J *2,* 1–5). This epistolary essay on Hölderlin, dated October 19, 1861, four days after Nietzsche's seventeenth birthday, is remarkable in the first place simply because Hölderlin, now recognized as one of the most gifted poets in German literature, was at that time relatively little known. Nietzsche's five-page essay comments on some of the today most famous poems and hymns, the novel *Hyperion,* and the truncated play *The Death of Empedocles.* Nietzsche obviously has read everything he can get his hands on, and his comments are succinct and trenchant. He remarks on the "richness of thought" in the poet's œuvre, noting that Hölderlin is a "kindred soul" of "Schiller and Hegel." Of Hölderlin's tragedy, *The Death of Empedocles,* Nietzsche writes: "In the never-completed dramatic elegy 'Empedocles,' the poet unfolds his own nature for us. Empedocles' death results from both the pride of a god and a contempt for humankind, from both weariness with the Earth and pantheism. Whenever I read this work in particular, the whole of it causes me to tremble. A divine loftiness lives in this Empedocles" (J *2,* 4).

Nietzsche's German teacher, Professor Koberstein, for whose class the essay was written, gave it a mediocre grade. He added the following remonstrance: "I'd like to give the author some friendly advice: stick to poets who are healthier, more lucid, and more German" (N *1,* 80).

Among the school essays, two others stand out: "Fate and History," and "Freedom of Will and Fate," both written in April 1862, when Nietzsche was seventeen. These essays point forward to many of Nietzsche's preoccupations as a mature philosopher. Even though their author still finds his way back to the piety that surrounds his upbringing, the doubts are virulent, the ferment potent:

> Great revolutions impend as soon as the crowd has understood that all Christendom rests
> upon suppositions: the existence of God, immortality, the authority of the Bible, divine
> inspiration, and other such things will have become problems once and for all. I have tried
> to deny everything. Oh, tearing down is easy, but constructing! And even tearing down

---

5. For the sake of those echoes of Hölderlin, we will cite here a number of lines from Nietzsche's German text, since it is impossible to know what Hölderlin would sound like in English. The scene shows Prometheus's father Iapetos urging his son to capitulate to Zeus's power and join him in performing sacrifice to the Olympians:

> Iapetos: Drum da ich fest glaube
> daß unsre Wesen jene Himmlischen
> Verachten wie wir sie—
> Prometheus: Ein eigenes Verachten,
> Wenn du die Macht derselben über unsere setzt.
> Dies du, ich nie.

A translation of the sense at least might run as follows:

> Iapetos: For the reason that, as I firmly believe,
> those celestial ones despise creatures like us
> as much as we despise them—
> Prometheus: We shall come to despise ourselves
> if you acknowledge their power over our own.
> This, for you; for me, never.

If the play "fails," it is because Nietzsche has its "Chorus of Human Beings" awkwardly straddling the epochs of Aeschylus and a much later nonspecific Christianity. Nietzsche is not yet able to do what William Butler Yeats will do so brilliantly in "The Resurrection." But then, most fourteen-year-olds do not try.

seems easier than it is: we are so determined down to the heart's core by the impressions of our childhood, the influence of our parents, and our upbringing, that those deeply rooted prejudices are not so readily eradicated by rational arguments or mere force of will. The power of custom, the need for something loftier, the rupture with all that subsists, the dissolution of all forms of society, the doubt as to whether or not a mirage has led humanity astray for two millennia, the feeling of one's own impropriety and boldness: all these things do battle with one another, and the battle is not decided until painful experiences and mournful events finally guide us back again to the old faith of our childhood. (J *2,* 55–56)

The same essay, "Fate and History," goes on to adumbrate Nietzsche's lifelong preoccupation with "becoming" rather than "being," his question concerning time and eternity, and his later "thought of thoughts," the eternal return of the same:

We scarcely know whether humanity itself is but a stage or period in universal history, or becoming; whether it is but an arbitrary epiphany of God. Is the human being perhaps no more than the development of stone through the medium of the plant, that is, an animal? Would not the fulfillment of humankind be achieved here, and would not history be a part of this development? Does such eternal becoming never come to an end? What are the mainsprings of this vast mechanical clock? They are concealed. Yet they are the same as those at work in the vast clock we call history. Events constitute the face of the clock. The hands move relentlessly forward from hour to hour, until they reach twelve and begin their course all over again: a new cosmic period commences. (J *2,* 56)

Across the entire range of his early writings, one is struck most of all by the following traits: fascination with the problem of the succession of the gods, the essential background of all tragedy; captivation by Byronic and Shakespearean heroes, by Manfred and Macbeth, the types he is already calling "superhuman"; an interest in the contrast between northern and southern Europe, the Nordic-tragic and the Italian-satiric characters, as in his short story "Capri and Helgoland"; an interest in prehistoric societies and in the origins of human memory, as in the essays "Hunters and Fishers" and "The Childhood of Peoples"; fascination with a kind of conflict that could have involved him only indirectly (or spectrally), that between father and son, as in the many poems, plays, musical compositions, and essays involving the Ostrogoth king, Ermanarich. His extended essay, "Ermanarich, King of the Ostrogoths: A Historical Sketch," completed in Naumburg on July 3, 1861, while he was still sixteen, he considered the best piece of work he had done at Pforta. A

Schulpforta. Detail of the chapel.

passage from this essay helps explain why the Ermanarich saga, which took him to the Nordic *Edda,* engaged him over a period of five years, pursuing him from Pforta to Bonn and Leipzig:

> It is a well-known fact that northerly peoples draw everything that in Germany still occupies the realm of historical luminosity and humaneness into the terrifying, the savagely sublime, and the mysterious. . . . That twilight of the gods, when the sun turns black and the earth sinks into the sea, when the cyclone of fire surrounds the all-nourishing world tree and its flames lick the sky, is the most grandiose invention that the genius of humankind ever devised, never surpassed in the literature of all periods, infinitely bold and fertile, yet dissolving in enchanting harmonies. (J *1,* 296–97)

Finally, it is regrettable that only the smallest fragments of Nietzsche's essay "On the Essence of Music" survive: for the composition of oratorios, *Lieder,* and pieces for piano accompanied all the literary production we have been citing here. We can assert perhaps only two things concerning his early views of music: first, he understood it to be the very heart of Greek tragedy, particularly in the choruses (J *2,* 374 ff.); second, in spite of his musical and religious conservatism, he defined the essence of music as "the *daimonic"* (J *2,* 172; B *1,* 293), no doubt related to what he would later call the *Dionysian.*

Both writing and composing seemed perfect occupations for a solitary. At age fourteen Nietzsche observed, "In general, it was always my plan to write a little book and then to read it myself. I am still possessed by this little piece of vanity" (J *1,* 11). He might have written those words at age forty as well: in a way, he was always writing books for everyone and no one. After once again describing his father's death (how many dozens of times does he invoke that death, in poems, journal entries, autobiographical sketches, and essays?), he concluded his *Curriculum vitae* with the remark: "That was the first period of my life, the fateful one, on the basis of which my entire life was formed—to be otherwise" (J *1,* 279–80). Nietzsche elaborated the "otherwise" of his infancy and childhood in the "Retrospect" to his very first autobiographical sketch, which shows both the pain and the piety that characterized his early life: "I have experienced many things by now, some joyful, some sad, some cheering, some depressing, but in all things God has led me securely, as a father leads a weak child. He has laid many painful things upon me already, but I acknowledge with devotion his tremendous power, which carries out everything so magnificently. I am firmly resolved to devote myself to his service forever" (J *1,* 31). "Forever" would last until the summer semester of 1864 at Bonn, although cracks in the façade of the little pastor's piety, as we have seen, had shown themselves many years earlier.

Nietzsche's judgments concerning his main personality traits did not alter substantially over the years. In a text written at age eighteen he noted: "Seriousness easily taken to extremes—I might almost say, passionate seriousness—throughout the many facets of my relationships, in mourning and in joy, even at play . . ." (J *2,* 120). Two years later, on the eve of his graduation from Pforta, he wrote: "I am convinced that precisely this death, the death of so exceptional a father, denied me all paternal assistance and guidance for my later life; further, it planted in my soul the seeds of seriousness and reflectiveness" (J *3,* 67). He added that an almost "fanatical zeal" propelled even his childhood play, citing the fact that he wrote a little book of instructions for each game in which he and his playmates engaged. Now, as he was preparing to graduate from secondary school and begin his university studies, Nietzsche reflected on the devotion to scholarship that had become his principal trait. The nineteen-year-old admitted that he was inclined in so many directions at once that he might well spread himself out too thin; he feared he would become an autodidact, a "Know-It-All," a Jack-of-all-disciplines, master of none. He was counting on an opposite tendency he saw in him-

Nietzsche as a university student in Leipzig, 1865–66. Photo: Stiftung Weimarer Klassik. GSA 101/7.

self, namely, the proclivity to trace every individual matter as far back to its origin and spawning ground as possible, hoping that this tendency to depth—the hallmark of the later genealogist—would overcome the temptation to dabble in everything. A letter to his mother, written years earlier, on May 2, 1863, expressed this same worry:

> As far as my future is concerned, it is the practical considerations that worry me. The decision about what I shall study will not come all by itself. Hence I myself must think it through, then choose; and it is this choice that is giving me problems. To be sure, I shall endeavor to devote myself wholly to whatever I study, but that only makes the selection more difficult, for I must choose the discipline in which I may dare hope to achieve something whole. And how deceptive these hopes often are! How easily one lets oneself be carried away by some momentary preference, a venerable family tradition, or someone's particular wishes, so that the choice of one's profession appears to be a lottery in which there are lots of losers but very few winners. Now, I am also in the particularly unenviable position of having interests in quite a few of the most distinct disciplines; satisfying them in a well-rounded way would make me a learned man but hardly a professional workhorse. It is clear to me that I must cast off some of these interests. It is likewise clear to me that I shall have to acquire some new interests. Yet which are to be the unlucky ones that I must toss overboard?—Perhaps the very children I love best! (B *1,* 239–40)

As we have seen, the tendency to be interested in too much was reflected in the drive to "universal knowledge," on the model of Alexander von Humboldt, the drive that Nietzsche says characterized him as a child; certainly his desire to inventory and classify his learning and his creative accomplishments reflected this drive, as did the hundreds of sketches by the budding philologist. While Nietzsche fulfilled the assignments Professor Ritschl gave him at Leipzig, his overweening desire was to write a history of Greek literature and philosophy—all of it. Later, when he felt that philology was too limited a discipline, he dreamed of returning to the university to study chemistry, physics, and medicine. Philosophers nowadays are fond of contrasting Nietzsche and Hegel, the latter a lover of systems and encyclopedias, the former ostensibly a dogged antisystematist. Yet the young Nietzsche often dreamed Hegelian dreams, and was fascinated by the word and the project of "encyclopedia" (J *4,* 3).

His retrospect on Schulpforta, composed at the end of his university career in Leipzig and on the eve of his career as a professor of philology in Basel, was both critical and affirmative: he suspected that the "homogenizing compulsion" of his schedule in the walled city-state of Pforta had forced him to neglect many aspects of his artistic development. Yet he also acknowledged that the discipline of philology had given him a center of scholarly gravity and a handful of models—a few teachers and advisors—whose example he could safely follow. His thoughtful look back at his education as a whole (he was now twenty-four years of age) reads as follows:

> My education in all its principal aspects was relegated to me myself. My father, a Protestant country pastor in Thuringia, died all too early: what I never had was the strict and skillful guidance of a manly intellect. When I started at Schulpforta, still a mere boy, I came to know only a surrogate for this paternal upbringing: the homogenizing discipline of a highly ordered school. However, precisely this well-nigh military compulsion, which treats the individual coolly and superficially because it is meant to work on the group as a whole, once again caused me to fall back on my own devices. I rescued my private inclinations and efforts from the monotonous regularity, lived by secretly cultivating particular arts, tried by means of an excessive striving for universal knowledge and enjoyment to shatter the paralysis of a schedule shaped by rules and regulations. A number of extrinsic contingencies were lacking, otherwise I would have tried back then to become a musician. For I had felt the strongest pull to music ever since I was nine years old. In that blessed state in which one does not yet know the limits of one's talent and assumes everything one loves to be attainable, I jotted down numberless compositions and developed a knowledge of musical theory that was somewhat more than that of a dilettante. Only in the final period of my life in Pforta, through correct insight into myself, did I surrender all plans for the life of an artist. Philology was now to fill the vacuum thus created. (J *5,* 252–53; cf. B *2,* 75)

Main portal of the chapel at Pforta. ". . . The lessons [in the afternoon] last until 3:50. Then we have our afternoon snack. . . . Then our monitor conducts a reading hour, during which we write exercises in Greek, Latin, or mathematics. At 5:00 there is recess, then recitation hours last until 7:00. . . . Then we can walk in the school garden until 8:30. After that comes evening prayer, and at 9:00 we go to bed. . . . That is the usual order of the day in Pforta" (Journal entry, Pforta, August 18 and 19, 1859; J *1,* 131). Photo: Stiftung Weimarer Klassik. GSA 101/598.

The Leipzig retrospective is largely negative and consistently self-deprecating. By the age of twenty, it seems, Nietzsche was a failed artist who had accepted sanctuary in academia. Yet if artistic endeavors and scholarship were the two poles of this retrospect, the reference to *philosophical seriousness* was already there:

> A certain philosophical seriousness has preserved me from a vague kind of dissolution into the many directions of my talents. That seriousness was never satisfied except in the face of naked truth and in the refusal to shrink back—indeed, in a proclivity for hard and harmful consequences. The feeling that universality would not allow me to reach the ultimate grounds of things drove me into the arms of rigorous science.
>
> There was also the longing to rescue myself from the abrupt emotional shifts in my artistic inclinations by sailing into the haven of objectivity.
>
> One is honest with oneself through either shame or vanity. (J 5, 250)

Thus, even on the verge of his move to Basel, Nietzsche had not wholly yielded to his fate, was not entirely "resigned to be a philologist"; he had not totally capitulated to the discipline that had saved him from theology. And yet the retrospect is all about resignation and renunciation. Ostensibly, both philosophy proper and art pertain to an earlier, already abandoned stage of his development: "When I look back and see how I moved from art to philosophy, and from philosophy to sci-

Nietzsche's fraternity at Bonn, "Franconia." Nietzsche (with the dramatic pose) is in the second row from the bottom. Note the fraternity's monogram, inscribed on a beer keg. Photo: Stiftung Weimarer Klassik. GSA 101/38.

ence, and in science to an ever narrower domain, it almost seems to me to be a conscious renunciation" (J *5*, 251). At the tender age of twenty-four he was ready to declare his formation finished: "I am inclined to think that a human being at twenty-four years of age has the most important aspects of his life already behind him, even if he only later brings to the light of day whatever it is that will have made his life worth living" (J *5*, 252). With two dozen years behind him, Nietzsche knew that even if his life was all over he would still have to count on being a late bloomer. What he could not know was whether the ends would justify the beginnings, which Hölderlin says are always "difficult."

Concerning the "wasted year" in Bonn little need be said. Nietzsche did follow some of the lecture courses taught by his future mentor, Friedrich Ritschl, professor of classical Greek philology first in Bonn then later in Leipzig. Yet he spent more time going to concerts and plays than attending classes, and in all things spent more money (for example, on a rented piano) than his mother could possibly afford to send him. In mid-November he wrote his mother and sister, "An hour ago I was at a supremely noble concert, fabulous luxury, all the womenfolk rouged a fiery red, everywhere English spoken *no speak inglich"* (B *2*, 19–20). Above all, it was a social year, spent with the students of the "Franconia," a fraternity to which many Pforta alumni were drawn. Many of his letters from these days sported the fraternity's spiffy monogram, which became Fritz's own. In Bonn, Nietzsche soon gained the reputation he deserved and even coveted: the students found him to be *moquant*, reserved at best, sarcastic at worst:

> Among the students I am taken to be an authority on music and an odd fellow besides, just like all the other Pforta alumni who belong to the Franconia. I am not by any means disliked, although my manner is somewhat *moquant* and I am taken to be a satirical type. This characterization of me in the judgments of other people will not be without interest to you. I may append my own judgment, which is that I will not let the *moquant* part prevail, that I am often unhappy, that I am too often morose, and that I am delighted to needle just a little bit—not only myself but the others too. . . . Hold me in your love, in spite of this letter. (B *2*, 43)

That mocking attitude prevailed when Nietzsche left Bonn for Naumburg at Easter in 1865 and refused to attend religious services: not only had he rejected the study of theology, which was his mother's long-standing dream for him, but he had also renounced the faith such study was meant to nurture. In a letter to his sister, young Nietzsche expressed his growing independence: "In our investigations, are we looking for repose, peace, happiness? No, only for the truth, even if it should be supremely intimidating and repulsive. . . . Here the paths that human beings will take diverge: if you wish to seek peace of mind and happiness, then believe; if you wish to be an apostle of truth, then investigate" (B *2*, 60–61). Not many months later, he expressed to his mother and sister his skepticism concerning duty in general, a skepticism that may only have disguised a fanatical rigor. He did so in terms that no doubt confused the sister and enraged the mother:

> "Do your duty!" Very well, honored friends, I shall do it, or strive to do it, but where does it cease? Whence do I know all that it is my duty to fulfill? And suppose I lived sufficiently in accord with duty: is a beast of burden more than a human being, inasmuch as it fulfills what is demanded of it more rigorously than human beings do? Has one done enough for one's humanity when one has satisfied the demands of those relations into which we enter at birth? Who commands us to let ourselves be determined by such relations?
>
> If we did not wish matters to be so, if we resolved to pay heed only to ourselves and to compel our fellow human beings to acknowledge us as we are, what then? What is it then that we want? Is it a matter of fabricating as bearable an existence for ourselves as we can?

The city of Bonn on the Rhine, viewed from the roof of the Hotel Royale. Photo: Stiftung Weimarer Klassik. GSA 101/513.

Two paths, my dears: either one makes a modest effort and gets used to living within the narrowest possible limits, with the candlewick of spirit nicely cropped, seeking wealth and enjoying the world's diversions; or one knows that life is squalid, that we are all the more life's slaves the more we want to enjoy it, so that one relinquishes life's goods, practices renunciation, is austere toward oneself and amicable toward others—because we feel compassion for our comrades in squalor—in short, one lives according to the stringent demands of original Christianity, though not the current saccharine-sweet fuzzy sort. Christianity is not something you can "go along with" *en passant* or because it is in fashion.

And is life then bearable? Yes indeed, because its burdens constantly diminish, and no cincture binds us to it any longer. It is bearable because it can be jettisoned painlessly. (B *2*, 95–96)

A year later, in Leipzig, he wrote his friend Carl von Gersdorff about his thoughts concerning duty, thoughts occasioned by an electrical storm: "What was man and his restless will to me! What was the eternal 'Thou shalt' and 'Thou shalt not' to me? How different the lightning, the storm, the hail, free powers, without ethics! How happy, how forceful they are, pure will, without the obfuscations of the intellect!" (B *2*, 122). At about the same time, his facetious letters home could not conceal how remote Naumburg was to him now: "I cannot reasonably ratiocinate a reason why I should write you any more. I don't have any news, my philological results don't interest you, philosophical discussions you dislike, I've already negotiated with you concerning a letter, money, and laundry, and the only thing that's left to say is hello-good-bye. . . . With that, I commend myself to you with a bow and a crook in my spine" (B *2*, 132–33).

While still at Bonn Nietzsche did manage to get himself a scar across the bridge of his nose, thanks to a friendly duel with a student named Delius. He also managed to lay a wreath on Robert Schumann's grave, Schumann being his favorite composer during the Pforta and Bonn years. With regard to more serious academic pursuits, one might add a revealing tendency on the student Nietzsche's part: whenever he did go to lectures and seminars, he paid less attention to the material being taught than to the manner in which it was being presented. This was yet another expression of his pedagogical drive, so strong in him from his earliest years, through the Pforta and "Germania" period, on into the decades of his Basel professorship and his nomadic wanderings. Concerning the year in Bonn and "Franconia," Nietzsche wrote the following in his Leipzig retrospect:

When after a six-year residence I bade adieu to Schulpforta, a strict but efficacious school-mistress, I went to Bonn. Here I noticed with astonishment how well taught but how miserably educated a state-supported pupil enters the university. He has thought through many things for himself, and now he lacks the skill to express these thoughts. So far he has experienced nothing of the formative influence of women; he believes he can get to know life from books and traditions, and yet everything now seems to him so foreign and unpleasant. That's how things went with me in Bonn: not all the means I selected in order to overcome that unfortunate condition may have been well chosen. . . . (J 5, 254)

To Hermann Mushacke in Bonn Nietzsche was more candid. He wrote Mushacke from Naumburg on August 30, 1865:

You can perhaps understand why I look back on Bonn with feelings of unpleasantness. True, I am still too close in time to the matters and the moods I experienced there. The bitter chalice of the present, the actual, does not allow me yet to appreciate the real core of it. For I hope that from the standpoint of memory this year too will happily be registered as a necessary link in the chain of my development. For the moment, that is impossible. It still seems to me that in many respects I wasted the year, that it was a mistake. My sojourn in the fraternity seems to me—to say it openly—a *faux pas,* at least for last summer semester. I transgressed my principle not to devote myself to things and people once I have managed to get to know them.

A thing like this is its own punishment. I am very upset with myself. (B *2,* 79–80)

And yet Bonn had not eradicated Nietzsche's familiar traits—his solitude, his tendency to meditation and self-observation, his earnestness, taciturnity, and even isolation. In December 1864, perhaps on New Year's Eve itself, Nietzsche wrote the following to his mother and sister:

I love New Year's Eves and birthdays. For they give us hours that we might often make for ourselves but only rarely do, hours when the soul stands still and can survey a stretch of its own development. Decisive leaps forward are born in such hours. My custom is to take up again the manuscripts and letters of the year flown by, and to jot down a few notes. For several hours one is sublimely beyond time; one almost steps outside of one's own development. One secures and certifies the past and receives encouragement and resolution to set off on one's ways once again. (B *2,* 34)

The move to the University of Leipzig in 1865 occurred because Nietzsche wanted to accompany his friend Paul Deussen there, and also because one of the most impressive of his Bonn professors, Ritschl, had accepted a professorship in Leipzig. Nietzsche noted with pride that

A view (taken at the turn of the twentieth century?) of the *Augusteum,* University of Leipzig. Photo: Stiftung Weimarer Klassik. GSA 101/544.

Goethe had registered at Leipzig a hundred years to the day before he himself had, and he embraced the Faustian precedent as an auspicious omen. During the period of transition between Bonn and Leipzig Nietzsche read widely in Hegel's philosophy. He wrote his friend Mushacke about his custom of washing Hegel down with coffee, noting that if he still got indigestion, he would take a David Friedrich Strauss pill, inasmuch as Strauss was only half a Hegel (B 2, 85). He had long been reading German translations of Ralph Waldo Emerson, who would remain a constant companion for many years. Yet Hegel's place was soon usurped by Kant and Schopenhauer. Nietzsche recounts his discovery of the latter's magnum opus in an old bookstore in Leipzig, above which he had his lodgings:

> At that time I was hovering in the air, all alone, with a few painful experiences and disappointments behind me, without anyone to help me, without principles to act on, without hopes, and without a single friendly memory. From morning till night I tried to fashion for myself a life that would suit me, a life that would be my own. . . . I was able to gather myself to myself in the blessed apartness of my apartment. If I met with any friends at all it was with Mushacke and von Gersdorff, who shared these intentions of mine.—Now, imagine in such circumstances what it must have been like to read Schopenhauer's magnum opus. For one day, while browsing through old Rohn's ancient books, I found that tome, which was utterly unknown to me, picked it up and leafed through it. I don't know what daimon it was that whispered to me, "Take this book home with you." At all events, it happened, despite my habit of not being too hasty with book purchases. At home I nestled into a corner of the sofa with the treasure I had found and began to let that vigorous, gloomy genius work his effects on me. Here every line screamed renunciation, denial, resignation; here I saw a mirror in which the world, life, and my own deepest soul were reflected back to me in horrific grandeur. Here the vast, disinterested solar eye of art gazed upon me. Here I saw sickness and recovery, exile and sanctuary, hell and heaven. The need for self-knowing, indeed, for self-gnawing, seized me violently. . . . Since I dragged all my qualities and all my endeavors before the forum of a gloomy self-contempt, I was bitter and unjust, I gave full head to the hatred I directed against myself. Bodily chastisements too played their part. Thus for two whole weeks I forced myself to stay up till 2 A.M. and to quit my bed at 6 A.M. on the dot. A nervous excitability overpowered me. Who knows to what degree of foolishness I would have goaded myself had not life's delectable decoys, the seductions of vanity, and the compulsion to regularity in my studies worked against it. (J 3, 297–98)

Nietzsche clearly adulated Schopenhauer as a man, Schopenhauer "as Educator," as he would later write. On January 31, 1866, he wrote his mother from Leipzig:

> I've set aside one evening a week on which Gersdorff and I read Greek together, and one evening every two weeks when he and Mushacke and I all go a-schopenhauering together. This philosopher has assumed a significant place in my thoughts and in my studies, and my respect for him waxes incomparably great. I also proselytize for him and lead certain other people (my cousin, for example) to him by the nose. Which hasn't been much use. For all dyed-in-the-wool Saxons follow one command alone: *primum vivere, deinde philosophari*, "live first, then philosophize" (B 2, 109)

To von Gersdorff, on April 7, 1866, he confessed that the three sources of recreation for him were Schumann's music, solitary walks, and his Schopenhauer (B 2, 121). Among the many things he admired about his dour mentor was the fact that Schopenhauer was clearly a good European. In the third of his *Untimely Meditations* Nietzsche was to write of Schopenhauer: "After a time, he was impervious to the limitations of nationality, and often quite acerbic concerning them; he lived in England, France, and Italy precisely as he lived in his homeland; he felt considerable sympathy for

The Philology Club of the University of Leipzig in 1867; Nietzsche is standing third from left, Erwin Rohde sitting second from right. Photo: Stiftung Weimarer Klassik. GSA 101/40.

the spirit of Spain. As a whole, he did not feel that it was a particular honor to have been born among Germans; and I really do wonder whether the recent political reconfigurations would have made him think any differently" (UB III, 7; *1,* 409). Yet no matter how genuine the adulation, Nietzsche resisted many of Schopenhauer's doctrines, especially his counsel of resignation in the face of life's tragic futility. For Nietzsche it was always a matter of a "pessimism of strength," a pessimism that could affirm the tragic character of existence and still say *yes* to its eternal recurrence.

At all events, the young philologist was thinking these kinds of thoughts while pursuing his linguistic and historical studies. Alongside his extensive notes on Hesiod and Homer, Aeschylus and Sophocles, Pythagoras and Democritus, as well as on the sources of Greek literature and philosophy generally, we find notes that can only be called "philosophical." Further, it is clear from letters of the last Leipzig years that Nietzsche became more and more concerned to develop a *style* of writing and thinking that was distinctively his own. He adopted as his motto the admonition of Pindar, γένοι᾽ οἷος ἐσσὶ, "Become the one you are!" For Nietzsche, such becoming would result less in an identity than in a style, or multiple styles. On April 4, 1867, he wrote to Paul Deussen:

> You will find it ridiculous that I devote so much energy to mixing the colors on my palette, ridiculous that I'm trying so hard to write in a tolerable style. Yet it is truly necessary, since I've neglected the matter for so long. Well, then, I avoid unnecessary erudition as strictly as I can. That takes a bit of self-overcoming. . . . My cerebral stomach gets upset when it is surfeited. Too much reading dulls the mind horribly. Most of our scholars would be worth more as scholars too if they were less full of scholarship. Don't eat too much at mealtime. (B *2,* 205–6)

On April 6 he wrote to von Gersdorff:

> I have to confess—and you will laugh at this—that what is costing me the greatest concern and labor is my German style (to say nothing of my Latin style: once I have confronted my mother tongue, I will turn to foreign languages). Now the blinders have fallen from my eyes: for too long I have been living in stylistic innocence. The categorical imperative,

"Thou shalt and must write" roused me. I tried something I hadn't tried since my years in the Gymnasium: I tried to write well, and suddenly the pen wilted in my hand. . . . Above all, a few cheerful spirits must be unfettered in my style, I have to learn to play, as on a keyboard, not merely pieces I have rehearsed but also improvised fantasias—as free as possible, yet still logical and beautiful. (B *2,* 208–9)

In August 1866 Nietzsche read Friedrich Albert Lange's *History of Materialism.* A letter to Mushacke written in November 1866 affirmed, "Kant, Schopenhauer, and this book by Lange—I don't need more" (B *2,* 184). The study of Kant became ever more intense during the years 1867–68. Nietzsche studied the third *Critique* of Kant, *The Critique of Judgment,* developing his own critique of its account of nature and the organism. Alongside notes on the recondite and fragmentary sources on pseudo-Suidas and Diogenes Laertius, and interspersed among essays written in Greek and Latin, one finds in Nietzsche's early writings an array of critical notes on the sad state of philology (culminating in his inaugural address at Basel, "Homer and Classical Philology") and agitated notes on the problem of teleological judgment and organic life in Kant's philosophy. At one point Nietzsche even considered writing a doctoral dissertation on the impact of physiological science on metaphysics since Kant (B *2,* 269; J *3,* 371–94).

The great friend of these Leipzig years was Erwin Rohde, the gifted classical Greek scholar. Like Nietzsche, Rohde was an enthusiast of Wagner; like Nietzsche, he was a loner. The letters of friendship they exchanged over the next decade are perhaps the most remarkable among Nietzsche's many correspondences. Only in the final years, after Nietzsche's break with Wagner, and after the radicality of Nietzsche's philosophy had alarmed Rohde, did they quarrel. Yet even in this relatively intimate correspondence one senses the reserve—ultimately the sense of radical isolation—that characterized Nietzsche from his earliest days.

In the fall of 1867 Nietzsche was called into the military service for one year. When his attempt to get himself stationed in Berlin foundered, he trained for the cavalry in Naumburg. He was certainly not immune to the heady Prussian spirit of the times, yet was never convinced by either blood or iron—not when the blood was for spilling, the iron for killing. When the war with Hapsburg Austria was declared, Nietzsche wrote: "One can learn a lot in such times. The ground that seemed firm and unshakable now trembles; masks fall from the faces they once concealed; selfish tendencies, now unveiled, reveal their repulsive physiognomy. Above all, however, one notices how slight the power of thought is" (B *2,* 138). The physical exertions of military life suited him, however, partly because they gave him a feeling of accomplishment, and partly because he still had plenty of time to continue his studies and concoct his "literary plans." He wrote to Rohde on November 3, 1867, signing off as "Friedrich Nietzsche, Cannoneer, 21ˢᵗ Batt., Cavalry Div. of Field Artillery Reg. No. 4":

Yes, my dear friend, if someday a daimon should direct you early in the morning, say, between five and six, to Naumburg and, as luck would have it, guide your steps in my direction: don't be petrified by the spectacle your senses present to you. Suddenly you are inhaling the atmosphere of a stable. In the faint glow of lanternlight phantoms loom. All about you there is a pawing of hooves, a whinnying, a brushing, and a clopping. In the midst of all this activity, a man decked out in the costume of a stable boy, as busy as he can be, is removing unspeakable and really quite untoward matter with his bare hands, or currying that old nag—I tremble when I look that figure in the face. By the dog! it is my very own figure.

A few hours later you see two steeds storming round the track, not without riders, one of whom resembles your friend quite closely. He rides his fiery, spirited Balduin and hopes that one day he will learn to ride really expertly, although (or rather, precisely because) he is now still riding on the blanket, using spurs and thighs, but *sans* riding-whip. He must also rapidly unlearn everything he once heard at the riding stables in Leipzig; above all, he must make every effort to sit in the saddle securely, the way a cavalryman ought. . . .

I assure you by the above-mentioned dog that my philosophy now has the opportunity to be of practical use to me. Every now and then I secretly whisper under the horse's belly, "Schopenhauer make haste to help me!" And when I come home exhausted and bathed in sweat, a glance at his portrait on my desk soothes me; or I open the *Parerga,* which, along with Byron, I now find more congenial than ever. (B *2,* 232–33)

He was proud to be the best rider among the thirty recruits in training, at least until in an over-enthusiastic leap into the saddle he shattered his breastbone on the pommel. The doctor located and repaired the torn pectoral muscles but failed to see the broken bone, and for five months Nietzsche did not recover from the severe infection that resulted. His "cure" at Bad Wittekind in the summer of 1868 and subsequent recuperation at home nevertheless granted him even more time for study.

As his competency in philology grew, so did his doubts concerning that discipline. He complained to Rohde about the "wriggling brood of philologists" at Leipzig, who scurried like moles after the worms and bugs of antiquity, never noticing what any of it had to do with "the compelling problems of life" (B *2,* 344). However, even though Nietzsche was doubtful about the state and status of philology, and the role he should play in it, he certainly preferred it to other fields of study. When he learned that his friend Paul Deussen had taken up theology in Tübingen, he expressed his horror in the face of his old nemesis—and then his relief when Deussen came to his senses and switched back to philology (B *2,* 145, 152, 161–63, and 202–3). Yet it was to Deussen that Nietzsche wrote in October 1868: "If I were to speak mythologically, I would say that I take philology to be a failed birth of the goddess Philosophy, a creature begotten upon her by an idiot or a cretin" (B *2,* 329). It was for the sake of this goddess, as well as the Muse of music, that Nietzsche eventually surrendered the science in which he had been so capably trained.

Nietzsche with Erwin Rohde and Carl von Gersdorff at the University of Leipzig, ca. 1867. Photo: Stiftung Weimarer Klassik. GSA 101/41.

Nietzsche's first meeting with Richard Wagner took place when he returned to his studies in the fall of 1868 at Leipzig. Wagner was visiting his sister and her husband, and learned of a young student who had been playing his music. He insisted on meeting him. Nietzsche was still ambivalent about "the music of the future," and only *Tristan* and *Die Meistersinger* received his unstinting acclamation. Yet this ambivalence was more generous than his earlier views: in October 1866 he had told von Gersdorff that the quality of the excerpts for piano from *The Valkyries* was "quite mixed"; the music was marked by both "great beauty" and "great ugliness," so that Wagner's final grade (A + -A = 0) was not very impressive (B *2*, 174). Yet when he finally met Wagner, who was born in the same year as Nietzsche's own father, he was fascinated by the man: his vitality, humor, and energy were overwhelming. "He is a fabulously lively and ardent man, he speaks very quickly and is quite witty, makes any small gathering a most cheerful occasion" (B *2*, 340). "Wagner, as I now know him, on the basis of his music, his poetic creations, his aesthetics, and last not least my fortunate meeting with him, is the liveliest illustration of what Schopenhauer calls a genius" (B *2*, 352). Nietzsche was ecstatic when at the end of the evening in Leipzig Wagner invited him to Tribschen, the villa he shared with Cosima von Bülow in Lucerne. Nietzsche would soon have the opportunity to pay such visits, since Lucerne was not far from Basel.

Meanwhile, Wagner's music was doing its work. Nietzsche wrote to Rohde: "I cannot calm my heart long enough to remain coolly critical of this music: every fiber, every nerve in me quivers; not for a long time have I experienced the lasting transport that occurs when I hear the *[Meistersinger]* overture" (B *2*, 332). Nietzsche, precisely as one who felt destined to be a hermit, envisaged the formation of a circle of intimate friends that encompassed Wagner, Rohde, and himself (B *2*, 356–57).

When Nietzsche studied Wagner's writings, he found them to be testimonies of a fellow Schopenhauerian. Wagner's plans to rejuvenate German culture as a whole struck a chord with Nietzsche's own strongly developed pedagogical drive. That drive ultimately vented itself in the kinds of cultural criticism we find in the *Untimely Meditations* of the early 1870s. Yet the culture critic vied with the philologist and the philosopher, and even with the enthusiast of the natural sciences. By 1869 Nietzsche had published several articles in well-known journals of classical philology. These articles attracted the attention of Ritschl's colleagues in Basel. At the very moment when Nietzsche was making plans (with Rohde, whom he earlier had urged to pursue a career in philology: B *2*, 275) to drop his philological studies altogether and take up the study of chemistry, the call to a professorship came from Basel. It was a remarkable call, since Nietzsche had not finished his doctoral dissertation, much less his second or "Habilitation" thesis. He was twenty-four years old, one of the youngest appointees to a professorship in German academic history. Nietzsche did not know whether to whoop or weep. In the end he did neither, but headed for Basel with a firm resolve to advance his discipline and reform the educational institutes of Germany and Switzerland. To Rohde, on January 16, 1869, he wrote:

> The prospects are probable, indeed certain, that in the near future I will be invited to become a professor at Basel University: I must prepare myself to assume the duties of an academic from this coming Easter on. . . . Now, of course, a little demon can really toss all this overboard, and if that happens, I'll be the last one to hang his head. . . . We really are the fools of fate. Just last week I was going to write you and propose that we study chemistry together, tossing philology where it belongs—up into the ancestral attic. Now old devil fate lures me with a philology professorship. . . .
>
> One more thing. Recently, Richard Wagner wrote me a most cordial letter—to my considerable joy. And from now on, Lucerne will not be out of my reach. Long live art and friendship! (B *2*, 358-60)

It is probably accurate to say that the impending professorship at Basel was neither a completely new beginning nor a proper end. It was a detour and a distraction, although one for which Nietzsche had to be grateful. He was obviously in high spirits when he wrote his mother and sister on January 17, 1869, insisting that they congratulate him on his appointment, signing off with this: "Ha ha ha! (He laughs.) Ha ha ha! (Once again he laughs.) Bang! (Door slams. Exeunt.) F N" (B *2*, 362). A month later he sent them his calling card (B *2*, 370), with the following exhortation:

Spread the news!

FRIEDRICH NIETZSCHE.
Specially Appointed Professor of
Classical Philology (with a salary of 800 Thaler)
at the University of Basel.

If his friend since Pforta days, Paul Deussen, could not conceal his jealousy, and if Nietzsche was merciless in pointing out to him the inanity of such jealousy (B *2*, 374–75), Carl von Gersdorff received this more thoughtful and more apprehensive missive from the new professor of classical Greek:

> The zero-hour is upon me: this is the last evening I will spend in my homeland. Tomorrow morning it's out into the wide wide world, to take up a new and unaccustomed profession, to enter into a heavy and oppressive atmosphere of duty and work. Once again I must take my leave: the golden age of free and unconstrained activity, of the sovereign present moment, of enjoyment of art and the world as a nonparticipant, or at least as a scarcely involved observer—this period is over, and it will never return again. Now the strict goddess Daily Duty rules. . . . So far I feel no trace of the obligatory professorial hunchback. To become a philistine, ἄνθρωπος ἄμουσος [an uncultivated human being], a man of the herd—Zeus forfend, and all the Muses! Farewell! (B *2*, 385)

"The zero-hour is upon me." Thus one is compelled to think of ends as well as beginnings. When we examine the medical records kept in the infirmary at Pforta, we are not struck by anything in particular concerning Nietzsche's health from 1859 to 1864. The common cold was common enough in young Nietzsche, yet all else seemed normal. There are disturbing references to migraine headache caused by eyestrain, as well as a nervous disposition inherited from his father—ironically, the nervousness seemed to be exacerbated by music, especially the "new music." Only long walks in the fresh air seemed to ameliorate those migraines. After treating Nietzsche for a serious bout of headache in 1862, the doctor noted:

> Nietzsche was sent home for further convalescence. He is a full-blooded, stocky man with a conspicuously fixed stare, myopic, and often plagued by headache at various places on the skull. His father, conceived when his own parents were already on in years, died young, due to liquefaction of the brain. Our young Nietzsche was conceived in the period when the father was already ill. There are not as yet any worrying symptoms. However, in the light of the antecedents, circumspection is called for. (N *1*, 129)

While it is untrue that Nietzsche was conceived during the period of his father's illness—Little Joseph may have been, but Friedrich Wilhelm and Elisabeth were not—the doctor's note remains disturbing. It adds one more cipher to the complex formula that will spell Nietzsche's end, or ends.

Nietzsche's letters home are perhaps more instructive than the Pforta medical records. Here is but a small sample: on January 30, 1861, he complains that he is very ill, that the headaches are "once

Friedmatt, "Tranquil Meadows," the Basel University Psychiatric Clinic.

again so intense" that he cannot work, adding that he is plagued by a sore throat and a laryngeal infection; on February 16 he writes that he is "fed up" with "these headaches," which are recurrent, and says that only long walks will cure them; on October 28 he writes, "I must unfortunately give you the unpleasant news that I once again have to go to the infirmary"; he complains of swelling in the throat, headache at the back of the skull, and rapid pulse; "along with that, a terrible cold sweat, and the general blahs"; in mid-February 1862 he reports, "I can't write any more, I am still exhausted, and my head is splitting"; on August 25 he complains once again of his "fatal headaches," which have put him in the infirmary for a week; he hopes that if he can avoid "all excitement" the headaches will go away (B *1,* 143, 147, 184, 196, 222). He complains less often about his eyes, although he is always demanding new and stronger spectacles to help him with his reading. During his final year at Pforta he notes, "My eyes are obviously worse: working by lamplight strains them and causes me a lot of inconvenience" (B *1,* 275). He plans to take better care of his eyes when he goes to the university. Yet more baneful illnesses await him there.

According to a number of accounts contemporary to Nietzsche, it was in Bonn—or, more precisely, in Cologne—that Nietzsche contracted the syphilitic infection that would eventually kill him. We know so little of Nietzsche's erotic life—about those "means" that he perhaps unwisely selected in order to expand his repertory of "formative influences" at Bonn—that it stretches the imagination to get him into a position where infection seems even remotely possible. One is driven to wonder, for example, whether the infection might have been picked up during his treatment of wounded soldiers during the Franco-Prussian War. In any case, his colleagues in "Franconia" proclaimed him a man "untouched by woman"; their raillery disturbs the otherwise confident diagnosis of syphilis.

An uncertain tradition has it that Nietzsche was treated twice during his first Leipzig year (1865–66) for syphilis—an "early luetic meningitis." Yet from the total lack of references to such an infection in Nietzsche's letters, diaries, or works, and from other remarks he *did* make later concerning the disease, one must surmise that if indeed he had syphilis he knew nothing about it. The medical records from his physical examinations in Basel and Jena two decades later, in 1889, leave little doubt that it was syphilis that caused his progressive paralysis.[6] Nevertheless, one has to concede that if ever a case of illness was "overdetermined," it was Nietzsche's. The pressure under which he worked was always intense: in 1888, the final year of his active life, he completed six books and many hundreds of pages of notes and fragments. His mood during those final months in Turin was "autumnal," yet also increasingly frenetic, as he finished the books he somehow sensed would be his last. There also remain nagging doubts, not only in his mind but also in ours, concerning the disposition to mental illness or cerebral infirmity inherited from his father. However, the symptomatology of luetic (syphilitic) infection defeats all other interpretations of Nietzsche's illness: too many symptoms confirm the diagnosis, no matter how skeptical one may be about the time or place or manner in which Nietzsche may have contracted the disease.

One should perhaps not linger on those final ten years of madness and worsening paralysis, the dreary sequence of dismal ends. They are defined by Nietzsche's decreasing control over and awareness of his behavior; his increasing torpor and regression; and his occasional aggression. Throughout these years, however, Nietzsche remained conscious, aware (though sometimes only vaguely, and always with confusion) of what was going on around him; only in the final months of the paralysis did he lose touch altogether. His parasympathetic nervous system remained intact, although some disturbance in his motor activity was noted by the doctors who examined him in 1889; by 1893 he was in a wheel chair, or sitting on a sofa or on a bench out on the veranda, or lying in bed. Above all, however, the spirochete wreaked havoc on his ability to gauge and control his emotional reactions—for example, when he listened to music or improvised on the piano—and it put a stop to his work. By the end of 1888 Nietzsche had ruptured relations with several old friends, had tried the patience of his publisher with countless demands and counterdemands, and had abandoned his philosophical plans in order to contrive grandiose political plots; by the end of 1889 there were neither plans not plots, except the ones that terrified him in his delirium. In the periods of apparent remission, during the years 1889 and 1890, Nietzsche dreamed of nothing more adventurous than a return to university teaching in Basel.

Franz Overbeck and Jacob Burckhardt received disturbing missives from Nietzsche during the first week of January 1889. Upon the urging of Burckhardt and Professor Ludwig Wille, head of the psychiatric clinic in Basel, Overbeck traveled to Turin on January 7. He found Nietzsche cowering in a room he had rented from Davide Fino, in the building that contained the Galleria Subalpina, located on the Piazza Carlo Alberto across from the Palazzo Carignano. Nietzsche had "deteriorated terribly" (N *3,* 39), a victim of the "sacred tumult" of his orgiastic god (N *3,* 42). Overbeck resolved to get Nietzsche back to Basel as soon as possible. With the help of a German-Jewish dentist practicing in Turin, they made the return journey on the afternoon of January 9. On the morn-

6. On this entire question, see Pia Daniela Volz, *Nietzsche im Labyrinth der Krankheit: Eine medizinisch-biographische Untersuchung* (Würzburg: Königshausen & Neumann, 1990), esp. pp. 365-70, 379-85, and 390-415.

Views of the Jena Clinic for the Care and Cure of the Insane. "The sky had cleared. Long, glistening rays played on the broad fields, with now and then the fleeting shadows of hurrying clouds. For a long time our eyes dwelled on the insane asylum, to which an unhappy chain of thoughts so readily attached itself" ("My Summer Trip," written in 1860 at age fifteen; J *1,* 195).

ing of January 10 Nietzsche was admitted to Professor Wille's clinic, "Tranquil Meadows," on the northwestern outskirts of Basel; he was diagnosed as having *paralysis progressiva* brought on by a syphilitic infection. The medical charts at Basel, drawn up during the eight days of his confinement there, referred to sleeplessness, nervous agitation, singing and yodeling, along with "uninterrupted motor excitation" (N *3,* 50).

On January 14 Nietzsche's mother visited him in Basel. She insisted that he be transferred to the Jena clinic headed by Professor Otto Binswanger, to allow her to be closer to her son. (Elisabeth was in Paraguay, founding "Nueva Germania" with her husband, Bernhard Förster; it was not until their leadership of the colony foundered, and only after her husband committed suicide on June 3, 1889, that she returned to Germany and assumed control of her brother's affairs.) The transfer to Jena occurred during the night of January 17–18. After a difficult train journey, during which Nietzsche several times exploded in rage against his mother and was restrained by Overbeck and two assistants, the patient arrived at his new home for the next fourteen months. The orange brick of the clinic building, with its turret towers and caged windows, enclosed snow white corridors, padded linoleum stairwells, and bolted doors. An English garden lay around the back, a rose garden in front.

Concerning Nietzsche's internment in the Jena clinic, we may solicit two witnesses, the first a fellow patient, the second a medical student. The fellow patient recalled:

> It was in the year 1888–89, when I was at the psychiatric clinic in Jena for treatment. What most interested me was a patient who was always quiet, off by himself, holding crumpled slips of paper in his hand. They read, "Professor Friedrich Nietzsche." He spoke this name many times each day. . . . What most interested him was one of the clinic caps, the so-called "progress caps," which he wore from morning till night, and which no one dared take from him. . . . What most irritated him was their checking up on him after he returned from a walk, when they would find stones and all sorts of things in his pockets. He loved to go bathing. . . . I once did a sketch of him as he sat there quietly. . . . When I was finished, I gave him the picture. He stood up, shook my hand, and said to himself, "Professor Nietzsche. . . ."[7]

7. This and the following quotation appear in Volz, *Nietzsche im Labyrinth seiner Krankheit;* Volz is here citing Sander L. Gilman, ed., *Begegnungen mit Nietzsche,* second edition (Bonn: Bouvier, 1985), vol. 98 of the series *Studien zur Germanistik, Anglistik und Komparatistik,* pp. 649-50 and 652-54.

The medical student, Sascha Simchowitz, reported:

> During the winter semester of 1888–89 I was a medical student in Jena, where I attended the lectures and visited the clinic of the well-known psychiatrist Professor Otto Binswanger. One day—it must have been in January 1889—a patient was led into the lecture hall. He had been admitted to the asylum shortly before. Binswanger introduced him to us as—Professor Nietzsche!
>
> The figure, of medium height, held himself stiffly at attention. His face was haggard. . . . Professor Binswanger began a conversation with him about his earlier life. We learned to our astonishment that he had become a professor in Basel at only twenty-four years of age . . . , and that chronic headache had later forced him to retire. Concerning his activities as an author he uttered not a word.
>
> Finally, he said he had lived in Turin, and began to praise the place, which had been especially pleasing to him because it united the features of both large and small cities. Quite spontaneously, he added some general remarks about the peculiarities of such cities. . . . Unfortunately, he did not bring his remarks to any sort of conclusion. In the middle of a sentence he lost his train of thought and sank into silence. Professor Binswanger now wanted to demonstrate to his listeners some disturbances in the patient's walk. He asked Nietzsche to walk up and down the room. But the patient responded quite lethargically, walking so slowly that the symptoms in question could not be seen. "Now, Herr Professor," Binswanger encouraged, "an old soldier like you surely can still march!" Nietzsche began to pace across the lecture hall with a firm gait.
>
> After that I saw Nietzsche many times, when we were doing our rounds. . . . His condition varied: sometimes he was quiet and amiable, but sometimes he had his bad days. The last time I saw him, he presented quite a different picture than the first time: he was now in a state of extreme agitation, and his consciousness was obviously turbid. He sat there, flushed of face, his eyes aflame with a wild pain, as he was being watched by one of the attendants.

On March 24, 1890, Franziska Nietzsche was granted custody of her son, who had grown more sedate. Mother and son remained in Jena for six weeks, until one day in May Nietzsche eluded her and tried to go swimming in a pond. A policeman found him, dressed him, and brought him home. Fearing that the police would force her to surrender her son to the clinic, Franziska and her Fritz left Jena surreptitiously on May 13, 1890, for Naumburg.

The widowed Elisabeth returned to Naumburg on December 16 of that year and began to play an active role in her brother's literary estate. On June 2, 1892 she departed once again for Paraguay, to try to salvage whatever she could of her possessions in "Nueva Germania"; by the fall of 1893 she was back, penniless, with plans to found a "Nietzsche Archive," which she would direct. Until 1897 the entire family survived on Nietzsche's meager pension from Basel, administered by Overbeck, which also paid all the patient's medical costs.

During the early years of Nietzsche's illness, both his mother and his sister firmly believed that their son and brother would recover. In the spring of 1889 Professor Binswanger expressed hope in some sort of "remission," but within the next few months he pronounced Nietzsche "incurable." The Jena charts noted the sudden outbreaks of excessive loudness, recurrent complaints concerning headache, visual and aural hallucinations, and accesses of compulsive nightmarish delirium and full-blown paranoia. Like Zarathustra in "The Convalescent," the patient slept beside his bed rather than in it, as though someone else were occupying it.

The most bizarre moments of Nietzsche's confinement in Jena occurred in October and November of 1890, when Julius Langbehn, the author of *Rembrandt as Educator,* descended on the clinic in order to achieve a "cure," more like a conversion, of the patient. After insinuating himself

Weingarten 18, taken from atop Naumburg's old town wall.

with both Nietzsche's mother and Otto Binswanger, Langbehn visited the clinic on several occasions over a two week period, trying—like Professor Lindner in Musil's *Man without Qualities*—to coax the lost lamb back into the fold. The attempted cure terminated when Nietzsche, enraged by Langbehn, who seemed to Nietzsche—even in his madness—yet another example of the good Christian anti-Semite who had plagued him for decades, upset a table onto him and threatened him with his fists. When Heinrich Köselitz visited Nietzsche in January and February of 1890, after the Langbehn fiasco had run its course, he found a patient who was delighted to see him, yet oddly excitable and strangely altered in his reactions and capabilities. "His laughter is usually cheerful, but it can also become uncanny" (N *3*, 109). When Overbeck visited the patient at the end of February, he noted that their friendship now had to feed on a past that was irretrievably gone: the fact that his friend talked of a return to teaching at the university only confirmed how remote the world had in fact become for him (N *3*, 110). Von Gersdorff and Köselitz, visiting him a year later, observed that he had slipped from madness into total stupefaction. He had lost all sense of rhythm at the piano. He often stared at his hands as though they were strangers. Köselitz too now feared that the patient might try to strangle his mother.

Franziska, with the help of her housemaid Alwine, cared for her son—who had once again become her little boy—from the moment she gained custody of him until her death on April 20, 1897. During those seven exhausting and disheartening years, with Alwine's help, she fed and bathed him. She read to him in a soothing monotone—sometimes *Tom Sawyer* in translation, sometimes her son's poem *O Mensch! Gieb Acht!* but the text scarcely mattered; the idea was to keep

Weimar. The Villa Silberblick today.

the patient quiet. "No one can understand a child better than his mother," she insisted (N *3*, 118). She took him on long walks through the nearby city park as long as he was able to negotiate the three blocks there, then on shorter walks in the sunny, park-like vicinity of the old town wall in front of the house. By 1894 trips to the local swimming pool had become impossible because of Nietzsche's rages and the waxing paralysis. The daily routine became increasingly monotonous. When Paul Deussen visited the patient on his fiftieth birthday, he recorded: "He sat there quietly, taking no part in anything, heeding nothing; only the flowers I had brought him roused his attention for a moment, and the cake they set before him he devoured eagerly" (N *3*, 176). Erwin Rohde reported the following to Franz Overbeck concerning his visit on December 27, 1894: "I saw the unfortunate man himself: he is totally apathetic; he no longer recognizes anyone apart from his mother and sister; months pass without his being able to *utter* a single sentence; he was also shrunken and bent over, having grown weak and small, although with a healthy skin tone—in short, he was a sight that brought tears to my eyes" (N *3*, 172). By 1895 the paralysis had spread to the chin, and eating became difficult. Nietzsche spent the better part of the day, weather permitting, sitting out on a veranda under a grape arbor. The grape leaves absorbed the occasional, unpredictable screams, or so Franziska hoped. When Overbeck visited Nietzsche for the last time, on September 24, 1895, he portrayed him as a "noble but mortally wounded animal, cowering in some corner, pondering only how it might perish" (N *3*, 178).

After Franziska Nietzsche's death from influenza and exhaustion in 1897, at seventy-one years of age, Alwine and Elisabeth assumed the care of her son.[8] The Basel pension now came to an end, and so did Nietzsche's "Naumburg." Soon after their mother's death, Elisabeth moved Nietzsche to the "Nietzsche Archive" she had relocated in Weimar in August 1896. In July 1897 both Nietzsche and the Nietzsche Archive were transferred to the "Villa Silberblick" on the outskirts of Weimar. "Silver View," a property given to Elisabeth by Meta von Salis, stood on a promontory that overlooked the glorious city of Goethe and Schiller. For the next three years Elisabeth kept him as comfortable as possible in a room on the second floor of "Silver View"; special visitors who came to the Archive, those she was counting on for financial support, were taken up to view the stricken philosopher. Harry Graf Kessler was one of the visitors. He recorded the following in his diary for August 8, 1897:

> He lay sleeping on a sofa. . . . His forehead was colossally broad, his great mane of hair still dark brown, as was his matted, enormous mustache; beneath his eyes were broad, dark brown lines, carved deep into his cheeks; one could still see in the dull, flaccid face a few deep folds, engravings of his thinking and willing. . . . In his expression lay an infinite weariness. The hands were waxen, the veins a greenish violet. His hands were somewhat swollen, as they are on a corpse. . . . Thus he seemed not so much a patient or a madman as a dead man.[9]

After another visit less than a year later, on April 17, 1898, Kessler recorded: "When we entered, he stretched out his hand, trembling somewhat, but quiet, and looking up as though in order to question, first to his sister, then to me. He looked at me too . . . seriously and quietly, like a beautiful, loyal animal. . . . The forms of civility and courtesy belonged among the very last human things that his spirit had retained. . . ."

Nietzsche spoke very little during those final years. Karl Böttcher jotted down a few phrases:

> He is sitting now . . . on a chair near the window. His broad shoulders are hunched over a thick book, which he seems to be reading, except that he is holding it upside-down. Large, animated eyes flash at me. . . . Sometimes he forces out a few words, as though talking to himself: "Lots of good people live in this house. . . ." "I wrote many fine things." He is given a small piece of pie; apparently it tastes good to him. "This is a lovely book," he says earnestly.[10]

During the final months of Nietzsche's life, the artist Hans Olde took a number of photographs of him on the second-story veranda of Silver View. The patient gazed vacantly, no longer even myopically, into the sunset.

Something like a mild stroke appears to have occurred during the summer of 1898. In May 1899 Nietzsche suffered a serious stroke. His right side was paralyzed; he became bedridden. After a bout with pneumonia and yet another stroke, he died in Weimar at noon on August 25, 1900. Elisabeth arranged a memorial service at the Archive in Weimar on August 27. She wanted to

8. Two years earlier, in December 1895, Elisabeth had pressured her mother to relinquish to her the post of literary executor. She now began to hire a series of editors, searching for one who would work fast enough for her, since she was driven as much by the need to sell books as by the desire to preserve the legacy of her brother's work; she was also searching for an editor who would conform to her ideas about editing, which she carried out as much with scissors and a box of matches as with a pencil.

9. Quoted in Volz, *Nietzsche im Labyrinth seiner Krankheit*, p. 491; the following quotation from Kessler appears on p. 495.

10. Quoted in Volz, *Nietzsche im Labyrinth seiner Krankheit*, p. 493.

Two views of the graves of Nietzsche, his father, his brother, and his mother; the photographs must have been taken between 1897 and 1935. Photos: Stiftung Weimarer Klassik. GSA 101/586 and 101/588.

bury him on the premises of her Archive, but the city health authorities balked. Nietzsche's remains were therefore transported to the *Vaterhaus* that had so often haunted his dreams. Friends and neighbors gathered on August 28, 1900, to inter him in Röcken alongside his father, mother, and infant brother.

Of course, there were speeches at the funeral. A cousin of Nietzsche's, on the Oehler side, reported to the assembled mourners that the last word "exhaled" by Nietzsche's "weary lips" was the name "Elisabeth," a detail he doubtless had from Elisabeth herself. Peter Gast (Heinrich Köselitz) concluded his funeral oration on the man who had said he would rather be a satyr or a clown than a saint by exclaiming, "Let your name be *holy* to all coming generations!" (N *3*, 354; 357).

At one point during his "wasted year" in Bonn a mocking Nietzsche could not resist quoting Juvenal to his mother: "Sometimes it is hard not to write satires" (B *2*, 67).

BEGINNINGS AND ENDS

Röcken

Naumburg

Pobles

Schulpforta

Jena

Weimar

Röcken. The church, the parsonage where Nietzsche was born, the barns and ponds of the parsonage.
Above right: Main door of the church.

The village of Röcken lies a half-hour's distance from Lützen right on the country road. Every traveler who passes down that road casts a friendly eye on the village. For it lies prettily there, with its surrounding greenery and ponds. Above all, the mossy church tower attracts the eye. I can still remember how I once walked with my father from Lützen to Röcken; when we were halfway there, the rising peal of the bells announced the beginning of Eastertide. This sound recurs in me often, and melancholy carries me off once again to the beloved but distant house of my father. In how lively a manner the cemetery stands before me now! How often I asked about the ancient, ancient mausoleum, about the biers and black satin bands, about the time-worn engravings and funeral monuments! But if there is one image that cannot be erased from my soul, surely I will never forget the familiar parsonage. For it was incised in my soul by a mighty stylus. The dwelling was first erected in

1820 [1825] and was therefore in very good condition. Several steps led up to the ground floor. I can still remember the study on the uppermost floor. The rows of books, with several picture books among them, rows upon rows of writing, made this room one of my favorite places. Behind the house was the large yard, with its grass and fruit trees. In spring part of it would be under water, and the cellar would usually flood too. In front of the house the courtyard encompassed the area from the shed and the barns over to the flower garden. I was almost always in the garden buildings or on the benches there. Behind the green fence were four ponds surrounded by willows. My greatest pleasure was to walk among these ponds, watching the rays of the sun dance on the mirror surface of the water, with the little fish playing busily below. . . . All about the cemetery lay the farmyards and gardens in tranquil familiarity. Accord and peace held sway over every cottage, and wild excitements remained at a far remove.

"From My Life," written August 18 to September 1, 1858, at age thirteen; J 1, 2-3

The increasing suffering of my father, his blindness, his haggard face and figure, my mother's tears, the doctor's portentous mien, and also the incautious remarks of some villagers must have given me a sense of impending doom. That doom in fact descended on us—my father died. —

I shall say nothing of my pain, my tears, my mother's suffering, the entire village's profound sadness. How his burial gripped me! How the dull funeral bells penetrated to the marrow of my bones! . . .

Some months later a second misfortune struck me. I had a premonition of it, thanks to a remarkable dream. It seemed to me that I could hear muffled organ music coming from the nearby church. Surprised, I open the window that looks out over the church and cemetery. My father's grave opens, a white figure emerges and disappears into the church. The gloomy, uncanny sounds surge on; the white figure appears again, carrying something under its arm that I did not clearly recognize. The grave yawns, the figure sinks into it, the organ goes silent—I awake. The following morning my younger brother, a lively and gifted child, is seized with cramps, and a half-hour later he is dead. He was buried right next to my father's grave. —

"My Life," version C, recorded at age sixteen; J 1, 281-82

Röcken. Church interior viewed from the choir loft.

The church of Nietzsche's maternal grandfather, Pastor David Ernst Oehler, at Pobles; the house at Weingarten 18, behind the Naumburg city wall (note the veranda on the far side of the house, where Nietzsche spent much of his time during the years of his illness).

We celebrated Grandpa Oehler's seventy-second birthday on August 2, 1859. A vast number of neighborhood children, in-laws, and grandchildren gathered. When I went downstairs early in the morning, Fritz came to me from the garden and told me that he had woken very early, on account of a strange dream: the entire parsonage in Pobles lay in ruins, and poor Grandma sat alone among the shattered beams and boards. The dream made him weep so much that he woke up and could not fall asleep again. Our dear mother forbade us to tell anyone else about this dream. Dear Grandpa was generally so vital and robust that anyone would have given him another twenty years. But late that summer he caught a cold and then became seriously ill. Grandpa, who had never had a doctor in the house except as a friend, had to call for help. It was influenza, and in midwinter (December 17, 1859) the man we loved so dearly died of it.

Elisabeth Förster-Nietzsche, quoted at N 1, 85

Schulpforta. The chapel, the approach to the main gate, and a school building.

It was a Tuesday morning when I drove out through Naumburg's city gates. Dusk still hovered over the meadows, and on the horizon only a few dimly lit clouds betrayed the approach of daylight. In me too a kind of dusk held sway: in my heart the sunlight of true joy had not yet risen. The terrors of a fraught night besieged me still, and the future ahead of me lay wrapped in an ominous gray veil. For the very first time I was to leave my parental home for a long, long period. I stepped forth to meet unknown dangers. My farewell had left me forlorn; I trembled at the thought of my future. Add to that the fact that an examination awaited me, which I had portrayed to myself in the grimmest of colors and forms; and the thought that from now on I could never give myself over to my own thoughts, that my schoolmates would drag me away from my most beloved preoccupations—this thought oppressed me terribly. And, pre-eminently, the thought that I was to leave my dear friends, that I would have to abandon congenial relationships in order to step forth into a new, unknown, unrelenting world—this thought crowded my heart, and every minute became more terrifying to me; indeed, as I saw Pforta shimmering in the distance, it looked more like a prison house than an alma mater. I drove through the gate. Then my heart overflowed with holy sensations, I was lifted up to God in silent prayer, and a profound tranquillity came over my spirit. Yea, Lord, bless my entry and protect me too, in body and in spirit, in this nursery of the Holy Spirit. Send your angel, that he may lead me victorious through the battles I go to fight, and let this place extend true blessings, blessings that will last me through times eternal. This I beseech Thee, O Lord! Amen. —

Text for Wilhelm Pinder, written at age fourteen; B 1, 50

Jena Clinic for the Care and Cure of the Insane, interior views. The long-necked fox brandishing a magic wand is actually a repair to the padded linoleum on a stair.

Then a shrill scream pierced our ears. It came from the lunatic asylum nearby. Our hands locked more tightly. It was as though an evil spirit had touched us with frightful, flitting wings.

"On My August Vacation," 1859, written at age four-teen, reporting on a trip to Jena; J 1, 143

To my room? But what do I see on my bed?
Someone is lying there—softly he groans, his throat
rattles—it is a dying man!

"A New Year's Dream," written at age twenty: J 3. 79

Weimar. Nietzsche in the "Nietzsche Archive" at Villa Silberblick;
the portraits were taken on the second-floor balcony in 1899 by
Hans Olde. Photos: Stiftung Weimarer Klassik. GSA 101/28, GSA
101/619, GSA 101/30, GSA 101/34.

63

Basel Badischer Bahnhof,
the point of embarkation for
Nietzsche's travels during
the Basel years.

TWO

"I'd rather be a Basel Professor than God..."

That, at least, was Nietzsche's retrospective view of the matter at the onset of his madness in 1889: a professorship in philology was preferable to divinity. Throughout the ten years and more that followed his retirement from Basel in 1879, he never ceased calling himself "Professor of Classical Philology," never surrendered his title. As we have seen, however, his acceptance of the call to Basel in 1869 was anything but a total conversion, anything but wholehearted. Not that Nietzsche refused to commit himself to his teaching and his other academic obligations. He threw himself into those duties with gusto, and in both his university and secondary school teaching (all the professors had to teach some advanced classes in the local Gymnasia) he earned the devotion of his students and pupils. During the next ten years, in spite of severe illness, he gave his profession everything it demanded of him, and more than it knew how to demand.

The university, founded in 1460, had, like the city it served, fallen on hard times. Most of its new faculty appointees were young men (none as young as Nietzsche, however) who would stay for several years and eventually move on to more prestigious institutions. Nietzsche arrived in Basel on April 19, 1869. He began to teach his first "summer semester" in early May, giving eight hours of instruction per week in the university and six at a local humanistic Gymnasium—or, as the Baslers called it, a *Pädagogium*—housed in the Mentelinhof on the cathedral square.

Although Naumburg too had been a city of burghers and bureaucrats, Basel was something new for Nietzsche. It was a city of citizens, thirty thousand of them, its cityscape *not* dominated by a fortress castle, a manor house, or any other appurtenance of aristocracy. When Nietzsche left behind him his Prussian citizenship and became a stateless resident of Canton Basel, he took a major step on the way to becoming a good European. The city itself was in the throes of rapid transformation: the walls of the town were coming down, especially at the points where railroad lines needed to gain access to the town center. Nietzsche took up residence near the Spalentor, the most splendid of the city gates, first at Spalentorweg 2, then at the nearby Schützengraben 45 (today number 47). At that time the latter dwelling, owned by a tailor's widow, was a modest row house in a neighborhood into which the university's mathematics and science faculties had recently expanded.

Nietzsche's classes were held not in this new university neighborhood, however, but in the oldest part of the university, on the "Rheinsprung," overlooking the swift-flowing river, with Germany's Black Forest in the distance. His secondary school classes were held in the Mentelinhof, a spacious

Schützengraben 45 (today number 47), where Nietzsche resided for the longest period during the Basel years; the house was soon nicknamed the "Poison Cottage," after a popular Basel wine bar. Photo: Stiftung Weimarer Klassik. GSA 101/508.

building with a cobblestone courtyard, directly across from the main entrance to the Münster, Protestant Basel's cathedral. Nietzsche would walk every day, quite early in the morning (his lectures began at 7:00 A.M.), across the Petersplatz and the bustling market and shopping streets, to the narrow, winding alleyways branching off from the Burghügel. At its summit lay the university buildings, the Münster, and the Mentelinhof. Whenever he walked out of the main entrance of the Mentelinhof, about to turn left toward the university buildings, he would see the statues on the façade of the Münster looming over him—there once again was the fearsome St. George, the terror of his youth, now spearing the dragon.

Over the next few semesters at the university, Nietzsche taught the history of Greek literature and pre-Platonic philosophy, Greek and Roman rhetoric, ancient Greek religion, Plato's life and teachings, Aeschylus's *Libation Bearers*, Sophocles' *Oedipus the King*, and Hesiod's *Works and Days*. At the Gymnasium he taught Plato's *Apology, Phaedo, Phaedrus, Symposium, Republic,* and *Protagoras;* selected books of Homer's *Iliad;* Aeschylus's *Prometheus Bound,* and Sophocles' *Electra*. His pupils had to read Euripides' *The Bacchae* on their own and write a paper on their impressions concerning the Dionysian cult.

Nietzsche's students and pupils were clearly impressed by their teacher's proficiency and enthusiasm. Their reports are in accord: he was the one teacher whose expectations they did not want to disappoint, and so they worked harder for him than for anyone else. As for Nietzsche himself, he prided himself on his ability to reach even the least talented and least motivated of his charges. In a late note toward his "autobiography," *Ecce Homo,* Nietzsche confessed:

At bottom, I belong among those involuntary educators who neither need nor possess pedagogical principles. The sole fact that in seven years of teaching the senior class in the Basel Pädagogium I did not have the occasion to mete out a single punishment, along with the fact that, as I was later assured, even the laziest pupils worked hard when they were in my classes, gives some indication of this. A clever little stratagem from my teaching days remains in my memory: whenever a pupil failed to recite adequately the matters that we had treated in the previous class, I always publicly blamed myself—I said, for example, that everyone had a right to demand of me further elucidation and commentary if what I had said was too cursory or too vague. A teacher had the obligation to make himself accessible to *every* level of intelligence. . . . I've been told that this little stratagem was more effective than any sort of scolding.—In my dealings with my high school pupils and university students I never had any real difficulty. . . . In the same way, when I was involved in doctoral defenses, I never felt I had to learn any new procedures or methods: what came to me instinctively was to be as humane as possible in such cases; indeed, I felt really good about the exam only when I had helped the candidate into smooth waters. A candidate in such circumstances has as much spirit—*or* as little—as the esteemed examiners. . . . Whenever I listened quite closely, it always seemed to me that ultimately it was the professorial examiners who were being *tested.*— (W *13,* 619–20)

While many Gymnasium pupils and university students have left us testimony concerning Nietzsche's eloquence and brilliance, few descriptions of his person remain. A remark by a pupil in the Pädagogium, reminiscing in 1941, is therefore of particular interest: he recalls that Nietzsche was

One of the oldest university buildings on the Rheinsprung in Basel.

St. George and the dragon, as portrayed on the Basel Münster, directly opposite the Mentelinhof.

Nietzsche in Basel, taken in late autumn 1873. Photo: Stiftung Weimarer Klassik. GSA 101/15.

"of a delicate and refined build, with a rather feminine way about him, in stark contrast to his martial mustache, which seemed to overcompensate for the rest of his characteristics" (N *1,* 522). While other testimony indicates that Nietzsche was actually quite stocky, and hardly delicate, the pupil may simply be giving an impression of Nietzsche's mannerisms. Whatever the case, we know that there was nothing coarse or even assertively masculine about the young academic.

Nietzsche's colleagues for the most part behaved amicably toward him. Indeed, they elected him dean of the faculty in 1874, which reflects confidence, if not friendship. He complained only that he had to invent excuses in order to escape from the endless succession of dinner parties (B *3,* 16). He much preferred to be out walking by himself—his solitude and his self-discipline perhaps being the fruits of what he would later analyze as the ascetic ideal. Among the most renowned of his colleagues at the University of Basel, and the most important to Nietzsche, were Wilhelm Vischer-Bilfinger, Ludwig Rütimeyer, Johann Jakob Bachofen, and, most important, Jacob Burckhardt.

Vischer-Bilfinger was a Greek specialist who had become a major force in the administration of the university; it was he who had contacted Ritschl in Leipzig and arranged for Nietzsche's hiring. Bachofen, best remembered today for his work *Das Mutterrecht,* the classic study of matriarchy, was a maverick ethnologist and a Romantic historian who focused on the communal origins of early humankind. In his book on ancient Greece, Bachofen referred to the oppositional pair "Apollinian-Dionysian" (though Jules Michelet was probably the more influential source for Nietzsche in this regard). In general, Bachofen emphasized the distance of modernity from the achievements of Greek antiquity; in all respects he resisted the rationalist historians' confidence that a sober and relentless methodology would enable them all to understand everything about ancient Greece. When Nietzsche delivered his two public lectures, "The Greek Music Drama," and "Socrates and Tragedy," which most of his colleagues thought an outrage against Plato and Socrates, he had the comfort of knowing that Bachofen had represented views almost as radical as his own.

Ludwig Rütimeyer was a geologist and paleontologist engaged in the battles over Darwin's work that characterize this period. Rütimeyer resisted Darwin's principle of natural selection from accidental variation, taking up the influential anti-Darwinian theories of Karl Ernst von Baer. Even though Nietzsche never got to know Rütimeyer personally, as he did Bachofen and Burckhardt, Rütimeyer helped nurture the scientific side of his thinking—the side Nietzsche and Rohde had wanted to develop at the time Nietzsche was summoned to Basel. In addition, Nietzsche came to learn a great deal from Rütimeyer's writings on the Alps; indeed, the title of one of Rütimeyer's books, *From the Sea to the Alps* (1854), sounds like Nietzsche's perpetual itinerary of the 1880s.

It was Jacob Burckhardt, the most famous of the three colleagues both in Basel and in the learned world at large, who developed the closest ties to Nietzsche. Twenty-six years Nietzsche's senior, Burckhardt nonetheless felt drawn to the brilliant young scholar; they shared passionate interests in music, art, and cultural questions generally. To be sure, Burckhardt remained a champion of Weimar classicism: if the young Nietzsche favored the music of *pathos* over *ethos,* emotion over mood, and thus Wagner and Beethoven over Haydn and Mozart, Burckhardt instinctively held to the classical scheme.[1] In later years Nietzsche would send Burckhardt every book he published, and Burckhardt would read and admire them all, without claiming to understand them. During their years together in Basel, each of the two knew how to appreciate their association without confusing it with the Aristotelian "friendship of equals."

If Beethoven overwhelmed Burckhardt, Wagner repelled him. By contrast, the first five years of Nietzsche's Basel period may also be called his Wagner period. Wagner was living with the baroness Cosima von Bülow in Tribschen, a villa on the outskirts of Lucerne, a train ride and a long walk from Basel. Wagner was fifty-six at the time, at the peak of his powers, with a stormy career behind him and Bayreuth ahead of him. The support of King Ludwig II of Bavaria and other proponents of the "music of the future" now made it possible for the construction of a special theater, the famous Bayreuth Festspielhaus, for the performance of Wagner's "collective art works." Meanwhile, Tribschen, Nietzsche's "Island of the Blessed," was Wagner's idyll, a place of escape from his turbulent life in Munich; it was also the place where he planned and discussed Bayreuth with—among others—the young academic and music enthusiast of Basel whom Wagner had first met in Leipzig.

Nietzsche first visited Tribschen—located on a forested knoll near the shore of Lake Lucerne, with Mount Pilatus in the distance—on May 15, 1869, less than a month after his arrival in Basel.

1. Yet Nietzsche's musical tastes eventually reverted to those of Burckhardt, so that, from this point of view at least, Burckhardt's lasting support of his strange young colleague can be understood. In February 1886 Nietzsche expressed the turn away from Wagner in his musical taste in the following terms: "A human being who has the character I have, *profondément triste,* cannot survive Wagnerian music over the long term. We need the south, sun 'at any cost,' bright, harmless, innocently Mozartian felicity and tenderness in tones. Actually, I ought to have people around me who possess the same character as this music that I love . . ." (B 7, 153).

"On the Saturday before Pentecost I took the early train to Lucerne; because my lake steamer wouldn't be leaving for a while, I walked out to Tribschen, uncertain about whether I should go. I stood quietly for a long time in front of the house, listening to a chord that was being played repeatedly, a chord expressing pain. They invited me in for lunch, but because of my trip to the Tellsplatte we postponed it until Monday" (N *1*, 295).

Over the next three years Nietzsche visited Tribschen many times, spending several holiday seasons with the family, putting up with the numberless household pets, running chores for Cosima, bowing to the master's whims, participating in Cosima's tableaus, mini-operas, and kitschy birthday celebrations with a devotion that in retrospect is difficult to understand—unless one accepts that Nietzsche was himself in love with Cosima, nine years his elder but as enchanting to him as she was to the Meister. In a letter written a decade later, after Nietzsche had seen Sarah Bernhardt perform on stage, he told his mother and sister that Bernhardt's mannerisms and beauty reminded him of Cosima Wagner (B *6*, 169). And in the very last autobiographical text we have from Nietzsche's hand, written in December 1888, he declared his hatred for his mother and sister, but confessed: "There is one single case in which I acknowledge my equal—I confess it with profound grat-

Richard and Cosima Wagner, taken in Vienna in May 1872. Photo: AKG London. 1-W9-K1872.

Ruins of the "Casseiopia" thermal baths, Baden-weiler, in the Black Forest region of Germany.

The landing dock and boat house at Tribschen, Wagner's idyllic residence on the shores of Lake Lucerne.

itude. Frau Cosima Wagner is the noblest nature by far, and, in order not to leave a single word unsaid, I say that Richard Wagner was by far the man most akin to me. . . . The rest is silence. . . ."[2]

Yet no matter how devoted he was to Cosima, and no matter how disquieted by Wagner's *dramatic* music, which always seemed to him to mistake the ears for the eyes, there can be no doubt that Nietzsche fell under the spell of the brilliant musician, librettist, stage manager, and public relations mogul, who had a touch of the charlatan about him. "No cloud ever darkened our sky," Nietzsche would later write of Wagner in *Ecce Homo,* after all the storms had passed. Much earlier, on June 16, 1869, he wrote to Erwin Rohde: "The world does not at all know the human grandeur and singularity of his nature. I am learning a great deal through my nearness to him: this is my practical course in Schopenhauerian philosophy" (B *3,* 17). And to Carl von Gersdorff, on August 4: *"No one* knows him or can judge him, because the whole world stands on a different foundation, and is not at home in his atmosphere. In him there prevails such an unconditioned ideality, such a profound and truly touching humanity, such a sublime seriousness of life, that in his proximity I feel I am close to the divine" (B *3,* 36).

Initially, Nietzsche's periods away from Basel were almost always vacations: Interlaken and Mount Pilatus in July and August 1869, with a brief stay at the Hotel Römerbad in Badenweiler in

2. EH I, 3; *6,* 268. An earlier version of this text—itself one of the final substitutions in the printer's manuscript of *Ecce Homo* at the very end of 1888—is more problematic, and more revealing, than the one we have only now cited. In the first draft of this passage Nietzsche wrote: "Frau Cosima Wagner is the noblest nature by far that exists, and, in relation to me, I have always interpreted her marriage with Wagner as adultery . . . the case of Tristan" (W *14,* 473). For more discussion of this substitute text for *Ecce Homo* I, 3, see chap. 11 of Krell, *Infectious Nietzsche.*

the Black Forest on August 14–15. In Badenweiler he no doubt visited the Roman baths dedicated to Casseiopia, built around A.D. 75, and the Fortress Baden, built in the twelfth century and destroyed during the Thirty Years' War. The next summer, in early June, he traveled with Rohde and his own mother and sister into the Berner Oberland, once again visiting Interlaken. He found his salary insufficient to support trips of this kind, however, and again his mother felt compelled to send him epistles on thrift. Still other forms of dissatisfaction were growing in him. He felt pulled in at least three directions: first, his teaching profession, which threatened to absorb all his energies ("This noble profession has something truly aggressive about it; in the evening, especially by Saturday, I am totally exhausted" [B *3, 20*]); second, the pull of Tribschen, inasmuch as Cosima and Richard would have loved to absorb totally the young Wagnerian's energies; and third, the pull toward something more encompassing than either philology or culture criticism, something larger even than academic philosophy—to wit, a kind of *thinking* that would also be a work of *art*.

In April 1870 a young theologian joined the university faculty, again as a result of the recruitment labors of Wilhelm Vischer-Bilfinger. It may have been Vischer who also arranged for rooms on behalf of the new professor, Franz Overbeck, in Nietzsche's house at Schützengraben 45. The two of them, along with Heinrich Romundt, who was writing his doctoral dissertation on Kant's *Critique of Pure Reason,* called their house "Poison Cottage," after a famous restaurant and wine bar in Basel with the forbidding name *Das Gifthüttli.* During the year in which Nietzsche's first *Untimely Meditation* appeared, 1873, Overbeck published his critical tract *On the Christian Quality of Theology Today,* a provocation that eventually forced Overbeck and his wife out of the church.

Franz Overbeck, Nietzsche's most loyal friend, taken during his later years. Photo: Stiftung Weimarer Klassik. GSA 101/362.

Basel. Rear entrance to the "Poison Cottage" (Nietzsche's residence).

Basel. "Das Gifthüttli," on Nietzsche's route from Schützengraben 45 to the university and the Mentelinhof. The "Little Poison Cottage" must have been the location, centuries ago, of arsenic mines; by Nietzsche's time it was a place for lunch or an evening glass of wine.

"Some day our house will be one of ill repute," Nietzsche boasted (B *4,* 140). Overbeck became the friend who would serve Nietzsche—and Nietzsche's mother, though not his sister—steadfastly and faithfully until Nietzsche's death. Of him Nietzsche wrote: "Overbeck is the most serious, candid, personally lovable, and least complicated person and researcher that one could wish for as a friend. At the same time, he has that radicality I need to have in all the people with whom I associate" (B *4,* 135). Many years later he would confess to Overbeck that Overbeck's loyalty and friendship had in fact saved his life: "In the midst of life I was 'surrounded' by my good Overbeck— otherwise that other companion would perhaps have risen to greet me: *Mors*" (B *5,* 456).

In July 1870 Nietzsche learned of the impending French declaration of war against Prussia. He wrote on July 16 to Erwin Rohde, perhaps the most talented of his philologist friends from Leipzig, and the one with whom he formed the most intimate friendship:

> We have had a terrible crash of thunder: *war between France and Germany* has been declared, and our entire threadbare civilization rushes to embrace the dreadful demon. What things we shall be forced to experience! Friend, dearest friend, we last met at the sunset of peace. How grateful I am to you! If existence becomes unbearable to you now, then come back to me. What are all our goals, anyway!
>
> We may already be at the beginning of the end! What a wasteland! We shall need monasteries once again. And we shall be the first *fratres.* (B *3,* 130–31)

He signed the letter "The Faithful Swiss," though he was neither Prussian nor Swiss. Both France and Germany needed several weeks to prepare for battle, and an ominous lull descended on Europe as they mobilized. No doubt, during these weeks, Nietzsche had intense conversations with Jacob Burckhardt, who was as prescient about politics as Nietzsche was surprised: Burckhardt knew that the Franco-Prussian War would not be a traditional skirmish between monarchical dynasties— it would be a war of industrialized nation-states, a rehearsal of total war. He wrote a friend in Baden of "a new element" in politics, to wit, the "deepening" impact of war: "One now tries to humiliate the conquered, to lower them as profoundly as possible *in their own self-esteem,* so that in the future they will no longer be capable of anything at all"; even if peace were restored, warned Burckhardt, it would be a matter of endless readiness for war, "and after a time no one will be able at all to say what life is for" (N *1, 367*).

Like Burckhardt, however, Nietzsche was filled with dread and uncertainty. His own friends Wagner and Cosima von Bülow were closer to Paris than to Berlin: at the time of the declaration, they were entertaining Catulle Mendès and Camille Saint-Saëns in Tribschen. Napoleon III might be an upstart, and the relic of an attenuated past thrice removed, but Bismarck's *Realpolitik* hardly seemed an acceptable alternative. In the midst of these foreboding events, the pope in Rome formally declared the doctrine of papal infallibility. To Nietzsche and his Tribschen friends, the tiara had become a fool's cap and bells, adding a jangle of comic relief to the frightening music being rehearsed in the rest of Europe. For his part, Nietzsche needed time to think. He had already decided—against Cosima's pleading—to participate in the war in some way, on the Prussian side, probably as a medic. For the time being he withdrew into a kind of retreat. With his sister, he traveled to Brunnen on Lake Lucerne, continuing on at the end of July to a lonely and spectacularly beautiful valley near Amsteg, north of Andermatt: the Maderanertal.

The Maderan Valley runs east and north from Amsteg in the Reuss Valley to the Hüfi glacier. The glacier feeds the mighty Chärstelenbach, the river that cuts through the steep valley down to the Reuss. Nietzsche and Elisabeth began their trip at Amsteg and advanced northeast by post coach toward Bristen, then continued on to Balmenegg and the Hotel Alpenclub. Today the Maderaner Hotel is a three-hour hike beyond Bristen, at some 1,350 meters above sea level. To the left, the gray cliffs of the Windgällen dominate the valley; to the right, the somewhat more distant peaks of the Bristenstock and Oberalpstock loom. The face of the Windgällen is spotted with scrub pine, and although it is dark gray rather than silver in hue, almost everything about it is reminiscent of Mount Parnassus at Delphi—a place that Nietzsche was never to see.

Immediately beyond his hotel, Nietzsche could stand on a promontory and survey the valley and no fewer than eight waterfalls, among them the "Milky," the "Bubbly," and, most impressive of all, the "Duster." Elisabeth and he occupied the new and more luxurious building of the Hotel Alpenclub, the so-called "English" quarters. There, even before they signed the registry, they made

Looking westward from the threshold of the Maderan Valley toward the towns of Bristen and Amsteg.

Hotel Alpenclub, today the Hotel Maderanertal. Nietzsche resided in the then recently completed "Engländerhaus," the building on the left.

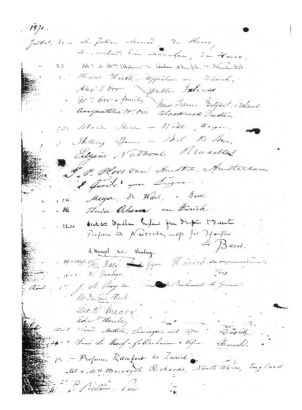

"The Duster," viewed from the plateau behind and above the Hotel Alpenclub, some 1,400 meters above sea level.

The hotel registry, showing at mid-page Nietzsche's signature, though no arrival or departure date. Beneath the registration of the prior guest, Herbert Wyndham from England, and the dates "28–30 Juillet 1870," he signs in as "Professor Dr. Nietzsche mit Frl. Schwester aus Basel."

the acquaintance of Adolf Mosengel, a landscape painter from Hamburg. Mosengel strengthened Nietzsche's resolve to join the Prussian medical corps (the *Felddiakonie,* a forerunner of the Red Cross), and in a week or so the two of them quit the Maderanertal for the battlefields of Lorraine. While on hikes through the isolated valley, Nietzsche worked on "The Dionysian Worldview," a text he would dedicate to Frau Cosima Wagner in December (she and Richard had been married on August 25, 1870) under the title "The Birth of the Tragic Thought." The text itself, like the god Dionysos, its object, represented two poles—one of sublime natural beauty and harmony, the other of dreadful destruction. When Nietzsche left the Maderanertal and traveled to Erlangen for medical training, he no doubt felt the tension between these two faces of the god. He abandoned vistas of splendor for visions of agony.

For ten days, August 13–22, 1870, Nietzsche was in emergency medical training at Erlangen. A few scattered notes from these days survive (W 7, 87–91), among them these jottings of August 20: "We just chloroformed a French soldier in order to apply a plaster cast (his hand is shot to pieces: he cried out when we applied the narcotic, *'Mon dieu mon dieu je viens';* before him it was a girl eleven years old, to remove a bone fragment from her leg. A couple of days ago . . . a boy with a severe head wound was chloroformed; very difficult. Yesterday a Prussian died in the hospital, shot in the lung, today another one. . . . Outbreak of diphtheria in the hospital." After arriving at Karlsruhe, Nietzsche and Mosengel crossed the Rhine into the Alsatian battlefields. Beginning on August 24, their *Felddiakonie* company traveled by train and on foot through the battlefields near Weissenburg, Sulz, Gersdorf, and Wörth. By August 29 they had reached Hagenau and Bischweiler, near Strasbourg, which the Prussians were holding under siege. By September 2 they had advanced beyond Nancy to Ars-sur-Moselle, near Metz, where the major front had formed: General von Moltke had driven a wedge between the two French armies, and a series of decisive and bloody battles ensued: Mars-la-Tour, Tionville, Gravelotte. In Ars, Nietzsche and Mosengel were assigned to two different cattle cars—each with six severely wounded soldiers—on a train that was to take them back to a military hospital in Karlsruhe. On the two-day, two-night journey, through rainy and cold weather, Nietzsche bandaged and fed the wounded. He wrote to Richard Wagner: "All six soldiers had bones that were shattered, several were wounded in four places. In two of them I found diphtheria" (B 3, 143). He himself was infected with dysentery and diphtheria, so that by the time he reported in back at Erlangen he collapsed. After a week of hospitalization Nietzsche was sent back to his mother's house in Naumburg to recuperate.

While in Naumburg he received a long letter from Carl von Gersdorff, written from the field. After a bitterly ironic account of a Mass celebrated on the eve of the battle of Mars-la-Tour, von Gersdorff recounted how he had stumbled across the grave of a mutual friend of theirs from Schulpforta days, Kurt Flemming (not the Henry Fleming of *The Red Badge of Courage,* who, it is true, also dreamed of heroic "Greek struggles," yet in some uncanny way related to him, as perhaps all the war dead are related):

> In Mars-la-Tour I came upon a small cemetery. In one corner there were nine fresh graves, one of which held my dear friend Kurt Flemming, who was mortally wounded in battle on August 16 in a costly attack by the Second Dragoneers' Regiment. I didn't have time to weep, but today tears come to my eyes when I think of that gentle, charming, and faithful friend. I can't help but remember many happy hours within those gray walls of old Pforta. . . . I cannot lay claim to glory, as others do, by having spilled blood with my own hands, but I believe that I acted as a Schopenhauerian ethics would require me to act: I prevented our soldiers, who were embittered in the extreme and wanted to destroy everything, from

Lorraine, near Mars-la-Tour.
Memorial of the Franco-Prussian
War, 1870-71.

firing on the village churches and nearby houses, which were filled with hundreds of French wounded. . . . There could be no joy over our victory, because its scope was still unknown to us, and the sacrifices we had made seemed so excessive. The regimental corps lost 10,000 men, my own division 5,500, many officers among them, my friends almost all dead or wounded. . . . The images of horror that haunt my eyes defy all description. . . . In terms of losses, Pforta has many of its pupils to mourn. . . . (N *1*, 379–80)

To a similar letter from Nietzsche—one of the many letters she would destroy when Nietzsche broke with the maestro after 1878—Cosima Wagner replied: "I know that there are experiences that stamp our inner life forever, like a red-hot iron branding the skin of a poor yearling!" (N *1*, 380). Once again, it was Schopenhauer alone who seemed to provide a moment of relief from, or comprehension of, the horror.

Nietzsche was too weakened physically and emotionally to return to the front. The meaning of human existence—or the lack of meaning—had become for him a burning question. If the wisdom of Silenus, that is, insight into the vulnerability and absurdity of human life, expressed itself in two sparse lines in the "The Dionysian Worldview," written in the Maderanertal before the war, the revised text in December expanded Silenus's grim wisdom to a full paragraph:

> Wretched, ephemeral brood of toil and calamity, why do you do me violence, so that I might tell you what it is more useful for you not to know? For in ignorance of your own misery your life will advance with the least suffering. As soon as one has become a human being, one cannot in any way become what is most excellent, one can have no share in the essence of the best. The most excellent thing for you—all of you, men and women alike— would be not to have been born at all. The next best thing, however, after you have been born, is to die as quickly as possible. (W *1*, 588; cf. 560 and 35)

Nietzsche feared that the wars of the future would be exercises in Silenic wisdom. His mood during these weeks seemed subdued but was in fact profoundly troubled. Only his mother was happy about the outcome: she was delighted to have her boy back home, and affirmed that the war had done him good, made him more practical, less bookish, and more dedicated to his family. Meanwhile, her son tried to lose himself in new approaches to the meter and prosody of ancient Greek poetry. Yet the seeds had been sown for Nietzsche's waxing skepticism concerning Prussia and Germany as a whole: in his first *Untimely Meditation* he would make public what his letters from this period express, namely, his belief that military power, imperialism, nationalism, and chauvinism stand in inverse ratio to all the works of civilization and culture.

In this time of trouble—for although Nietzsche had returned to his teaching in Basel he had not yet recovered from the exertions and exactions of the war—he sought solace in Burckhardt's lectures on world history, which he attended each week. He also looked to the ancient figure of Empedocles of Acragas, as Hölderlin had, seeing in him the very model of a tragic thinker. Many of the traits he found in Empedocles would be celebrated years later in Zarathustra.[3]

Toward the end of 1870 one of the chairs of philosophy at Basel was vacated. Nietzsche hatched the plan of assuming that chair himself and filling his own vacated chair of philology with his friend Erwin Rohde. The scheme betrayed Nietzsche's naïveté concerning academic affairs. Without giving a thought to the other philosophers at Basel, who would have preferred to die three deaths than to have Nietzsche as a colleague (among them was the conservative Christian philosopher Karl Steffensen, who had heard Nietzsche on Socrates and was determined not to hear any more), Nietzsche pleaded with his patron and friend, Professor Vischer-Bilfinger, in January 1871:

> Most Esteemed Councillor,
>
> By now my doctors will have been in touch with you about the extent of my suffering; they will have reported that overwork is responsible for these unbearable conditions. Now, I have asked myself time and again how to account for this exhaustion that always intervenes before we reach mid-term; I've even had to contemplate the necessity of abandoning my work at the university altogether, as though it were a mode of life not suited to my nature. But now I have finally arrived at another conception of the problem in question, and this is what I would like to propose to you here.
>
> I am living out a peculiar conflict, and it is this that has so exhausted me and even caused me physical distress. By nature I am compelled by the strongest necessity to think things through in a unified philosophical way, to stick with a problem, persisting at it undisturbed, pondering it over long stretches of time. What with the many day-to-day responsibilities bound up with my profession, I feel as though I am tossed from side to side, diverted from my proper orbit. The juxtaposition of university and secondary school duties is something I cannot sustain much longer, because I feel that my proper task, which is *philosophical,* suffers from it, and indeed is reduced to being a mere avocation, something I do on the side. . . . For this reason I request permission to apply to you for the *philosophical professorship* that has opened up due to Professor Teichmüller's departure.
>
> My personal justification of this effort to attain the philosophical chair . . . is that I feel I am capable and knowledgeable in that area; in fact, all in all, I feel I am better prepared for that job than for a purely philological one. . . . As long as I have been studying philology I have never wearied of maintaining close contact with philosophy. Indeed, the principal thrust of my involvement was always on the side of the philosophical questions. . . . It is only by accident that I didn't plan my university studies in the direction of philosophy right from the start: the accident in question was that I never had a significant and truly inspiring teacher in philosophy. Given the current state of philosophy in our universities, that should come as no great surprise to you. . . .
>
> If I may sketch out more fully for you the combination I have in mind: I believe that in *Rohde* you would find a thoroughly suitable successor both for my chair in philology and for my secondary school position. . . . I can't tell you how much my existence here in Basel would be alleviated by the proximity of my best friend.— (B *3,* 175–77)

3. On Nietzsche's Empedocles fragments, see Krell, *Postponements: Woman, Sensuality, and Death in Nietzsche* (Bloomington: Indiana University Press, 1986), esp. chap. 2, "Corinna."

Nietzsche signed as a professor of classical philology, and, given the opposition from Steffensen, a philologist is what Nietzsche would officially remain until his retirement in 1879. The plan to bring Erwin Rohde to his side, and to move into a field that was closer to his calling, failed. His disappointment can be measured by the enthusiasm with which he had developed the scheme. In early February he had written to Rohde (B *3*, 183):

> My dear friend,
>
> Grand transaction, transfiguration, transubstantiation, the likes of which the world has never seen!!
>
> *Maybe* there is a prospect of our enjoying the next semester working together. You *as my successor,* and I—*as a university philosopher!!*
>
> . . . I shall write no more about it. Let's hope for the best, but *keep it quiet!*
>
> . . . Show no one this letter, including Vischer.
>
> > *Freude, schöner Götterfunken!*
> > Amicus.

Now, two months later, he was abashed. His letter to Rohde in early April (B *3*, 192–93) betrayed the new mood:

> Dear friend,
>
> I suffer under the bitter feeling that I have excited hopes in you that I shall now have to dash. . . . Now for once you have good reason to be seriously angry with me. What a stupid stunt I've pulled! And how certain I was of the combination! I dare not try to shield myself behind my sickbed, although it was a thought produced during a sleepless, feverish night. And I believed that I had discovered an elixir against illness and nerves—being together with you, my dear friend!—when all I'd done was banish it into the haziest remoteness. . . . Forgive me, dear and faithful friend, I meant well, but what can we do against the demons?
>
> > FN.

Nietzsche had sensed a split in his existence from his earliest school days, especially at Schulpforta, where the call to art and music had been muffled by criticism; or at Bonn and Leipzig, where philology had rescued him from theology but condemned him to a life of "renunciation" and "resignation"; or, finally, at Basel, where the daily grind absorbed his energies, and where even the visits to Tribschen forced him to make so many compromises of intellect and taste. As the bottleneck narrowed, Nietzsche's health showed signs of serious deterioration. He had read the situation correctly: "I am living out a peculiar conflict, and it is this that has so exhausted me and even caused me physical distress." A crisis was in the making—not the first, nor the last—on the scene of Nietzsche's health and illness. Sometimes he described it as a monstrous pregnancy: "Science, art, and philosophy now grow together in me, to the extent that some day, it seems, I will give birth to Centaurs" (B *3*, 95). His reaction to the crisis—always his first reaction—was to shift ground, to travel.

After applying for sick leave in February 1871, Nietzsche headed south for Lugano. Illness was compelling him in the direction of solitude and isolation. After an adventurous crossing of the St. Gotthard Pass in a horse-drawn sleigh, Nietzsche and Elisabeth took up residence for six weeks in the Hôtel du Parc in Lugano, on the shores of the lake that bears the same name.[4] Here his health

---

4. Today the once elegant Hôtel du Parc, later called the Grand Palace, is a ruin. A green construction screen covers its entire façade, while the city fathers and the land speculators try to decide what to do with it. It is located at the center of the boardwalk on the lake, adjacent to Santa Maria degli Angeli church.

Lugano. The Hôtel du Parc (later renamed the Grand Palace),
today in ruins, abutting the church of Santa Maria degli Angeli.
First photo: Stiftung Weimarer Klassik. GSA 101/547.

A photo (in Nietzsche's own collection) of the Hotel
Schilthorn, Gimmelwald, in the Berner Oberland.
Photo: Stiftung Weimarer Klassik. GSA 101/530.

was gradually restored. Here too he worked on the first manuscript proper of *The Birth of Tragedy from the Spirit of Music,* a book whose working title, to be sure, was less imposing: Nietzsche called it "The Origin and Goal of Tragedy" (W *7,* 167; cf. 93; B *3,* 189).

Nietzsche's summer vacation with Elisabeth in the Hotel Schilthorn, in the Gimmelwald section of Lauterbrunnen Valley in the Berner Oberland, was a relatively carefree and pleasant one, in spite of stormy weather. The autumn in Naumburg and the "greeting of the daimons" that he celebrated in November in Basel with Jacob Burckhardt—a large glass of Rhône wine, half poured into the streets, half drunk, with the concluding cry, χαίρετε δαίμονες, "Hail to the Daimons!"— were happy occasions, perhaps the most congenial of his Basel years (B *3,* 244, 246, 248). He returned to his teaching, happy and reinvigorated. At the end of the year, on December 17, 1871, he accompanied Cosima to a concert conducted by Richard Wagner in Mannheim. As a Christmas gift he dedicated to her a piano piece for four hands, "Echoes of a New Year's Eve." He did not dare travel to Tribschen himself for Christmas, fearing the Meister's judgment of his music, and perhaps fearful of which four hands would mingle over his piece. Cosima's and Richard's judgment of the music oscillated somewhere between scorn and condescending sympathy, but they remained discreet, and Nietzsche never really learned how his gift had been received.

The Birth of Tragedy, Nietzsche's first major work, published during the first week of 1872, was the result of several years' work. Five significant stages on the way to the first half of it may be identified: first, Nietzsche's two public lectures at Basel, "The Greek Music Drama," presented on January 18, 1870, and "Socrates and Tragedy," delivered on February 1; second, the manuscript "The Dionysian Worldview" (W *1,* 551–77), presented in 1870 as a Christmas gift to Cosima Wagner under the title "The Birth of the Tragic Thought" (W *1,* 579–99); third, his plan entitled "Tragedy and the Free Spirits," sketched out on September 22, 1870, in Naumburg (W *7,* 103–4), which considerably expanded the scope of his inquiry; fourth, the new version of the opening sections of *The Birth of Tragedy,* written in Lugano in January-February 1871; and fifth, "Socrates and Greek Tragedy," from the spring of 1871, a draft of sections 11–15 of *The Birth of Tragedy* (W *1,* 601–40).

In another sense, *The Birth of Tragedy* represented much more than the fruits of several years' work. It pointed back to Nietzsche's earliest experiences, which were profoundly dark. When Nietzsche glanced behind the shimmering veil of Olympian appearances, he saw a gaping tomb in the cemetery of his infancy. As evangelical as God's green acre appeared to be, Dionysos Zagreus, the god torn to pieces by the Titans, haunted that space. So did the duplicitous Socrates, who as logician and dialectician brought tragedy to an end, but who as the music-practicing and dying human being portrayed in Plato's masterful dialogues continued to seduce the youths of every Athens in Western history. *The Birth of Tragedy* also pointed far ahead to all the work Nietzsche would do in the future, inasmuch as he continued to think about tragedy—especially about the tragedy of all thinking.

The responses to the book were long in coming, and Nietzsche awaited them with trepidation. When the wait grew too long, and when the outraged voices were finally heard, he suspected that one opponent was right when he claimed that the philologist Nietzsche was, "in terms of our discipline, dead." Concerning his beloved, derided newborn he exclaimed, "It is as though I had committed a crime" (B *4,* 71). He was drawn into a polemic with Ulrich von Wilamowitz-Moellendorf, who lambasted Nietzsche's *Birth of Tragedy* as bad philology and tasteless Wagnerian fluff. The peroration of Wilamowitz's "Philology of the Future" read: "I demand one thing: let Herr N. keep his word, let him take up the thyrsus and sweep across India to Greece; but he should step away from the lectern, where he is supposed to be teaching a science. Let him gather tigers and panthers about his knees, but not Germany's young philologists, who are supposed to be learning the *askese* of self-denying work" (N *1,* 469). Wilamowitz's ban appeared almost simultaneously with a positive review by Erwin Rohde, but it was not until Rohde's reply to Wilamowitz, entitled *Afterphilologie,* which may be variously translated as "second-rate philology" or "anal-compulsive philology," that the polemic exploded. Even Ritschl began to distance himself from his most promising student, and Nietzsche's own students in Basel stayed away in droves. Nietzsche retaliated by spoofing Wilamowitz's name in letters to his friends: there we find references to German equivalents of "Will o' the Wisp's whisk at Fritz Nietzsche's Fritsch wits" (Fritsch was Nietzsche's publisher), "William without Wits," and "Willy Whamo-wuss" (B *4,* 14, 30). Yet Nietzsche knew well that such polemics would only distract him from his proper task. In letters written some months later he urged himself to cease and desist: "Meanwhile, I must extract from myself everything polemical negative hateful torturous"; and he posed the rhetorical question, "How will I feel once I have purged all the negativity and outrage that lie concealed in me?" (B *4,* 224; 268). Several years later he confessed to Hans von Bülow that such purgation was the primary purpose of all his planned *Untimely Meditations:* "The next five years I have determined as the period in which I will work out the remaining ten *Untimelies,* so that I can cleanse my soul of all its passionate, polemical waste" (B *5,* 3). His mood during this period of birth (the birth of tragic thinking) and death (the slow and painful death of a philologist) was best expressed in a letter of condolence that he wrote to Carl von Gersdorff, whose brother had died after spending several years in an insane asylum: "He has gotten over it, this existence of ours—you and I still have to do so, and among the most difficult things we have to get over is the ever-greater isolation that advances with relentless footfall—our siblings parents friends—they all slip away, everything eventually becomes a part of the past, as do we ourselves" (B *4,* 100).

The next five years found the renegade philologist making his way from philology to philosophy—either to the early Greek philosophers he was lecturing on, or to Schopenhauer, who was for him a "physician of culture," and Wagner, the very incarnation of Schopenhauerian genius. Already in Lugano, working on the final manuscript of *The Birth of Tragedy,* Nietzsche felt the pressure of a split, a schism or schizophrenia, in his professional, professorial self: "I live with a keen sense of alienation from philology, the most aggravated sort of alienation one could think of: praise and blame, indeed, all the highest hymns of praise that I receive on this side, make me shudder. Thus I live by gradually moving toward my philosophical existence, and already I believe in myself; and even if, on top of it all, I should become a poet, I am ready for it" (B *3,* 190).

The first phase in this transformation was the series of lectures "On the Future of Our Educational Institutes," whereby the "Our" was a misnomer, inasmuch as it was principally the German Gymnasium that Nietzsche had in mind, not the educational institutes of the Swiss cantons. The five lectures, which the "Voluntary Academic Society" of Basel had invited him to deliver during the months of January through March 1872, were marked by a lively, dramatic style; the young academic freely borrowed aspects of his own experiences at Pforta and Bonn in order to develop his criticism of all educational practices that stifle genius. He delivered the lectures to some three hundred listeners, who were disappointed, however, when Nietzsche proved unable to devise a sixth and final lecture with concrete suggestions for educational reform. Jacob Burckhardt waxed enthusiastic over these lectures, but noted the "profound melancholy" that permeated them, and the missing proposals and dim prospects for improvement (N *1,* 447). Just as Nietzsche was unable to confront in a sustained way the socioeconomic transformations that were revolutionizing the social order of his times, he had little to say about the role of schools and universities in such a world. His passion for pedagogy, his desire to be a teacher of teachers, would never die, but it would assume odd forms in

Nietzsche's growing isolation. Having planned to publish these lectures as his second major work (B *3, 296*), he eventually let the project die (B *4, 127*).

Nietzsche's four *Untimely Meditations,* further way stations, were written during the years 1873–75. Rather, they were *dictated,* since Nietzsche's eyes were usually too weak for reading and writing once atropine treatments began in the spring of 1873. The first, a polemic against David Friedrich Strauss, written at Wagner's behest in the spring of 1873, is perhaps best remembered because of Nietzsche's insistence there that the Prussian victory over France in 1870 was by no means accompanied by advances in German culture. The second, originally planned as an essay on "the plight of philosophy," became Nietzsche's major meditation on history, "On the Use and Disadvantage of History for Life." It is noteworthy that even Jacob Burckhardt felt defensive about his own practice of historical research after reading his young colleague's attack on "antiquarian" and "monumental" approaches to history. The third, "Schopenhauer as Educator," largely ignored Schopenhauer's teachings and focused instead on his heroic struggle to resist academic philosophy.[5] Finally, "Richard Wagner in Bayreuth" was a celebration of the *effort* in which Wagner was engaged, but was riddled with doubts about both the "Wagnerians" and the Meister himself, who sometimes seemed more showman than artist. Another projected *Untimely Meditation* was "The Plowshare," a project never realized. Indeed, according to several of Nietzsche's plans, there were more than a dozen unfulfilled *Untimely Meditations:* "I am duty-bound to fertility said the cat, as she dropped a litter of thirteen" (B *4, 230*).

A third way station was Nietzsche's text *Philosophy in the Tragic Age of the Greeks,* which at one point he also planned to publish as his second major work. "The path from Thales to Socrates," he exclaimed to von Gersdorff, "is simply extraordinary" (B *4, 139*). Yet the assignments he received from Wagner distracted him from his work on this very rich text, which he left behind as a highly polished piece of literary remains. The same must be said for the essay "Truth and Lie in a Nonmoral Sense," philosophically speaking the most far-reaching of Nietzsche's early pieces. It is related to the earlier "Pathos of Truth," one of his *Five Prefaces to Five Unwritten Books,* a Christmas present to Cosima Wagner in 1872. "The Pathos of Truth" and "Truth and Lie" contain an almost identical passage, one of the most memorable in Nietzsche's œuvre: "In some remote corner of universal space, glimmering with the numberless solar systems that were spilled out into it, there was once a star on which clever animals invented *knowing.* It was the most arrogant and mendacious minute of universal history, but still only a minute. After nature drew a few breaths, the star congealed, and the clever animals had to die" (W *1, 759; 875*).

Finally, Nietzsche's notebooks of the early 1870s exhibit his fascination not only with the Greek philosophers but also with Kant's metaphysics and aesthetics, along with issues in contemporary chemistry, physics, cosmology, and biology. They also contain notes that resist classification, notes in Nietzsche's own voice, so to speak, which we discern amid the voices of Prometheus, Ermanarich, and Empedocles. For an instant in these notebooks, Nietzsche's voice is that of Oedipus.

In the spring of 1872 a young colleague at the University of Freiburg-im-Breisgau, Karl Mendelssohn-Bartholdy, son of the composer, invited Nietzsche to travel with him to Athens,

5. To Cosima Wagner Nietzsche wrote on December 19, 1876: "Will you be astonished if I tell you that I have to confess a difference that I have with Schopenhauer's doctrine, a difference that developed quite gradually, but of which I have suddenly become aware? In terms of almost all his general claims I do not take his side; even while I was writing about him I noticed that I was already beyond all questions of dogma. For me, what was important was the *human being*" (B *5, 210*). The same rejection of Schopenhauer's teachings was declared to Paul Deussen in even stronger terms: see Nietzsche's letter of early August 1877 (B *5, 264–65*).

OEDIPUS

Talks

of the Last Philosopher

with Himself.

A Fragment

from the History of Posterity.

I call myself the last philosopher because I am the last human being. No one talks to me other than myself, and my voice comes to me as the voice of a dying man. With you, beloved voice, with you, the last vaporous remembrance of all human happiness, let me tarry an hour longer. With your help I shall deceive myself about my loneliness; I shall lie my way back into society and love. For my heart refuses to believe that love is dead, cannot bear the terror of the loneliest loneliness: it compels me to talk, as though I were two.

   Do I hear you still, my voice? You whisper as you curse? And yet your curse should cause the bowels of this world to burst! But the world lives on, gazing at me all the more brilliantly and coldly with its pitiless stars; lives on, as brutish and blind as it ever was; and only one dies—the human being. And yet! I hear you still, beloved voice! Another besides me dies, another besides me, the last human being in the universe: the last sigh, *your* sigh, dies with me—the prolonged *Woe! Woe!* sighed about me, the last of the men of woe, Oedipus. (W 7, 460–61)

Crete, and Naxos. Fearful of offending the Wagners, Nietzsche declined the invitation. Wagner had written a tract against Mendelssohn and Meyerbeer, *Judaism in Music,* and Wagner's young epigone did not want to be associated with the Meister's enemies. Indeed, Nietzsche's letters at this time, especially those to his mother or to Richard and Cosima Wagner, did not shy from ugly and slighting remarks about Jews and Judaism. Only when he had gained distance from Bayreuth and from the Wagners, from 1876 onward, and especially after he had befriended Paul Rée during the winter of 1876–77, did Nietzsche's appreciation of Jewish culture and his hatred of the anti-Semitism that was so strong in the German lands begin to prevail. Elisabeth's marriage to one of the leading German anti-Semites, Bernhard Förster, only confirmed Nietzsche's long-term development toward philo-Semitism. While his relation to the religion and the moral codices of Judaism remained ambivalent, Nietzsche came to identify European high culture as largely the creation of the Jews. Yet in 1872 he was still under the shadow of Bayreuth. Nietzsche's early resistance to things and people "Jewish" deprived him of his one chance to see the snows of Cretan Mount Ida or the coasts of Ariadne's Naxos. The Maderanertal was as close to Parnassus as he would get—except perhaps for Paestum, which he presumably visited in 1876–77 and which would have to communicate to him the sense of all the sites of ancient Greece.

Entrance to the Hotel Fantaisie near Bayreuth, where the Wagners sojourned from April to August 1872.

In April 1872 the Wagners moved from Tribschen to Bayreuth. The abandonment of his "Isle of the Blessed" left Nietzsche disconsolate. Once again he was homeless. He and Rohde visited the Wagners in their delightful summer residence outside Bayreuth, the Hotel Fantaisie, where the Meister and his entourage stayed from April to August. Wagner laid the cornerstone of the Festspielhaus in Bayreuth on his fifty-ninth birthday, May 22. While Nietzsche was convinced of the importance of the event, he remained uncertain as to whether the cultural world was ready for the Wagnerian challenge; at bottom, he was not sure Wagner could withstand the temptation to turn it all into show, to betray music with spectacle, and to capitalize on the betrayal.

Meanwhile, Nietzsche distanced himself more and more from his own musical compositions. Wagner had teased him about his passionate improvisations at the piano, although this was an area in which Nietzsche could not abide teasing. Nietzsche sent one of his last compositions, his "Manfred-Meditation," which was based on his early admiration of Byron, to Hans von Bülow, who replied in hyperbolic fashion: "Your 'Manfred-Meditation' is the very extremity of extravaganza and phantasmagoria, the most unregenerate and antimusical thing I've seen put to staff paper in a long time" (N *1,* 479). Nietzsche's reply was surprisingly mellow and meditative: "You must realize that since my *earliest* youth and up to the present moment I have been living under the craziest illusion: I've taken *so much* joy in my music! . . . It has always been a problem for me to know whence this joy arises. There was something so irrational about it: in this regard I could turn neither left nor right, the joy was always there in front of me" (B *4,* 79). Curt Paul Janz suggests that in these late pieces Nietzsche's music became heavier, more cumbersome, less formally refined, and less lyrical—in spite of his tendency to "Impressionism" (N *1,* 480). Apart from the fact that one can as easily speak of Nietzsche's "Expressionism," there is some truth in thinking of Nietzsche's own music as wandering a path from Schumann to Satie—but a Satie who has lost his capacity for whimsy.

In the last days of September 1872 Nietzsche enjoyed a brief holiday in Splügen and Chiavenna, to which he traveled by way of Chur and the nearby Bad Passugg. For the first time he traveled the spectacular Via Mala, from Bad Passugg via Thusis to Splügen, heading toward that part of the Swiss Alps—in the canton of Graubünden (or Grisons)—that would become so important to him. He communicated to his mother his first impressions:

> The city of Chur is at Sunday rest, the mood defined by the afternoon. I ascend the country road easily: everything reposes before me in the golden transfiguration of autumn, as I saw it the day before. Splendid views to my rear; continuously changing, ever-expanding outlooks. After half an hour I take a small side path that leads me into lovely shade—for by then it is fairly warm. On this path I arrive at the gully through which the *Rabiusa* surges: I cannot praise it adequately. Across bridges and along narrow paths that cling to cliffs, after another half-hour, I make my way to Bad Passugg, which is announced by a little flag. . . . The valley is utterly charming, and for a geologist, replete with minerals, minerals for every mood. I found veins of graphite, but also quartz with ochre, and the man who owned the land even had fantasies of gold deposits. One sees the most variegated veins of stone and all kinds of rocks—twisted, contorted, creased. . . . (B *4,* 53–54)

The next day he took the post coach to Splügen, deep into Graubünden, almost as far south as St. Moritz in the Engadine, the valley farther east that would be a home to him in the 1880s. His letter continues to report his discoveries of Alpine splendor and solitude:

> It was the most beautiful coach ride I have ever taken. I can write nothing that is adequate to the magnificence of the vast *Via Mala.* It is as though I had never been in Switzerland before. That is *my* kind of nature. And as we came close to Splügen, the wish to stay there overwhelmed me. . . . This valley in the high Alps (about 5,000 feet) is to my taste: bracing air, hills, cliffs and boulders of all shapes, surrounded by the mighty snowcaps. Yet what I like best are the splendid country roads on which I hike for hours, sometimes toward the Bernardino, sometimes up to Splügen Pass, without having to pay any attention to the road surface. Every time I turn my head I am bound to see something splendid and unexpected. It seems that it will snow tomorrow: I look forward to it with joy. . . .
>
> You cannot imagine how much I like it here. Since coming to this place, I find that Switzerland has a new charm for me; now I know a corner where I can live in a way that invigorates and refreshes me, but without any form of society. Human beings strike one here as remote shadows. (B *4,* 55–56)

Two weeks later, again to his mother, he offered a summary report on his Alpine idyll: "I have nothing to tell—the air of the heights! the air of the high Alps! the air of the central high Alps!" (B *4,* 67). Nietzsche did of course *see* where he was; yet he traveled mainly in order to *breathe.* He now possessed one of the two places to which he would regularly repair, once the professorship at Basel had been laid to rest. He had not yet swum in the sea, but he had breathed in his mountains.

The next summer, during July-August 1873, he was in Flims-Waldhaus with his friends Romundt and von Gersdorff, staying at the Hotel Segnes-Post. Von Gersdorff reported that what they most enjoyed at Flims were long walks through the shadowy forests of pine and larch and swims in the milky green Caumasee. The lake lay several hundred meters from their hotel, down a steep, winding path. "We undress and dress to the insistent croaking of a huge frog," added von Gersdorff, noting also that the lake was "said to have curative properties" (N *1,* 543). The friends then sprawled on moss and larch needles, reading Plutarch, Goethe, and Wagner, and indulging in lengthy discussions; it was at Flims that Nietzsche dictated to von Gersdorff his essay "On Truth and Lie in a Nonmoral Sense," based on notes jotted down the previous summer. He had green curtains hung in his room at the Segnes; green was also the color he would later choose for the wallpaper and for the tablecloth in his room at Sils—always green, for the sake of his light-sensitive eyes. Yet the friends spent most of their time in the verdant outdoors, where Nietzsche no doubt sported his green sun visor. Von Gersdorff reported: "The region is splendid: a gradually ascending mountain valley of quite broad dimensions, covered with abundant forest, bordered by foothills and high mountains. Across from our hotel, off to the left, towers the Flimser Stein, a picturesque cliff that faces us, having nothing of the oppressive breadth of the gray Mönch. . . . The beautiful larch forest stretches right up to our house, giving us shade against the sun all day long. . . . There is a superabundance of brooks, rushing by, gurgling lustily. . . . An endless multiplicity of colors and forms in nature—that is the magic of our place here" (ibid.). On August 9 the first published copy of Nietzsche's first *Untimely Meditation* reached him; the friends swam out to a large rock in the Caumasee and carved into it: U. B. I. F. N. 8./8. 1873: *Unzeitgemäße Betrachtungen I,* by F. N., with the publication date.

When he returned to Basel, Nietzsche continued to give his eyes a rest, or continued *trying* to do so. He worked on a second *Untimely,* "The Plight of Philosophy," but the essay would not jell. Later in the fall, after composing a tract for Wagner's Bayreuth group (a piece the committee eventually rejected, however, so that Nietzsche had wasted his time), he began to write the best known of the four *Untimely Meditations,* "On the Use and Disadvantage of History for Life." Von Gersdorff helped prepare the printer's manuscript in December 1873. In January 1874 Nietzsche was elected dean of his faculty for that year. How he found the time to read and take notes on a whole range of works in theoretical physics and cosmology, wrestling especially with the *problem* of time, no one knows.

In the summer of 1874 he traveled with his friend Romundt to Bergün, farther east than Splügen and much farther south than Flims. Bergün lies nestled in another of Switzerland's breathtaking and breath-giving valleys, the Albula Valley *(Albulatal),* at the point where, at 1,400 meters, it begins its long climb toward the pass that opens onto the Upper Engadine *(Oberengadin).* In the Hotel Piz Aela, Nietzsche was working on the third of his *Untimely Meditations,* "Schopenhauer as Educator." He wrote his mother:

Coat of arms on the Hotel Piz Aela in Bergün, Albulatal. It mentions the important local family *Salis,* the name of Nietzsche's future friend, Meta von Salis-Marschlins. Concerning his first trip to the Albula Valley, Nietzsche wrote to Franz Overbeck in Basel on July 30, 1874 (B *4,* 252): "Here we are living in a fine hotel, where we are well taken care of, and not overcharged. . . . Up to now we have seen a cliff near the Albula bridge, which connects and surveys two lonely valleys in the high mountains, a place where I would like to build myself a tower, and a sulphur spring in one of the side valleys—we brought some of the water home with us in bottles in order to eliminate any bowel obstructions that our consumption of Veltliner wine may induce."

My dear and good Mother, I am sitting here in the mountains and want to write you a little note. . . . Dreary rain has fallen for a few days now, and all the people here are very
impatient—that's the general state of mind in this isolation, except for me, inasmuch as I
am thinking about how I can finish up this new text of mine. I am living somewhere else,
somewhere where the rain does one no harm. Otherwise one enjoys the invigorating air
of the Alps without even thinking about it; one has escaped from the city and the daily
grind; things occur to one here that do not stir down below, in the humid summer of the
city. (B *4*, 248)

Writing to Carl von Gersdorff on July 26, 1874, Nietzsche related some more details of his and
Romundt's life in the Albulatal:

Here (in Bergün: take a look at Baedeker) I am with Romundt in a heavenly area. We are
the sole guests in a hotel that hundreds of travelers pass by every day on their way to or
from St. Moritz. Of course, we do not have a lake like the one we had at Flims: recently
we located one about three hours up the mountain, at about 6,000 feet, bathing and swimming in it until we almost froze, emerging a fiery red color. Today we went looking for a
sulphur spring that has not yet been developed; on the way home a goat gave birth to her
kid before my eyes. It was the first birth of a living thing I had ever seen. The kid was
much more agile than a small child is, and also looked better; its mother licked it and in
general behaved in a very rational manner, while Romundt and I stood there looking like
a couple of hopeless dummies. (B *4*, 247)

To his sister he wrote in a less sanguine and bucolic fashion, confessing to her his exhaustion:
"Yet it is a terrible thing, always having to swim against the tide, and sometimes I am weary of life"
(B *4*, 250). After returning to Basel, he described his state of mind in greater detail to Erwin Rohde
on October 7, 1874:

It's not that I am discouraged or lack confidence: I brought courage and confidence back
with me from the tranquillity of the mountains and lakes. Up there I soon noticed what my
life was missing, or rather what I had in excess, namely, self-centeredness. And that comes
from this everlasting brooding on myself, and my continuous suffering. In the end one *feels
oneself continuously,* as though one had a hundred scars, as though every movement hurt. But
truly, I'll soon be thirty, and a few things have to change: I have to become more manly and
more stable, so it isn't always a matter of these damned ups and downs. (B *4*, 261–62)

On August 4 he traveled to Bayreuth, where the Wagners' splendid new residence, "Wahnfried," had been largely completed. He made the mistake of taking with him a piano version of
Johannes Brahms's "Triumphal Hymn," which he had heard at a concert in the Münster at Basel and
once again in Zürich. He had suddenly fallen in love with Brahms's music and did not see why
Wagner too should not confess his admiration. Cosima prevented Wagner's fury from leading to an
open break between the two. Yet perhaps for the first time Nietzsche saw the Meister, the Schopenhauerian genius, as a jealous petty tyrant.

Nietzsche attempted several cures at spas before taking up his teaching duties in Basel for the
academic year 1874–75. His health was poor: stomach trouble now joined the migraines and the
severe myopia and eyestrain to plague his existence. From this year on, Nietzsche was never truly
well again. He tried to work on a fourth *Untimely,* "We Philologists," yet found that he was now so
little a part of the "we" that the work was doomed. Other things happened that contributed to his
dour mood: Gustav Krug's father died on the eve of his son's wedding, and as Nietzsche wrote a letter of condolence he touched an old scar of his own, worried a still-open wound:

Today, my dear friend, you must hear also from me a few words of heartfelt sorrow. To be
sure, on the basis of my own experience I know almost as little what it means to lose a

The house in which Nietzsche resided during his cure at Steinabad bei Bonndorf, Black Forest, Germany.

father as to have one. For that reason my early inner life was more difficult and oppressive than anyone's should be. Precisely out of the often-felt need for a truly intimate and loving counselor, I dare say I understand today the degree and scope of your loss.

When I see you now in my mind's eye, two words seem to be tied together in an enigmatic way: death and marriage. These two words follow one another so quickly that it seems there can be no end to the period in which we live and flourish. . . .

And so the wondrous and monstrous question that the word "death" poses may have the other word as one of its answers. *One* possible answer. For perhaps there are several.—(B *4*, 240)

At the end of June 1875 Nietzsche wrote Carl Fuchs of the "atrocious crisis" in his health, stemming principally from a stomach ailment, which was beginning to "rattle the fortress walls" of his existence (B *5*, 66). He consulted his doctors, then chose a spa in the Black Forest region of Germany, not far from Basel. On July 16, 1875, Nietzsche headed for Steinabad, near Bonndorf. He could not really compare Steinabad and the Schwarzwald to Bergün and the Albulatal: the sublimity of the high Alps of Graubünden was nowhere seen or felt in the verdant, velvet textures of the Black Forest. Yet he could not help but compare Steinabad to Flims-Waldhaus, which he had visited with von Gersdorff and Romundt two years earlier: the many walking paths in Steinabad were broader and more level—the descent from Flims-Waldhaus to the Caumasee had been quite narrow and steep. He conceded that the beauty of Flims had been more powerful, but praised the way in which the Black Forest was remarkably dense, intimate, and absorbing—a body could lose

The Roggenbacher ruins, a robber baron fortress dominating the valley near Steinabad.

himself and all his cares in it. The forest was especially beneficial to his eyes: he spent many hours walking in the shade of giant white and red pines, oaks, birches, beeches, and ash trees. He ambled by the trout pond in the clearing and entered into the deep shadows of the forest. He took longer hikes to a medieval fortress, the Roggenbacher ruins, whose mighty walls and towers had been destroyed during the Peasant Rebellion of 1524–25. He wrote to his mother and sister on July 25, 1875, "I walk a lot through the woods here, and amuse myself very well, so that I haven't had a single hour of boredom; I am thinking things over, thinking them through, full of hope and confidence, sometimes about the past, but much more often about the future; it is my style of life, and it is my style of recuperation too" (B 5, 89).

One of Nietzsche's pupils, Louis Kelterborn, visited his esteemed teacher at Steinabad, and recorded the following:

> Of course, I could see from his facial expression and his skin tone that he was in poor health. He also told me in detail of his regimen at the spa. . . . He then took me on a tour of the entire establishment and the surrounding park area; he tried to get me to go swim-

ming, but I declined. After we ate, we hiked for several hours through the magnificent forests thereabouts. Nietzsche was always a sturdy hiker, and his steady pace and stride—taking very long steps, and moving always in a regular rhythm—seemed to do him good. We met only a few other hikers, and our path took us through some small villages. . . . We felt liberated from everything hectic, and in this mood of profound contentment and equanimity I enjoyed my conversation with him twice as much as usual—and my conversations with him were always uncommonly stimulating and significant for me. Finally, our talk turned to personal matters . . . , but then veered back again to questions of music, music in general and Wagner in particular. They were holding the rehearsals in Bayreuth just then, and so we were thinking about them. (N *1*, 617)

Nietzsche hoped that his summer cure in Steinabad would make him "Bayreuth-fit," that is, capable of traveling to Bayreuth for the Festspiel at summer's end (B *5*, 75). In this respect, the cure failed. In other respects it had very beneficial effects. He found plenty of time—and sufficient eyesight—for reading: on July 19 he wrote to a friend of the "streaming rain" that was drenching the Black Forest. Like a "Hungarian grain speculator," Nietzsche estimated that it would be "a lovely twelve-hour rain," surely a minimal estimate for the Black Forest! At the moment of writing he was studying an area in which he had done little work in the past: the development of world trade, commerce, and social and political economy.[6]

Nietzsche began to write "Richard Wagner in Bayreuth," the fourth of his *Untimely Meditations*, precisely because he himself could not be there: his text proved to be an exercise in enforced distance from Wagner. The summer of 1875 was also a time of plans for future studies—Nietzsche at one point referred to his "basketful of work for the next seven years," including studies in the historical and natural sciences. To Carl von Gersdorff he wrote: "We still have a good stretch of the way to climb, and we shall climb slowly, but on and on, in order to attain an unobstructed view of *our superannuated civilization*. And one must make one's laborious way through several of the sciences, above all, the *strict* sciences properly speaking. Yet such patient progression is our kind of happiness, and I don't want much more than that" (B *5*, 87). In other letters he spoke of his "big plans," not only for future study, but for the *writing* that would grant his life the coherence it craved. His thoughts about the style of his earlier writings, the *Untimely Meditations* and *The Birth of Tragedy*, were also becoming more critical. In a letter to a French colleague who had complimented him on his *Birth of Tragedy*, Nietzsche expressed nagging doubts "whether with the style of my writings—their endless monologue—I have drawn the best from myself as an author" (B *5*, 107). The fourth *Untimely*, on which he began to brood in Steinabad, would take longer to write than all the others put together, but it too would be in the style of monologue. A very different kind of style, however, a style of multiple voices and traces, was preparing itself in him. Meanwhile, Nietzsche decided that even if he were to live for others, he would have to write for himself—*mihi scribo, aliis vivo*, he wrote to Romundt (B *5*, 116)—and that he would not publish "Richard Wagner in Bayreuth" even

6. B *5*, 82. These Steinabad studies did not find expression in Nietzsche's works until the second part of *Human, All-Too-Human*, published at the end of 1879: see especially aphorism 286 of "The Wanderer and His Shadow," on private property, under the title "Whether possession can be brought into equilibrium with justice." Nietzsche's views on social theory and practice are more complex (and more noteworthy) than commonly supposed. Consider the conclusion to MAM II, WS, 286: "In order that possession can from now on enjoy greater confidence and become more moral, one should keep open all the avenues of work that lead to *small amounts* of acquisition; one should hinder effortless and sudden enrichment; one should withdraw from private hands and private corporations every branch of transportation and commerce that leads to the accumulation of *large amounts* of wealth, including all the branches of finance and banking. — One should see both those who possess too much and those who possess too little as equally dangerous" (W *2*, 681).

if he should manage to complete it. It was also a time of personal reflection, especially on the importance of friendship. He closed a letter to Rohde dated August 1 with some thoughts about Bayreuth—where his friend was already in attendance at the summer festival:

> Desperation everywhere! And yet I am *not* desperate! Even though I am not in Bayreuth! Can you figure that one out? I am almost unable to. And yet in spirit I spend three-quarters of my day there, hovering always like a ghost over Bayreuth. Don't worry about teasing my mind: tell me a little bit about everything, dearest friend. Often enough on my walks I direct whole sequences of the music, which I know by heart, humming away like crazy. Give the Wagners my warmest greetings! (B *5,* 94)

Finally, the letters from Steinabad all reflect Nietzsche's concern with the relation of illness to one's lifework: on the one hand, periods of illness force us to take our lives and our limitations more seriously, and thus give us an opportunity to focus and to plan carefully; on the other hand, illness can so weaken and depress us that we lose the courage to engage in any serious planning, so that we dither and dwindle. "It isn't death I'm most afraid of," he wrote to a musician friend, "but a life of illness, in which one mislays the *causa vitae*" (B *5,* 100). On August 11, 1875, he wrote to Malwida von Meysenbug in Paris:

> I am once again making plan after plan, trying to bring my life into some kind of order—there is nothing I am more inclined to do and am happier to do as soon as I am by myself. This serves as a genuine barometer for my health. Such as we, I mean you and I, *never suffer in body alone,* but all is profoundly permeated by spiritual crises, so that I cannot imagine how I could ever regain my health by frequenting pharmacies and kitchens. . . . The secret of all convalescence for us is to develop a thick skin, the sole antidote to our massive inner vulnerability and capacity for suffering. At least nothing *from outside* should be able so easily to collide with us and do us harm. At any rate, nothing is more painful for me than to be held against the fire on both sides at once, on the inside and the outside.— (B *5,* 104)

Perhaps the most remarkable letter mailed during this Steinabad summer, a summer rich in letters, is the one dated August 2, 1875, to Frau Marie Baumgartner. The mother of one of Nietzsche's students, residing in nearby Lörrach, Marie Baumgartner proved to be one of Nietzsche's most generous and capable friends during the Basel years, helping him with manuscripts, proofs, translations, and similar matters. In a letter to Erwin Rohde, Nietzsche called her "the best mother I've ever known" (B *5,* 93). To Marie herself he wrote:

> You mustn't believe that I was ever in my life spoiled by an excess of love. I believe you have noticed this fact about me, too. In this regard I bear traces of resignation, ever since my earliest childhood. Yet it may be that I never deserved anything better. Now, however, I *do* have it better, no doubt about it! Sometimes I am astonished by it even more than I take joy in it, it is so new to me. Now a number of things are growing in me, and from month to month I see things more clearly with regard to my life's task, although I do not have the courage to tell anyone about it. A calm but quite decisive advance from stage to stage—that is what promises to take me very far. It occurs to me that I am a born *mountain* climber.—You see how *proudly* I can talk.— (B *5,* 95)

Back in Basel, Nietzsche moved into more spacious lodgings on the Spalentorweg. His sister was still with him, the sister who had kept house for him over so many years now, whom he praised for a temperament that matched his own (B *5,* 112). He crawled into his "snail's shell" and wrote. His health continued to deteriorate during that fall and winter, becoming critical during the Christmas holidays—always a time of crisis for Nietzsche throughout his adult life. In January 1876 he wrote von Gersdorff from Naumburg:

It is laborious for me to write, and so I shall be brief. Dearest friend, I've just put the most terrible, painful, uncanny Christmas of all behind me! On Christmas Eve, after many preliminary attacks, which supervened with increasing frequency, I suffered something like a total collapse. I could no longer doubt that I am plagued by a serious illness of the brain, and that my stomach and my eyes suffer only because of this illness in the central nervous system. My father died at age thirty-six of an inflammation of the brain; it is possible that matters will move more quickly in my case. . . . There is as yet no real reconvalescence; my uncanny state has *not* been alleviated; at every instant I am reminded of him. (B *5*, 132)

He was given permission to find a temporary replacement for his secondary school teaching, and it was all he could do to teach his lecture courses and seminars at the university. For spring break, he and von Gersdorff traveled to the eastern shore of Lake Geneva, visiting Veytaux and the castle of Chillon, near Montreux, staying in the Pension Printannière. In spite of the cold, rainy weather, the friends took daily walks for five or six hours at a stretch. They visited Bex, in the Rhône Valley southeast of the lake; there too they set out on vigorous walks, in spite of Nietzsche's ill-health. Nietzsche seems always to have possessed a high energy level, no matter how sick he was—probably a result of his robust constitution, which his illness would batter mercilessly over many years before it finally dragged him down (N *1*, 627). He visited friends in Geneva during the month of April, and, after a brief acquaintance, proposed marriage to Mathilde Trampedach, a young musician from the Baltic region, whom one contemporary described as a creation of Fra Lippo Lippi. The proposal came so suddenly that one suspects that Nietzsche was inviting the rejection he duly received.

During these years, Nietzsche struck up acquaintanceships and developed friendships that remained important for the rest of his life and work. For example, with Heinrich Köselitz, a musician and composer who assumed the pseudonym *Peter Gast*. Gast would be remembered as one of Nietzsche's editors—or, rather, as an editor used and abused by Nietzsche's sister. Nietzsche's friendship with Köselitz too was a friendship of unequals. The philosopher tried to publicize "Peter Gast's" musical productions, today fallen into oblivion, while Köselitz transcribed endless manuscripts and corrected countless pages of proof for Nietzsche. By contrast, Paul Rée would be a friend—and rival—of the most intimate sort. He first arrived in Basel in the spring of 1873 as a friend of Romundt's, but Nietzsche and Rée became firm friends during Nietzsche's year off in Sorrento. Malwida von Meysenbug, a Wagner enthusiast and intellectual who became one of Nietzsche's most loyal friends, invited the two of them to travel with her to Sorrento, near Naples, in the autumn of 1876. Von Meysenbug, along with Marie Baumgartner, was destined to be a "mother" to Nietzsche, one who was sympathetic to his work as well as personally supportive of him. In Sorrento, Rée worked on his book *The Origin of Moral Sensibilities,* a project that influenced Nietzsche more by its intent than its content.[7] It was during the autumn, winter, and spring of 1876–77 in Sorrento that Nietzsche's studies took a definitive turn to questions of values and moralities. His notes, eventually taken up into *Human, All-Too-Human,* exhibited the most decisive turn in Nietzsche's career: "we philologists" were now becoming genealogists of morals.

Perhaps the best insight into Nietzsche's friendship with Malwida von Meysenbug—a remark-

7. To be sure, Nietzsche always denied Rée's influence, not only in the fourth paragraph of his preface to *On the Genealogy of Morals* (W *5*, 250-51), written and published in 1887, but already, and in the strongest possible terms, in a letter to Erwin Rohde in mid-June 1878 (B *5*, 333). It is nevertheless true that the influence was mutual. Rée dedicated a copy of his *Moral Sensibilities* to Nietzsche with the phrase, "To the father of this text, most gratefully, from its mother." Yet it was Paul Rée more than anyone else who encouraged the move that Nietzsche himself was making, from philology to genealogy—the genealogy of morals.

Malwida von Meysenbug (1816-1903), Nietzsche's friend since 1872, Wagner enthusiast, idealist, educator, and emancipator. Photo: Stiftung Weimarer Klassik. GSA 101/293.

Paul Rée (1849-1901), author of *The Origin of Moral Sensibilities* (1877), Nietzsche's friend since 1873 and eventual rival for the affections of Lou von Salomé. Photo: Stiftung Weimarer Klassik. GSA 101/385.

able woman, too little known in the English-speaking world—comes from a letter Nietzsche sent her after having read her *Memoirs of an Idealist*. On Good Friday, April 14, 1876, Nietzsche wrote her from Basel:

> About two weeks ago, of a Sunday, I hied off to the shore of Lake Geneva and spent the entire day, from early dawn to moonlit dusk, quite close to you: with my senses restored to health, I read your book to the end, saying to myself over and over again that I'd never experienced a more consecrated Sunday; the mood of purity and love did not forsake me, and all nature on that day was the the mirror image of this mood. You passed before me as a higher self, a *much* higher self—but more encouraging than disheartening: thus you hovered in my imagination, and I measured my life against your exemplary one, asking myself about the many things in me that are wanting. . . . For me your book is perhaps a more stringent judge than you yourself would be in person. What must a man do in order not to prove unmanly in the face of this image of your life?—this question I have asked myself many times. He would have to do all the things you have done, not one whit more! Yet in all probability he will not be able to do them, lacking as he does the unfailing guiding instinct, and the love that is always ready to lend a hand. One of the supreme motifs, one I have come to be aware of only through you, is that of maternal love without the physical bond of mother and child: it is one of the most splendid revelations of *caritas*. Bestow on me a portion of this love, my most esteemed friend, and look upon me as a son who needs such a mother—and I mean really needs her! (B *5,* 148–49)

Hotel Römerbad, Badenweiler. This old print shows how the concert hall and dining room was arranged in the 1870s.

The letters to Marie Baumgartner and Malwida von Meysenbug invite us to consider whether the *Vaterhaus* that Nietzsche suddenly found so empty in his early childhood was actually empty of a mother as well. Or, if that is too harsh a judgment, they invite us to ask whether the mother Nietzsche sought was not really there for him until he was released on probation from the Jena asylum in March 1890.

It was Köselitz, the musician and Wagner enthusiast, who encouraged Nietzsche to publish the fourth *Untimely,* which appeared in July 1876. Nietzsche finished the manuscript during the weekend of June 17–18, residing once again in the magnificent Römerbad Hotel in the Black Forest town of Badenweiler. It may have been with some trepidation that Wagner thanked his young associate for the book: "Friend! Your book is gigantic! Where in the world did you learn all those things about me?" (N *1,* 714). Wagner would have been shocked by many of the notes Nietzsche had been jotting since the spring of 1874 (W *7,* 754 ff.), notes that were far more critical than anything he allowed himself to write—or publish—in "Richard Wagner in Bayreuth." Nietzsche traveled to Bayreuth in August for the Festspiel, yet immediately became disgruntled with the high society of "Haus Wahnfried" and the pomp and circumstance of the festival; he fell desperately ill, left Bayreuth before the second cycle of the *Ring* was performed, returned, then left again, now for the last time. He later claimed that the first sketches of his future work *Human, All-Too Human,* at that time still under the title *The Plowshare,* were written in Klingenbrunn, "a small village in the woods" to which he made his escape from Bayreuth (B *5,* 338). He explained to Wagner himself that the great events of the summer of 1876 were marred for him by "a vein of the darkest melancholy," and that he had become "fed up" with his illness—"I want to live a healthy life or no longer live at all" (B *5,* 191). Some months later he wrote Cosima from Sorrento: "From year to year one grows quieter and quieter, and in the end one says not a serious word more about personal matters. . . . Practically every night I am involved in dreams with people long forgotten, preeminently with the dead. Childhood, boyhood, and my school years are quite present to me" (B *5,* 209). The only consolation offered by that last visit to Bayreuth was his meeting Frau Louise Ott, originally from the Baltic region also but now residing with her husband and child in Paris. She was perhaps the most beautiful and congenial of the women who moved him deeply in his life; their brief correspondence is one of the tenderest in Nietzsche's collected letters.

Back in Basel he took up his secondary school teaching once again, but now for the last time. He moved from his spacious apartment on the Spalentorweg back to the "Poison Cottage" at Schützengraben 45, and applied for a year's leave of absence due to illness (B *5,* 158–59). Malwida had extended the invitation to come to Sorrento, and Nietzsche and Rée were now planning the journey. The three of them, along with a consumptive student of Nietzsche's, Albert Brenner, would undertake to live in a "kind of monastery for free spirits" (B *5,* 188), a "school for educators," an "ideal colony" or *université libre* (B *5,* 216). Nietzsche was granted a Swiss passport or letter of protection from the Basel canton, even though he was not Swiss but stateless, or, as the official designation had it, *heimatlos,* "homelandless."

On October 1 Nietzsche traveled with Paul Rée to Bex, the town in the Swiss canton of Valais that he had visited with von Gersdorff that spring. They stayed for two weeks in Bex, where Nietzsche worked on a projected fifth *Untimely Meditation,* "The Free Spirit." That work was never realized either, though fragments of it appear in the book that marked a turning-point for him, *Human, All-Too-Human.* On October 19–20 the two friends moved on to Geneva, where young Brenner joined them, and then on to Genoa, via Mount Cenis and Turin. For the first time in his life, Nietzsche beheld the Mediterranean. He voyaged from Genoa to Naples by ship, stopping in Livorno for a side trip to Pisa. The three arrived in Naples during the night of October 25–26. Brenner reported that the sea voyage was smooth except for the final twenty-four hours, and that Nietzsche had "held out for a long time" before he too succumbed to seasickness. (The return trip the next May would be more eventful in this regard.) In Naples the three friends joined Malwida von Meysenbug, who promptly accompanied them to the promontory of Posillipo, south of Naples, overlooking the bay toward Vesuvius, Sorrento, and Capri. Two days later they traveled to Sorrento, there finding lodgings for the winter. Malwida wrote her foster-daughter, Olga Herzen, on October 28, 1876:

> The day before yesterday, in the evening, I drove with my three gentlemen to the top of the Posillipo. The light was heavenly, the kind in fairy tales. Storm clouds had gathered majestically over Vesuvius; from the lightning bolts and the gloomy dark red of the clouds a rainbow formed; the city glistened as though it were built of pure gold, and on the other side the sea was a deep blue. . . . It was so wonderful that the gentlemen were well-nigh intoxicated with rapture. I never saw Nietzsche so lively. He laughed aloud from sheer joy. After

Sorrento. A night in early spring.

Sorrento. Gate and stairway
of the Villa Rubinacci.

> quite a bit of discussion, we determined to go to Sorrento. Yesterday we came here, in
> splendid weather, and looked at a *pension allemande* not far from the road, the Villa Rubi-
> nacci. The gentlemen liked it so much that we immediately decided to stay. It is very beau-
> tiful here, and convenient too, since the gentlemen have their own part of the pension, so
> that I can move about as freely as I like. We were at the Wagners [who are staying for a
> month close to Sorrento] yesterday evening, and they were miffed that we hadn't taken
> rooms in a building with a sunny disposition that is adjacent to their hotel; but it is more
> expensive there and we would be less independent. Here we are our own masters, and the
> German landlady is an agreeable person. Trina [Malwida's servant] is as busy as can be. . . .
> There are terraces on all sides of the Villa. The windows in the salon look out over Naples,
> now in resplendent sunlight, my beloved island, Ischia, and Mount Vesuvius. In front of the
> house stands a veritable forest of olives and orange trees, which form a green foreground to
> our painting. (N *1*, 744–45)

Malwida and her three gentlemen visited the Wagners many times over the next few weeks
for sightseeing trips or soirées. The most adventurous of their outings was the trip by donkey to Il
Deserto, at the tip of the peninsula on which Sorrento is located, in order to celebrate Malwida's
birthday. Yet Cosima's terse diary entries and Nietzsche's almost total silence indicate how great
the distance between Nietzsche and the Wagners had become. No doubt Nietzsche's friendship
with Rée, who Cosima, after "closer inspection," discovered was an "Israelite," offended her. At all
events, the von Meysenbug party experienced a little relief once the Wagners had departed for
Rome on November 7. Wagner went off to complete *Parsifal;* Nietzsche remained in order to
write *Human, All-Too-Human.*

Albert Brenner painted for his family back home a picture of daily life at the Villa Rubinacci—once the four would-be free spirits were able to devise their own way of life:

> We are living a short distance from Sorrento, in a part of the region where only gardens,
> garden houses, and villas prevail. The whole section is like a monastery. The alleyways are
> narrow, bordered on both sides by stone walls about a man's height. Soaring above the
> walls are orange trees, cypresses, fig trees, and grape arbors, framing the expanse of blue sky
> in a charming way. Because the few homes here are mostly inside the walls, it seems as
> though one is living in a labyrinth. . . . A small citrus orchard separates our villa from the
> sea. From the orchard you have to descend almost vertically to the shore, as Sorrento is

View from the patio in front of the Villa Rubinacci. Mount Vesuvius looms above the roof of a local Sorrento church.

built on a cliff. . . . We have two large terraces, one overlooking the sea, the other the mountains. Yet the house is not at all expensive, neither relatively nor absolutely; there is nothing elegant about it. (N *1,* 748)

The friends swam, walked, or worked, depending on the weather. Sometimes they hiked over the mountains south of Sorrento to the Gulf of Salerno. In the evening, Paul Rée read aloud to the group. From fall to spring their reading and discussion program was quite extensive: they began with notes from Jacob Burckhardt's lectures on Greek civilization, with commentary by Nietzsche, who had discussed the lectures with Burckhardt in great detail; they went on to read the two great Greek historians, Herodotus and Thucydides, along with Plato's massive late work, *Laws.* "How mild, how conciliatory Nietzsche still was back then," Malwida observed in a later supplement to her autobiography. "His generous, amiable nature was in equilibrium with his acerbic intellect. How cheerful he could be, how heartily he could laugh" (N *1,* 749).

At Christmas time Malwida presented Nietzsche with a large fan to use as an eye shade, and a red satin sleeping cap with a long red tassel to help keep his head warm night and day, in an effort to fend off headache (B *5,* 212). To Rée, who claimed that vanity lay at the root of all moral systems, she gave a gilded mirror. While Nietzsche, his eyes protected behind the visor, reclined in his easy chair, and Malwida and Brenner sat close to the hearth, peeling oranges, Rée, seated at a table with a lamp, read to the group. Malwida saw them as "an ideal family" living in a kind of "mission house," preparing to "scatter seed for a newly spiritualized culture." During the day, Rée and Nietzsche searched out grottoes along the rocky coast where the fledgling missionaries might instruct

Gulf of Salerno. The rocky
shoreline south of Sorrento.

"The day is blue and warm, and this afternoon we want
to row a boat past all the beautiful grottoes" (B 5, 200).

Lava formation not far below the summit of Mount Vesuvius.

A glimpse of oscillation at the main temple of Paestum.

their pupils, women and men alike, in the ways of enlightenment and emancipation. By Christmas time the reading program had shifted, perhaps due to Rée's influence, but certainly in line with Nietzsche's own desires, to the French moralists and skeptics: Montaigne, La Rochefoucauld, Vauvenargues, La Bruyère, and Stendhal—although the great Voltaire, to whom *Human, All-Too-Human* was eventually dedicated, cannot have been neglected. Finally, in spring, the four read and discussed Afrikan Spir's *Thought and Reality,* Ranke's *History of the Papacy,* and the New Testament. Once again, Nietzsche delivered the principal commentary on the last-mentioned text, for his study of philology had shed light on this fateful book as well. Quite late in his active life, as he was writing *The Antichrist,* Nietzsche had occasion to remember those discussions in Sorrento.

Nietzsche's health seemed to be improving gradually, but he suffered some serious relapses and was ill for many days at a time. On the good days he traveled—to Naples, in order to undergo a medical examination, to Pompei for ten days at the beginning of March, to the Isle of Capri on March 23. He almost certainly visited Paestum also, the site of some of the best preserved of the ancient Greek temples, only fifty kilometers south of Salerno. In his notes from the spring and summer of 1875 he observed the "unmathematical oscillation" of the temple columns, which seemed to be equidistant but in fact were not. He called such architectural oscillation "an *analogon* to the modification of a tempo: genuine animation in the place of mechanical movement."[8]

Brenner and Rée left the group in April, and the Sorrento idyll soon dissolved. Nietzsche himself departed on May 8, 1877. He returned to Switzerland, traveling by ship from Naples to Livorno and Genoa, and then by train from Genoa to Milan, Chiasso, and Lugano, where once again he resided in the Hôtel du Parc. The sea voyage to the north was more adventurous than the trip south had been. On May 13, 1877, Nietzsche wrote from Lugano to Malwida, who was still in Sorrento:

> The way people suffer on a sea voyage is terrible and yet truly ridiculous; that is the way my headaches sometimes seem to me now, inasmuch as the illness may come precisely when the body is otherwise bursting with good health.—To be brief: today I am once again "the cheerful cripple," whereas on the ship [from Sorrento to Livorno] I entertained the most foreboding thoughts—the only doubt I had about suicide was whether I could locate the deepest part of the sea, so that I wouldn't be fished out straight away and have to cough up a frightful amount of cash and credit as a tip for my rescuers. . . . In the harbor of Livorno it rained all night. I wanted to go out on deck anyway, but the most bloodcurdling warnings of our captain held me back. Everything on shipboard was rolling noisily back and forth, the chamber pots cracked and came to life, children screamed, the storm howled. Eternal sleeplessness was my lot, as the poets would say. . . . I went on to Switzerland, taking the train on the first stretch of the Gotthard railway line, which is not yet complete, from Como to Lugano. How did I come to travel here to Lugano? I didn't really plan to, but here I am. As I crossed the Swiss border under heavy rainfall, there was incredible thunder and lightning. I took it as a good omen. Nor can I conceal the fact that as I drew closer to the mountains I felt better and better. . . . I found a good porter who spoke Swiss German. I was touched when I heard him, for I suddenly realized that I prefer to live among Swiss Germans rather than German Germans. The man took such good care of me: he dashed about in a most fatherly way—all fathers are somewhat awkward—and managed to get all my scattered luggage back together again. I went on to Lugano. . . . This morning I saw all my beloved mountains before me, each one a mountain of memory. (B *5*, 235–37)

Nietzsche soon made his way, via Thun, Interlaken, Brienz, and Meiringen, to Bad Ragaz, where he stayed for three weeks in the Hotel Tamina as a "cure" guest. On June 10, having derived no benefit from the "cure," he left Bad Ragaz for Rosenlaui. There, in a pine-studded valley of the Bernese Alps, surrounded by snow-covered mountain peaks, he spent the rest of the summer, perhaps trying to recuperate the Maderan Valley experience of 1870 or the Flims-Waldhaus experience of 1873. His "cure" in Rosenlauibad consisted mainly of mountain air, dairy products, and feverish work on the book begun in Sorrento, *Human, All-Too-Human*. Once again Nietzsche proclaimed his affinity for the Alps: "It is *my* kind of nature" (B *5*, 247). His impending return to Basel and to teaching evoked ambivalent responses from him. On the one hand, the very thought of returning to Basel was repulsive to him; he wanted now to dedicate himself to his philosophy and his writing (B *5*, 248). On the other hand, he realized that it was his philosophy that was killing him, and so his teaching obligations appeared to be his salvation:

> I am resolved to return to Basel in October and take up my old activities. I can't hold out unless I feel *useful,* and my people in Basel are the only human beings who communicate

8. W *8*, 63; cf. M 169; *3*, 151. There are no references to a trip to Paestum in Nietzsche's letters, as far as we know, nor does Curt Paul Janz mention such a trip. Yet our reading of the working notes concerning Paestum (cited above, but see also the Paestum passage in the portfolio to the present chapter, below) convinces us that Nietzsche was in fact there during the winter and spring of 1876–77. These notes, we suggest, are not based on secondhand experience.

Hotel Rosenlaui, in the Berner Oberland, where Nietzsche spent the summer of 1877.

to me the fact that I am useful to them. My altogether problematic broodings and scribblings have until now only made me ill; as long as I was an actual *scholar,* I was also healthy. But then came the nerve-racking music and metaphysical philosophy, cares concerning myriad things that don't mean anything to me. So, I want to become a teacher again: if I cannot survive it, then I want to perish *practicing my craft.* (B *5,* 250)

Yet something had changed once and for all. Philology now seemed to be a layer of moss smothering the plants he genuinely wanted to thrive—his burgeoning *thoughts*—even if the cost of removing the moss and cultivating those thoughts, as his doctors warned him, would be chronic migraine and eventual blindness (B *5,* 276; 288). By December 3, 1877, the title and contents of *Human, All-Too-Human* were ready for the printer. It was the book in which metaphysical questions would be subordinated to psychological ones; or, better, the book in which Nietzsche's penchant for investigating the family tree of metaphysics and morals would finally blossom: "Humanity loves to deflect from its mind all questions concerning the provenance and the beginnings of things: wouldn't one have to be almost dehumanized in order to sense in oneself the opposite inclination?" (MAM I, 1; *2,* 24). Several weeks later, Wagner sent Nietzsche the libretto of what proved to be his last great music drama, *Parsifal.* Nietzsche, who had known about the project in detail for years, was repulsed by its lugubrious piety; it seemed to him more a piece of Counterreformation propaganda than a work of art. In a later letter Nietzsche derided *Parsifal* as "Hegelianism in music" (B *6,* 224); still later, he noted that *Parsifal* and Bismarck were engaged in the same diplomacy— making secret pacts with Rome. *Human, All-Too-Human,* for its part, struck Cosima and Richard as impious and cruel. The long-impending break now occurred, and it was irreversible. At about

View along the road that leads from Meiringen to Rosenlaui.

the same time, Nietzsche's old friends von Gersdorff, Rohde, and Overbeck either married or sought alliances of their own, so that they all became more distant. Nietzsche set up his household, once again run by Elisabeth, in an apartment at Gellertstrasse 22, near St. Alban's gate, on the out-skirts of Basel. It was a time of *crisis,* in the original Greek sense of *separation.* "The *crisis* of my life is here: if I did not feel the superabundant fertility of my new philosophy, I could be terrifyingly lonely. Yet I am *at one with myself*" (B 5, 331).

While passing through Meiringen, Nietzsche had met Dr. Otto Eiser, a physician and Wag-

Nietzsche in Basel, ca. 1876. Photo: Stiftung Weimarer Klassik. GSA 101/17.

nerite. After a brief examination, Dr. Eiser asked Nietzsche to go to Frankfurt for a complete physical. This Nietzsche did from October 3 to 7, 1877. Dr. Eiser and his colleagues noted the deterioration in Nietzsche's retinas; they could only speculate that the patient's "excessive intellectual activity" was the cause of his migraines and stomach disorders. They cautioned him against "heroic" cures of any kind, and urged nothing more than a radical decrease in his workload (N *1,* 787).

Nietzsche now requested a permanent replacement for himself at the Pädagogium in the Mentelinhof. At the end of March 1878 he was officially released from his high-school teaching obligations, which in fact he had not fulfilled since October 1876. He held out at the university until the beginning of the summer semester of 1879. By that time his existence in Basel was slowly disintegrating. In April 1878 his friend Köselitz, who had copied out the printer's manuscript and corrected the proofs of *Human, All-Too-Human,* departed for Venice. The next month, Nietzsche's young student and friend, Albert Brenner, who had been with him in Sorrento for the greater part of a year, died of tuberculosis after the most painful agony. Then his sister was called back to Naumburg: their mother believed that her son's chances of marrying would be improved if Elisabeth were back in Naumburg doing what every dutiful daughter should do—taking care of her mother (the Thuringian version of *Like Water for Chocolate*). Elisabeth left Basel on July 8, whereupon Nietzsche moved into a Spartan apartment on the other side of town, at Bachlettenstrasse 11, not far from the zoological gardens. He devised a number of detailed plans and schedules for his work day, with a view to conserving his rapidly ebbing strength.

At the end of April, his new book was published: *Human, All-Too-Human: A Book for Free Spir-*

its, Dedicated to the Memory of Voltaire on the 100ᵗʰ Anniversary of His Death on May 30, 1778. Many of Nietzsche's friends—among them the Wagners, as we have seen—showed open hostility to the work; others, including the acerbic Rohde and the gentle Overbeck, were put off by its trenchancy. Still others, however, celebrated this turn in his writing; among these were Jacob Burckhardt, who could only bless Sorrento for having, as he believed, rescued Nietzsche from the Nordic malaise of Wagner, and Paul Rée, who was there for the better part of the book's gestation. Cosima snarled that in this book Judea had once again slyly betrayed Germania, and she burned all of Nietzsche's letters; Rohde complained that the book's readers were "plunged into an ice-cold *frigidarium* immediately after having been baked in a *caldarium*"; Richard Wagner and even Malwida von Meysenbug bemoaned the fact that their friend was now a "Réealist"; finally, Wagner took up the pen to condemn the apostate in the August-September edition of the *Bayreuther Blätter* (N *1,* 820; 827; B *5,* 351). Some otherwise sympathetic readers were no doubt fooled by the book's "aphoristic" style, believing it to be a jumble of notations and opinions. In fact, the nine chapters of aphorisms were very carefully ordered and orchestrated: Nietzsche had taken a scissors to the final manuscript, reordering, renumbering, and supplying a title for each aphorism. The result was a rich, multichrome fabric, far more carefully woven than any of the older "monological" texts. Yet because Nietzsche had renounced the Wagner circle, and had not yet created for himself a new circle of readers, the book was a failure for its publisher, Ernst Schmeitzner.

Nietzsche spent the summer of 1878 in the Berner Oberland. He stayed in the mountaineers' lodge on the Männlichen, near Grindelwald, enjoying a view of the Jungfrau. It was not a fortunate choice for his health: the weather conditions changed rapidly and radically, and Nietzsche suffered repeated attacks of headache and nausea. By late summer he was in Interlaken at the Hotel von Unterseen, his health still problematic. After a month in Naumburg, he returned to Basel for what would be his last semester of university teaching. Frau Marie Baumgartner helped him prepare the printer's manuscript of an "appendix" to *Human, All-Too-Human,* entitled "A Miscellany of Opinions and Maxims," published on March 12, 1879. Burckhardt read the appendix too with delight, and congratulated his young colleague in a way that Nietzsche would never forget: he called him a wanderer on dizzying mountain peaks, and even though Nietzsche had never been able to ascend to the peaks because of his eyes, he embraced Burckhardt's hyperbole as the truth about himself. His reading during these dire months—and reading was possible for him for only a half-hour each day—was rather more appropriate: he called Fontenelle's *Dialogues with the Dead* a "blood relative" (N *1,* 843).

In May he traveled to Geneva and to Wiesen, near Davos, in the hope of improving his health; he had already submitted his request to be released permanently from all university teaching duties. On May 6, 1879, he wrote to Paul Widemann: "I have resigned my professorship and am going into the mountains—brought to the point of despair, scarcely daring to hope. The suffering was too intense, too protracted" (B *5,* 412). The next day, to Marie Baumgartner: "I have suffered **mightily.** Things have gone as far as they can go, I have surrendered my professorship. In a few days I shall leave Basel forever. My furniture is up for sale. Saturday my sister is coming" (B *5,* 413).

A restlessness now overtook him. Once again he was homeless, having surrendered his sole claim to Swiss "citizenship." He fled ever farther into the mountains, in search of a new morning. He became the very wanderer he had portrayed in *Human, All-Too-Human:*

> *The wanderer.*—Whoever has attained even the slightest freedom of reason cannot but feel like a wanderer on Earth—though not like a traveler who *heads for a final goal,* inasmuch as there is no such thing. In contrast, the wanderer will take a good look, will have an open

eye for the way everything in the world actually transpires; for that reason the wanderer cannot let his heart grow too attached to any particular thing; the wanderer's heart must itself be a wanderer, taking its joy in change and transiency. To be sure, evil nights will befall such a wanderer, when he is weary and finds that the gates of the city that was to have offered him hospitality are locked; it may be too that, as in the Orient, the desert sands extend to the very gates of the city, that the prowling beasts of prey in the desert howl at first from afar, then quite close, that a fierce wind whips up, that thieves drive off his pack animals. Then the night falls upon him as a second desert, a redoubled desert, and his heart wearies of wandering. When the sun rises in the morning, glowing like a god of wrath, and the gates of the city gape, he may see in the faces of those who live there even more desert, even more filth, deception, and hazard than he saw when he was outside the gates—and the day proves to be all but worse than the night. That is how things may go for the wanderer. By way of compensation, however, there may dawn the splendid mornings of other regions and other days, when he espies already in the gray light a swarm of Muses dancing in the mountain mist quite close by, when later that morning he walks quietly beneath the trees, feeling the equanimity of his forenoon soul, as all kinds of dazzling and nourishing fruits are tossed his way from treetop and leafy ambush—the gifts given to all free spirits who are at home in mountains, forests, and solitude, and who, like him, in their sometimes joyous, sometimes brooding way, are wanderers and philosophers. Born of the secrets of the dawn, they allow their thoughts to drift toward a question—the question as to how the day, between the tenth and twelfth strikings of the clock, can show such a pure, translucent, and cheerfully transfigured face:—they go in search of the *philosophy of forenoon.* (MAM I, 638; *2,* 362–63)

I'd rather be a Basel Professor than God . . .

Basel

Maderan Valley

Lorraine

Tribschen

Bayreuth

Flims-Waldhaus

Steinabad

Badenweiler

Sorrento

Paestum

Pompei

Rosenlaui, Bernese Alps

Views of Basel. The main entrance to the Mentelinhof, where Nietzsche taught his secondary school classes; the Spalentor, near which Nietzsche first lived in Basel; the Rhine, not far from the university.

To Friedrich Ritschl in Leipzig; from Basel, May 10, 1869; B 3, 7

On Tuesdays and Fridays I teach two classes at the secondary school, on Wednesdays and Thursdays one class. So far, it is a pleasure. Because we are reading [Plato's] *Phaedo*, I have the opportunity to infect my pupils with philosophy.... In my university lectures I have seven students, which they say is quite normal around here. The students are all hardworking; they attend an insane number of lectures each week. The concept of 'hookey' they know only by hearsay."

A messenger [in Euripides' *The Bacchae*, lines 690-714] recounts how in the noonday heat he drove his herds up to the mountain peaks: it is the right moment and the right place to see things as yet unseen. Now Pan sleeps, now the sky is the undisturbed backdrop to a *gloria*, now the day *blossoms*. The messenger espies three bands of women scattered across an Alpine meadow, reclining, but the very picture of dignity. Many of the women are leaning against the trunks of pines. All sleep. Suddenly, Pentheus's mother begins to cry out in joy, sleep is cast off, all leap up, models of noble form. The young girls and women let their hair fall to their shoulders; those whose fawnskins have become undone at the strap or pin fasten them again. They gird themselves with snakes that lovingly lick their cheeks. Some of the women take young wolves

and fawns into their arms and suckle them. All bedeck themselves with garlands of ivy. One stroke of the thyrsus, and water bubbles forth from the rocks; one stroke of the staff upon the earth, and a fountain of wine wells up. Sweet honey drips from their staffs, and if anyone so much as grazes the ground with the tips of her fingers, snow-white milk flows forth. — It is an utterly enchanted world; nature celebrates her feast of reconciliation with humanity.

"The Dionysian Worldview," written in summer 1870: W 1, 558-59

Views of the Maderan Valley, where Nietzsche worked on "The Dionysian Worldview." The Chärstelenbach, with the Hotel Alpenclub visible in the distance; *above,* the meadow directly below the cliff on which the hotel is built.

Kurt Flemming, a Pforta alumnus, among the thousands killed on
the Lorraine battlefields during August and September of 1870.
The photograph of Flemming is to be found in Nietzsche's personal
collection of photographs, housed today in the Nietzsche Archive
at Weimar. Photo: Stiftung Weimarer Klassik. GSA 101/143.

To Carl von Gersdorff in France; from Naumburg, October 20, 1870; B 3, 148-49

The atmosphere of these experiences wrapped me round like a gloomy fog: for some time
all I could hear were painful cries, laments that never seemed to end.

To Carl von Gersdorff in Berlin; from Basel. May 1, 1872: B 3, 317

Tribschen has now come to an end. We walked about as though through ruins, everything about us was so touching; it was even in the air, in the clouds. The dog wouldn't eat; whenever you talked with the family of servants, you found that they were sobbing the whole time. We packed up the manuscripts, letters, and books—how disconsolate I was! These past three years, during which I lived so close to Tribschen, visiting it twenty-three times—how meaningful it was to me! Had I not made these visits, what would I be! I am happy that in my book *[The Birth of Tragedy]* I have carved into stone for myself the world of Tribschen.

To his sister in Basel; from Bayreuth. August 1, 1876: B 5, 181

Yesterday I could listen to *The Valkyries* only in a darkened room outside the hall; my eyes have become altogether impossible! I long to leave, it is pointless to remain. I shudder before each one of these long concert evenings; yet I do not stay away.... I'm fed up. Nor do I want to attend the premiere. I'd rather be anywhere else, only not here, where everything tortures me.

Tribschen, on Lake Lucerne, then and now; *below*, views of the Bayreuth Festival Theater. Photo: Stiftung Weimarer Klassik. GSA 101/615.

At noon. — Whoever in his life has been granted an active and stormy morning finds that an odd craving for tranquillity overtakes his soul at life's noontide, a craving that can last for many moons, many years. It grows quiet about him, the voices fade away, and are now far off; the sun shines straight down upon him. On a concealed meadow in the forest he sees Great Pan sleeping; all the things of nature have nodded off with him, an expression of eternity on their faces—at least, that is the way he thinks of it. He wants nothing, is troubled about nothing, his heart stands motionless, and only his eye still lives—it is a death with vigilant eyes.

MAM II, 308; 2, 690

Caumasee, at Flims-Waldhaus, where Nietzsche spent part of the summer of 1873, working on "Truth and Lie in a Nonmoral Sense."

The forest of Steinabad bei Bonndorf, where Nietzsche spent the summer of 1875, taking a cure for his stomach and contemplating "Richard Wagner in Bayreuth."

To Erwin Rohde; from Steinabad. August 1, 1875; B 5, 91-92

I had several really wonderful days, with the weather cool and fresh, as I hiked through the hills and forests all around me here, always alone, but with a pleasure and a joy that words cannot express! I wouldn't dare even try to express the hopes, probabilities, and plans I crave to realize, imagining them down to the smallest detail! And then, almost every day was graced by a wonderful letter, a letter full of love. I am proud and touched whenever I think that all of you belong to me, you, my dear friends! If only I had some happiness to dispense! Care and discouragement plague me most when I realize that I am good for nothing, and that things will have to go the way they are going, no matter how merciless they are. But then sometimes it seems to me I'm really a lucky devil, and have so far managed to escape the most vicious attacks of illness and suffering. In particular, the stupidities and mean tricks of fate have so far caused me no labors, and I have no right to think of myself as one of the truly unfortunate ones. What I want to say is this: I really do have a bit of joy to expend. If only I knew how!

Römerbad Hotel, Badenweiler, with a view of the cupola of the concert hall. Nietzsche first stayed at the hotel in August 1869; in June 1876 he worked there on the final sections of "Richard Wagner in Bayreuth."

To be sure, ours is a life full of manifold pain and shame: to feel restive, to feel that we are not at home in a world, and yet to have to talk to it, demand of it; to despise it and yet not be able to dispense with what we despise—that is the proper calamity of the artist of the future. The artist, unlike the philosopher, cannot chase after some obscure angle for himself: for as a mediator of the future the artist needs human souls, needs public institutions as guarantors of that future, bridges between "now" and "some day."

"Richard Wagner in Bayreuth." UB IV. 10; 1. 500

To his sister in Naumburg: from Sorrento, October 28, 1876: B 5, 197

Here we are in Sorrento! The whole trip here from Bex took eight days. In Genoa I was sick in bed. From there we took a three-day voyage, and guess what, we somehow avoided getting seasick. I much prefer to travel by ship than by train, which I hate. We found Fräulein von Meysenbug in a hotel in Naples and traveled together yesterday to our new home, the Villa Rubinacci, Sorrento, *près de Nâple.*

I have a very large, high-ceilinged room, with a terrace in front. I just came back from a swim: Rée assures me that the water is warmer here now than in the North Sea in July. Yesterday we visited the Wagners, who live five minutes away in the Hotel Victoria. They plan to be here through the month of November.

Sorrento and Naples are beautiful—that is no exaggeration. The air here is a mixture of mountain and sea air. It does one's eyes good. In front of my terrace I have a huge green orchard (it stays green even in winter), with the dark, dark sea beyond, and, beyond that, Mount Vesuvius.

Views of the Gulf of Salerno, near the Amalfi Coast; Sorrento, the Villa Rubinacci; citrus orchards of the Villa.

115

Paestum, southeast of Sorrento. Nietzsche in all probability visited the temple site during the early spring of 1877.

Whatever is perfect should not have had a becoming. — We are accustomed to drop the question of becoming when it is a matter of something perfect. Rather, we take joy in the present thing as though it sprang from the earth after some magic wand had struck. Probably we are still operating under the impact of a primeval mythic sensibility. We *almost* feel (when, for example we are in a Greek temple, like the one at Paestum) as though one morning a god playfully constructed his dwelling out of these monstrous supports. At other times we *almost* feel as though a soul suddenly inspired stone and now wants to speak through it. The artist knows that a work will achieve its full effect only if it creates the impression that it is an improvisation, that it was excited into existence with miraculous suddenness.

MAM I. 145; 2. 141

The animal with a good conscience. — I am not blind to the vulgarity in everything that pleases us in the south of Europe, whether in Italian opera ... or in the Spanish picaresque novel.... Yet here the vulgarity does not offend me. Just as little am I put off by the commonness that one encounters everywhere on a stroll through Pompei, or, at bottom, even while reading any ancient text. How to explain this? Is it that in such music or fiction a sense of shame is missing, that everything vulgar enters on the scene with the same self-assurance and confidence that is displayed by any other noble, lovely, and passionate trait? "The animal has

its rights, just as humans do. So let us allow it to circulate freely! And you, my dear fellow human, you too are still an animal, in spite of everything!" — That seems to me to be the moral of the story, and the peculiarity of southerly humanity.

FW. 77: 3, 432-33

Interior views at Pompei, which Nietzsche visited in early March 1877.

118

Rosenlaui, where Nietzsche spent the summer of 1877, continuing work on the first part of *Human, All-Too-Human: A Book for Free Spirits.*

To his mother and sister in Naumburg, from Rosenlauibad, June 25, 1877: B 5, 247

Village, surroundings, room and board—all are very good. Mild and pleasant air from morning to night. I have to be careful about hiking for *too long*, however: I had to pay the penalty twice, insomnia and nervous exhaustion—it took two days before I felt halfway decent again. Every time a storm hangs in the air I have a headache. Perhaps I am not at a sufficient altitude? (I am at an elevation of over 4,000 feet.) I am *very much* alone, though enough English pass through: my residence here will no doubt do me good over time. This is *my kind* of nature.

Oberengadin. The path from Sils-Maria
to the Chastè Peninsula.

THREE

THE SOLITUDE
OF
HIGH MOUNTAINS

That is something—to be the
most independent spirit in Europe.

Nietzsche to Carl Spitteler

It is as though he came from a country
where no one else dwelled.

Erwin Rohde to Franz Overbeck

At some point in our account of the final ten years of Nietzsche's active life, the years after he resigned his professorship and became a philosopher-nomad, we shall have to break with the chronological order we have up to now tried to respect. For Nietzsche's nomadism proved to be cyclical. He spent his winters on the Mediterranean, first in Genoa, then in Nice, and his summers in the mountains of the Upper Engadine, almost always in Sils-Maria. Only during the final winter of his productive life did he move inland, to Turin, as though combing the hills of Aosta for the most archaic of seas. Before we surrender chronology altogether, however, we shall offer an account of Nietzsche's work places from 1879 onward based on the chronology of his *publications.* We shall begin with "The Wanderer and His Shadow" and end with the six books he prepared for publication in 1888.

"The Wanderer and His Shadow" was published in December 1879. In a letter to Georg Brandes on February 19, 1888, Nietzsche recalled the period between the *Untimely Meditations* and *Human, All-Too-Human* as "a crisis and a change of skin" (B *8*, 260). He began and ended "The Wanderer," which along with "A Miscellany of Opinions and Maxims" became the second part of *Human, All-Too-Human* in its second edition (1886), with something like a Platonic dialogue. Except that here Socrates was Nietzsche's own shadow. In effect, all the books that followed this one were dialogues of this kind, whether as the fruits of his solitude in the mountains or his intimate converse with the sea. "The Wanderer" was the first text Nietzsche composed in the Oberengadin. He had pushed farther south and higher into the mountains, moving from Wiesen near Davos, via Tiefenkastel and the Albula and Julia passes, high into the Upper Engadine, 1,800 meters above sea level. He took a room in a private house somewhere near the village of Champfèr, about a half-hour's walk from St. Moritz, the resort town that was too expensive and too crowded for him. (The administration of the

A rocky cleft and pocket of summer snow on Mount Corvatsch, south of Lake Silvaplana, in the Oberengadin.

University of Basel had granted him a pension of 3,000 Swiss francs, barely sufficient for his meager needs; his greatest single expense would be for transportation.) His diet was simple: practically no meat but a great deal of milk and cheese. When the weather permitted, he took seven- or eight-hour hikes through the hills and around the lakes of St. Moritz, Silvaplana, and Sils. His letters to friends and family affirmed that the Engadine was a discovery of special importance to him, not least because of the promise it held for his health. By the end of 1879 he had experienced 118 days of severe illness—a "lovely statistic," as he wryly commented to Elisabeth on December 29 (B *5,* 475).

To Franz Overbeck, Nietzsche wrote on June 23, 1879, "But now I have taken possession of the Engadine, and am as though in **my** element, quite marvelously! I am *related* to *this kind* of nature. Now I sense an alleviation. Oh, how I have longed for it!" (B *5,* 420). To his mother he wrote in early July, "Woods, lakes, the best walking paths (which always have to be specially arranged for me, half-blind as I am), the most bracing air, the best in Europe—these are the reasons I love this place" (B *5,* 424). To his sister, on July 12, he exclaimed, "These splendid forests! I am out-of-doors seven or eight hours a day. . . . St. Moritz is the *only* place that is decidedly *good for me*—every day, in good and bad weather, I am grateful for this **air.** I shall be traveling here in the future, I can tell that already" (B *5,* 427–28). Finally, the following two letters, the first to Franz Overbeck on July 11,

1879, the second to Paul Rée at the end of the month, demonstrated the dire state of Nietzsche's health and the desperation that the Engadine would have to help him confront if not overcome:

> I am as ill here as everywhere else, and have been in bed for the past eight days. The same old litany, as disgusting to me as it is to you! Nevertheless—St. Moritz is the right place, well adapted to my sensibilities and my sense organs (my eyes!), as though created for patients. The air is almost better than that of Sorrento, and is full of fragrances, the way I like it. The way I divide my day, my life-style, my diet—these things would not have dishonored a wise man of old: everything *very simple,* and yet a system of fifty sometimes very delicate considerations. (B 5, 425)

The second letter, to Paul Rée, written at the end of July 1879:

> My dear friend, do you really know how things as a whole have been going for me? Several times I narrowly escaped the portals of death, but was fearfully tortured—that is the way I live from day to day, with each day having its own chapter in the book of my illness. I now have Europe's best and mightiest air to breathe, and I love the place where I am staying: St. Moritz, in Graubünden. Its nature is akin to my own: we do not astonish one another, but are intimate together. Perhaps the place will do me good—in any case, I can hold out *here* better than anywhere else. (B 5, 430)

It was between hope and despair that "The Wanderer and His Shadow" came to be—virtually all of it written in pencil in six pocket-sized notebooks that Nietzsche carried on his walks with him. One projected title for those notes was "Thought Paths of St. Moritz" (W 8, 610). Nietzsche claimed it was his precarious health that condemned him to "this accursed telegram style" of composition (B 5, 461). Although the claim may have been disingenuous, Nietzsche's health certainly did not encourage expansive, discursive treatment of any subject. Economy of means, brevity of wit, steady aim, and a single cut of the scalpel—these were the characteristics of Nietzsche's prose in "The Wanderer." Later, when Köselitz returned the printer's manuscript to the author for a final check, Nietzsche cut it into strips, altering the order of the aphorisms and supplying each with a title—as he had done for the first part of *Human, All-Too-Human.* Schmeitzner agreed to publish the new book, even though the last had been a commercial failure.

Nietzsche meanwhile wearied of the loneliness of the Engadine. In the very letter to his mother in which he praised St. Moritz as the only place that did him good, he proposed to return to Naumburg in order to become her gardener, an occupation his father—no doubt facetiously—had predicted for him. "A real *job* that takes time and causes me *toil,* without taxing my brain—that is what I need" (B 5, 427–28). On September 11, 1879, he described his plan to Heinrich Köselitz in terms redolent of midlife crisis:

> I am at the end of my thirty-fifth year; the "middle of life" they have called it now for a millennium and a half. Dante had his vision during this period; he speaks of it in the opening lines of his poem. And now in the very midst of life I am so "surrounded by death" that it could seize me at any hour. Given the nature of my illness, I am forced to think of a *sudden* death, due to convulsions (although I would a hundred times prefer a slow, lucid death, during which one could still speak to friends, even if it should be a more painful one). Thus I now feel like the most ancient of men, also in the sense that I *have fulfilled* my life's work. A good drop of oil has been pressed from me, I know, and they will not forget that about me. . . .
>
> I won't be coming to see you. . . . I'm in a state where it seems more suitable to settle down close to my mother, my hometown, and my childhood memories. (B 5, 441–42)

Oberengadin. The summit of Mount Corvatsch. "To climb as high as any thinker ever climbed, up into the pure, icy, Alpine air, where no fog rises to veil things over, and where the fundamental constitution of things expresses itself in a rough and lapidary fashion, but with inescapable intelligibility!" ("Schopenhauer as Educator," UB III, 5; *1, 381*).

He asked his mother to make arrangements for him to dwell in a tower in the old town wall close to Weingarten 18. In September 1879 he returned to Naumburg, though not to dwell in the town wall. In Naumburg he suffered the worst autumn and Christmas season of his life. During a particularly severe attack of migraine, he lost consciousness. His thoughts were close to death. In January 1880 he wrote to Dr. Otto Eiser, who had examined him three years earlier:

> My existence is a *terrible burden:* I would have cast it off long ago if I hadn't been conducting the most instructive tests and experiments in the intellectual and ethical domains precisely during this period of illness and almost total deprivation—this joyfulness, thirsting after knowledge, brings me to heights where I triumph over all martyrdoms and all hopelessness. On the whole, I'm happier than ever before in my life. And yet! Constant pain, a feeling of being half-paralyzed, a condition closely related to seasickness, during which I find it difficult to speak—this feeling lasts several hours a day. For my diversion I have raging seizures (the most recent one forced me to vomit for three days and three nights; I thirsted after death). Can't read! Only seldom can I write! Can't deal with my fellows! Can't listen to music!
>
> . . . My consolations are my thoughts and perspectives. On my walks here and there I scribble something on a sheet of paper; I write nothing at a desk; my friends decipher my scribbles. (B *6*, 3–4)

At the same time, and in much the same vein, he wrote to Malwida von Meysenbug in Rome:

> Although writing is one of my most forbidden fruits, you must nevertheless have a letter from me, you whom I love and esteem as an older sister. This will no doubt be my last! For the terrible and all but unrelenting martyrdoms of my life make me thirst after the end; according to certain symptoms, it seems that the saving brain stroke is close enough to grant me hope. As far as torture and deprivation are concerned, my life during the past few years can measure up to that of any ascetic of any period; nevertheless, I have attained much during these same years toward the purifying and polishing of my soul—and I no longer need either religion or art to that end. (You will notice that I am proud of the fact; indeed, the abandonment of everything first allowed me to discover my own sources of rescue.) I believe that I have fulfilled my life's work—admittedly, as one who was not given the time. . . . No pain has been able to seduce me into bearing false witness against life, *life as I know it,* nor should it ever be able to do so. (B *6*, 4–5)

Riva. „Hotel Seevilla".

An old print of the Hotel Seevilla, today the Hôtel du Lac et du Parc, in Riva del Garda.

As though in flight from death itself, Nietzsche left Naumburg on February 13, 1880, heading for Riva, on the northern shore of Lake Garda in the Trentino-Alto Adige region of Italy. Riva, cradled in the snow-streaked Dolomites, was an oasis of trees and flowers. The spacious grounds of Nietzsche's hotel, the Seevilla (today the Hôtel du Lac et du Parc), extended to the Lido of Lake Garda. Yet the weather on the lake was unpropitious: the South Tyrol, especially in February, was not far enough south.

Daybreak was published in June 1881. From now on it would be either the sea or mountains and lakes that dominated Nietzsche's landscapes. "I no longer want insights without danger: let the researcher always be surrounded by the treacherous sea or the merciless mountains!" he exclaimed in one of his notebooks (N *2,* 43). The autumn and winter in Naumburg had taught him that the dream of homeland, of a nest in a tower in the city wall, was a pipe dream, that his would have to be a life of nomadic solitude. He did take pleasure in Köselitz's company for four months, the first month at Riva, the remaining three in Venice. Köselitz's apartment, near the Campo San Canciano, was in the working-class neighborhood of Cannaregio: number 5256 on the narrow Calle Nuova. After staying with his former student for several weeks, Nietzsche found an apartment for himself not many blocks away, with a view onto San Michele, the island cemetery of Venice. The friends' relationship was not without tension: Nietzsche grew impatient with many of Köselitz's mannerisms; Köselitz complained that Nietzsche's presence was "all-absorbing," not so much because of the work that Nietzsche demanded of him but because of the sheer intensity of the man. What united the two was their devotion to music and their mutual capacity for an utterly ascetic life-style, simple to the point of monasticism. Yet if the weather in Riva was too rainy and blustery, that of Venice was too unpredictable, with many days of Scirocco wind. Nevertheless, a number of the notes that became aphorisms in *Daybreak* were written under the title "L'ombra di Venezia" (W *9,* 47–102). These notes proved to be continuous with those of "The Wanderer," focusing on the history of religion and morality.

When the temperature began to rise, Nietzsche sought a summer residence. He wanted to return to Champfèr near St. Moritz, but worried about the expense. After a period of indecision, he opted for the "Eremitage" of Marienbad in the Bohemian Forest. It was the rainiest of summers, however, and the only memorable event of the season was the arrest of the owner of the "Eremitage," who was accused of producing counterfeit notes in his basement. Nietzsche's mood was deplorable, and once again his solitude seemed to him unbearable. The estrangement from Wagner was particularly burdensome.

After the miserable weeks in Marienbad, Nietzsche tried to recover for five weeks in Naumburg, as though forgetting the wretched winter he had recently spent there. On October 8, 1880, he left Naumburg for Stresa, on the southwestern shore of Lago Maggiore. He found the lake region too chilly, "not southern enough," shivering already at "the frosty breath of winter" (B *6*, 40). Yet it was here, in view of the romantic Isles of Borromeo, that he resumed work on *Daybreak,* still under the title *The Plowshare,* a title he had chosen during the period of the *Untimely Meditations.*

Quite suddenly, without adequate preparation, Nietzsche moved to Genoa for the winter, arriving there on November 8. During the first week he changed his lodgings four times. The work on *Daybreak* continued, and, in spite of Nietzsche's ill-health and restiveness, his notes assumed the form of what we identify as his characteristic style, or styles, with impressionistic portraits of landscapes (especially the high mountains) and cityscapes (especially cities on the sea), expressionistic sequences and uncanny alignments of stark images, along with far-ranging reflections on the origin and impact of moral and religious systems—all of it laced with an irony sometimes cheerful, sometimes hilarious, and sometimes virulently sardonic. Perhaps the most powerful image of *Daybreak* was the one Nietzsche supplied for the second edition of the book in 1886, an image of his own life *beneath* mountains and seabeds:

> In this book you will find a "subterranean" creature at work, burrowing, digging, subverting. You will see him, presupposing that you have eyes for such work in the depths; you will see how slowly, how reflectively, with what gentle implacability he moves forward. He scarcely betrays the destitution that prolonged lack of light and air imply; one could even say that in his obscure toil he is content. Does it not seem as though some sort of belief guides him, some sort of consolation grants him recompense? As though he perhaps wants to have his own long obscurity, his unintelligibility, his concealment and riddlesomeness, because he knows what he will also have: his own morning, his own redemption, his own *daybreak?* . . . Oh yes, he will turn back; do not ask him what he wants to do down there; he will tell you himself soon enough, this seeming Trophonios, this subterranean creature, as soon as he has "become man" again. For one forgets silence altogether when one has been, like him, for so long a mole, for so long alone— — (W *3*, 11)

Recoaro Terme. Detail of the main building of the Fonti Centrali.

Nietzsche and Köselitz corrected the proofs of *Daybreak* during May and June of 1881 in the South Tyrolean spa of Recoaro, in the Dolomites east of Lake Garda, where Nietzsche was also taking the famous Recoaro waters. The two friends resided in the Albergo Tre Garofani ("The Three Carnations"), an elegant yet unpretentious hotel not far from the Fonti Centrali. The rugged beauty of the Dolomites once again affected Nietzsche deeply; as before, however, his health and the weather conspired to frustrate the purposes of his stay. In spite of Köselitz's companionship and considerable help, Nietzsche's solitude, which was both inevitable and willed, oppressed him. He wrote to his mother and sister, begging them *not* to read his new subterranean book (B *6,* 91). The mole, the all-but-blind rodent that subverted the fields, and the ancient oracle of Trophonios that granted mortals insight into the nature of their impending death, were both dreaming of a new dawn. Such were Nietzsche's images and dreams as the decade of the 1880s commenced.[1]

The Gay Science was published in August 1882. Even though this book was initially conceived as a continuation of *Daybreak* (Nietzsche described it as Books 6–10 of that work), its contents turned out to be markedly different. *The Gay Science* reflected Nietzsche's reading in the natural sciences during the past several years, especially in mechanics, thermodynamics, and theoretical biology. It also contained some of Nietzsche's most memorable literary and philosophical passages, including one of his most prescient poems:

> *Ecce Homo*
>
> I know the place whence I stem!
> Insatiable as any flame,
> I glow and consume myself.
> All grows bright when I arrive,
> All is cinder when I leave:
> Flame is surely what I am.

Further, *The Gay Science* presented some of Nietzsche's most radical reflections on our (in)capacity to know the world ("Let us be on guard!" FW, 109), on the much-discussed but really quite complex topic of the death of God ("The madman," FW, 125), on the need for tragic affirmation and love of one's fate ("For New Year's," FW, 276), and finally, on Nietzsche's "thought of thoughts," the eternal recurrence of the same ("The greatest burden," FW, 341). The earliest public appearance of Nietzsche's most stirring doctrine occurred in his most dogmatically antidogmatic book—a happenstance that suggests that eternal return is not a doctrine or theory at all but a *thought,* one of those things that comes on dove's feet but moves the world. It is also a possibility that stalks us into the shadows of our loneliest loneliness. In July 1881 Nietzsche wrote, "Meanwhile, it is as someone long dead that I gaze on things and people—they move me, terrify and delight me, yet I am altogether remote from them" (B *6,* 101–2). Most striking of all the aphorisms of *The Gay Science* was the final one in the first edition, which introduced the figure of Zarathustra and announced that "the tragedy commences" (FW, 342).

In the retrospect of the 1886 preface to the second edition of *The Gay Science,* Nietzsche called his book a work of *convalescence,* and he identified the convalescence with his life in Genoa, the city of Columbus; the tragedy and tragic affirmation contained in such convalescence, however, belonged at least as much to the mountains and lakes of Sils-Maria. For after his unsuccessful effort

1. For a discussion of the Trophonios and mole images, see Krell, *Infectious Nietzsche,* chaps. 3 and 5, "The Decadence of Redemption" and "Der Maulwurf/The Mole."

during May and June 1881 to reside in Recoaro in the mountains east of Garda, Nietzsche returned to the Upper Engadine. He traveled westward, first to Milan and Como, then up the western shore of Lake Como, through the splendid towns that dot the lake, to Chiavenna, and up the steep Maloja Pass onto the high plain of the Oberengadin. On a postcard to Heinrich Köselitz—filled from edge to edge with a minuscule script, as were all of Nietzsche's post cards—he told how he had made his way to the village of Sils-Maria by a happy accident. Champfèr and St. Moritz reminded him too strongly of his terrible illness there two years before; he was so repelled that he was about to flee the Engadine altogether. "In the end, thanks to an earnest and exceedingly kind Swiss gentleman with whom I had traveled through the night, a man who was returning from Naples to his homeland, I found lodgings in the loveliest corner on Earth: I have never had it so quiet, and all the fifty conditions of my squalid life seem to be fulfilled here" (B *6*, 100). To that nameless Swiss gentleman Nietzsche owed the great gift of Sils-Maria; perhaps he also owed him the tip to seek lodgings in the house of Gian Durisch, which from now on would be his principal summer residence. On July 7, 1881, he wrote to Elisabeth in Naumburg:

Sils-Maria, Oberengadin. The house and tea-and-spice shop of Gian Durisch, today the "Nietzsche-Haus."

> Of all the places on Earth, I feel best here in the Engadine. To be sure, the attacks come to me here as they do everywhere else; yet they are milder by far, much more humane. I am continuously calmed here, none of the pressure that I feel everywhere else. Here all excessive stimulation ceases for me. I would beg of mankind, "Preserve for me but three or four months of summer in the Engadine, otherwise I really cannot bear life any longer." . . . Yet the Engadine summer is so short, and by September's end I will return to Genoa. I have never had such tranquillity, and the paths, woods, lakes, and meadows are as though made for me; the prices are not altogether beyond my means. . . . The place is called Sils-Maria. Please keep the name a secret from my friends and acquaintances; I don't want any visitors. (B *6*, 98–99)

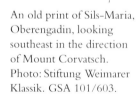

An old print of Sils-Maria, Oberengadin, looking southeast in the direction of Mount Corvatsch. Photo: Stiftung Weimarer Klassik. GSA 101/603.

Genoa. Salita delle Battistine, bordered on the left by the park of the Villetta di Negro. On November 27, 1881, Nietzsche wrote to Heinrich Köselitz (B 6, 143), "I was in my garden, that is, the garden of the Villetta Negro, which is close to where I live (Stendhal once called it 'one of the most picturesque places in Italy'), and I thought of you most affectionately."

After an eventful summer of work on *The Gay Science,* including his "vision" of eternal recurrence of the same at Surlej on the Lake of Silvaplana (W *9,* 494), Nietzsche left Sils-Maria. He headed for Genoa on October 1, 1881, which was quite late in the season. At the end of November he heard for the first time Bizet's *Carmen,* with a libretto based on the novella by Prosper Mérimée; its "southern" flavor enchanted him; it was the light, bright music he needed to counter the cumbersome, cloudy Wagnerian music that rubbed his nerves raw. Yet Mérimée's tale seemed to be a rehearsal of his own desperate love for Lou von Salomé during the following summer.

The greatest single joy of Nietzsche's winter (1881–82) in Genoa was the visit from Paul Rée, his boon companion of Sorrento days, who would also soon be drawn into the Lou debacle. February in Genoa was so warm that the two friends once again swam in the sea, even though the autumn had been chilly.

A note from this period comments on the Spartan character of Nietzsche's life, whether in Genoa or in the Engadine: "The need for luxury always seems to me to indicate a profound lack of *esprit,* as though one surrounded oneself with stage props precisely because there is nothing complete, nothing actual, there. . . . Whoever is spiritually rich and independent is the most powerful human being, any way you look at it; it would be reprehensible, at least in our humane times, were one to want anything more—one would be insatiable. Simplicity in food and drink, hatred of all liquorous spirits—that pertains to such a one as well" (N *2,* 95).

He was still constantly changing his dreary, unheated rooms, often writing in cafés when the lighting in his lodgings was too poor or the weather too severe. He finally located the house that would suit him: Salita delle Battistine 8 (interno 6). Rée described Nietzsche's rented room as an "amiable" one, located "in the middle of the city, but very quiet, close to a monastery where no coaches are permitted to pass" (N *2,* 96). Nietzsche nevertheless entertained reveries of Tunisia and the highlands of central Mexico as places of even more profound solitude and silence. By March it was so warm that once again he determined to head for the mountains, toting his *Gay Science* with him.

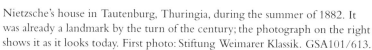
Nietzsche's house in Tautenburg, Thuringia, during the summer of 1882. It was already a landmark by the turn of the century; the photograph on the right shows it as it looks today. First photo: Stiftung Weimarer Klassik. GSA101/613.

Curiously, inexplicably, Nietzsche escaped the frying pan of Genoa by hopping a freighter to Messina, Sicily. At the end of April he made his way up to Rome in order to visit Malwida von Meysenbug and Paul Rée. There the fateful meeting with Lou von Salomé took place—in the less than propitious surroundings of Saint Peter's Basilica. Nietzsche spent the summer not in Sils but in Tautenburg, close to his birthplace. It was to this secluded village in the Thuringian Forest that he repaired with Lou von Salomé. In the woods of Tautenburg the proofs for *The Gay Science* were corrected; in Tautenburg the first copies of the published book arrived on August 25. Nietzsche was delighted to have found a "disciple" with so scintillating an intellect, even at the tender age of twenty-one, and the three friends, Nietzsche, Rée, and von Salomé made elaborate plans to live together (as free spirits, though not as free lovers), whether in Paris or Vienna, Munich or Leipzig. Nietzsche fell head over heels in love, and his letters between April and December of 1882 showed how desperately he could crave and how totally jealousy could consume him. They also showed how relentlessly his mother and sister were willing to intervene in order to protect his chastity—which, to be sure, was never at hazard. Franziska and Elisabeth hammered in a wedge that would never be removed: they were bent on becoming what Nietzsche later called the "infernal machine" that knew precisely when and how to hurt him most. By the fall of 1882 he was writing drafts of nasty letters to Franziska and Elisabeth, drafts he never sent. On one scrap of paper he reported the fact that ground ginger is good for the soul: he would be sending his mother and sister a pound of it (B *6*, 267). Sils-Maria now served as a refuge from Naumburg. He wrote from Sils to Elisabeth in Naumburg early in July 1883: "Sils-Maria is in a way the end of the world. In Naumburg one is much closer to 'the world'; unfortunately, also closer to 'the wicked world,' as I perceive with sadness from your letter" (B *6*, 389).[2]

None of that was apparent during the summer of 1882, however, with Nietzsche arriving in Tautenburg on June 25 and not departing (except for brief interludes) until August 27. He was aware that something of a "crisis" was building up in him, or, as he said in a letter to Malwida von Meysenbug, an ἐποχή or *Epoche,* that is, "a condition of being in between two crises," presumably

2. To Franz Overbeck Nietzsche wrote on March 6, 1883: "Dissolving the ties with my family now is proving to be a true blessing. Oh, if you only knew all the things I have had to overcome under this rubric (since my birth)! I don't like my mother; and to hear my sister's voice grates on my nerves. I was *always* ill when I was with them. We have not 'quarreled' much, not even last summer; I know how to handle them; but it doesn't agree with me to have to do so" (B *6*, 338-39). To Heinrich Köselitz he reported on August 26 of the same year that his mother and sister had driven him to the verge of madness, and that he was caught in a labyrinth of *ressentiments* and desires for revenge (B *6*, 435; cf. 437).

Tautenburg, Monday, June 26, 1882

My dear friend,

A half-hour from Dornburg, where the elderly Goethe enjoyed his solitude in the midst of lovely forests, lies Tautenburg. Here my good sister has arranged an idyllic little nest that is to shelter me this summer. Yesterday I took possession of it. Tomorrow my sister will depart and I shall be alone. Yet we've agreed on something that perhaps will occasion her return. Granted, that is, that you have no better way to spend the month of August and would find it fitting and meet to live with me here in the woods; in that case, my sister would conduct you hither from Bayreuth and live with you here (for example, in the house of the local pastor, where she is now staying: the community has a good selection of lovely and inexpensive lodgings). My sister, whom you may ask Rée about, would need a great deal of solitude during this period in order to brood on her little novella-egg. She is mightily pleased by the thought of being in your and my proximity.—So! And now, let us be upright "unto death"! My dear friend! I am committed to nothing here and could quite easily alter my plans in case *you* have other plans. And if I am not to be together with you, then simply tell me so—and you don't even need to give any reasons! I trust you *implicitly:* but you know that. —

If we get along well together, then so will our states of health, and in some secret way this visit will do us both good. Prior to this, I've *never* thought that you might "read aloud and write" for me; but what I very much wish to be permitted to be is your *teacher.* Finally, to tell the whole truth: I am now seeking the human beings who could be my inheritors; I bear about me some things that are not to be read in my books—and for these things I am searching for the finest, most fertile soil.

You see my *selfishness!* —

Every time I think on the threats to your health and your very life, as I do again and again, my soul is filled with tenderness; I don't know if anything else could bring me so quickly to your side.—And then I'm ever so happy to know that you have Rée, and not only me, as a friend. It is a genuine pleasure for me to think of walks and talks together with the two of you. —

The Grunewald was far too sunny for my eyes, anyway.

My address is: Tautenburg near Dornburg, Thuringia.

Yours faithfully,

Friend Nietzsche

P. S.: Yesterday Liszt was here.

The Tautenburgerwald above the village, where Nietzsche and Lou von Salomé walked during August 1882.

the past crisis of his illness and the imminent crisis of his unrequited love (B *6, 223*). He stayed in a modest farmhouse owned by the Hahnemann family. Lou was there for three weeks in August. Elisabeth, now thirty-six years old, was in attendance as chaperone—in spite of the fact that she and Lou, in Bayreuth for the premiere of *Parsifal,* then later in Jena, had quarreled bitterly. They had fought *before* their sojourn together in Tautenburg with Nietzsche, who was of course the object of the row. Nietzsche and Lou tried to shake their chaperone. They walked through the woods; Nietzsche introduced Lou to his philosophy; Elisabeth, neglected, went into a slow burn. For their part, the local authorities were pleased to have a famous professor in their midst: they erected five new benches in his honor along the shady paths through the woods that he and Lou frequented, and invited him to have brass plates made for as many of them as he liked, a task he promptly assigned his mother back in Naumburg. By summer's end, Elisabeth had told their mother everything she never wanted to know about Lou and their Fritz; Franziska made the mistake of telling Nietzsche that he was causing his father to turn over in his grave; Nietzsche fled to Leipzig, where Lou and Paul joined him for the month of October. With Lou's and Paul Rée's departure for Paris on November 5, without Fritz, the fiasco was over, except for the desperate letters that flew back and forth for several more months. Whether Franziska ever had the brass plates made we do not know. Yet among Nietzsche's notes, the "Tautenburger Sketches for Lou" have a special place, if only because so few of Nietzsche's notes were addressed to anyone other than himself.[3]

All four parts of *Thus Spoke Zarathustra* were written and published (or, in the case of Part Four, privately printed) during the years 1883–85. Every indication we have from Nietzsche's letters and from his philosophical autobiography, *Ecce Homo,* tells us that *Thus Spoke Zarathustra* was his greatest achievement, his magnum opus. If in the years that followed Nietzsche worked on a *philosophical* magnum opus under titles such as *Midday and Eternity, The Will to Power,* and *Transvaluation of All Values,* the watershed of his creative life doubtless remained *Thus Spoke Zarathustra.* The central

3. See W *10,* 37-42; also printed in part in B *6,* 242-45. Most of the notes are on questions of style and matters of love. The sixth note reads, *"Love,* for *men,* is something altogether different than it is for women. For most men, to be sure, love is a kind of *obsession to possess;* for other men, love is adoration of a suffering and veiled godhead. [¶] If our friend Rée read this, he would take me to be crazy. [¶] How are you? There never was a more beautiful day in Tautenburg than today. The air is clear, mild, and bracing: which is the way we all should be" (W *10,* 37; B *6,* 243).

The "Zarathustra Stone," on the shores of Lake Silvaplana near Surlej, as it looked early in the twentieth century. Photo: Stiftung Weimarer Klassik. GSA 101/612.

thought of that work, eternal return, he associated with Sils-Maria, and particularly with a vast boulder on the southern shore of Lake Silvaplana. Even though the thought had struck him early on while he was studying the fragments of the ancient Greek thinkers, and perhaps even as far back as "Fate and History," he pinpointed a particular time (August 1881) and a specific place (the cleavage of that gigantic boulder not far from the village of Surlej) in which the thought suddenly alighted on him. In the course of recounting why he wrote such good books, Nietzsche announced in *Ecce Homo:*

> I shall now relate the history of *Zarathustra.* The fundamental conception of the work, *the thought of eternal return,* which is the highest formula of affirmation that can ever be attained, belongs to the month of August in the year 1881. The thought was jotted onto a page that bears the following signature: "6,000 feet beyond humanity and time." On that day I went walking through the woods near Lake Silvaplana; I stopped near a mightily towering pyramidal boulder not far from Surlej. There the thought came to me.— (W *6,* 335)

If the thought of eternal return had its home in the mountains of Sils, *Thus Spoke Zarathustra,* Part One, was born on the Italian Riviera. After Rée and Lou had departed for Paris, Nietzsche traveled south, seeking solace with the Overbecks in Basel, then continuing on to Genoa. He arrived at Genoa to find his former lodgings on the Salita delle Battistine occupied by someone else, and so he moved farther south along the coast to Rapallo. During the months of December 1882 and January-February 1883 he worked on the first part of *Thus Spoke Zarathustra*. Most of the first draft was written in only ten days at the end of January. At the very moment he was about to mail the manuscript to his publisher, Ernst Schmeitzner in Chemnitz, Nietzsche learned of Richard Wagner's death in Venice on February 13, 1883. News of that death ripped open old wounds in him— the deepest, the festering wound being his (incorrect) suspicion that Wagner had accused him of pederasty (B *6*, 365). He fell ill for days.

Nietzsche was aware that *Thus Spoke Zarathustra* constituted a watershed in his life, a Continental Divide that began to rise with the fourth book of *The Gay Science,* "Sanctus Januarius." Even before the first part of *Zarathustra* was written, on September 9, 1882, Nietzsche wrote to Franz Overbeck:

> If you have read "Sanctus Januarius," you will have noticed that I have already come to a *turning point*. Everything lies new before me, and it will not be long before I am able to see the *frightening* face of my life's future task. This long and rich summer [in Tautenburg] was for me a time of *rehearsals;* it is with the greatest confidence and pride that I now take my departure from it. For during this stretch of time I found that I was able to *bridge* the otherwise horrid gap that separates willing from accomplishing. There were *hard* claims on my humanity, and in the most difficult circumstances I found that I was sufficient unto myself. This entire condition "in between" what once was and what one day will be I call *in media vita*. (B *6*, 255)

Upon completing the first part of *Zarathustra* in Rapallo, Nietzsche celebrated it in a letter to Heinrich Köselitz, calling it a "kind of homily" and his very best work, one that had "rolled a stone" off his soul: "There is nothing more serious or more cheerful from my hand; with all my heart, I wish that *this* color—which need not be used in combination with any other color—be my 'natural' color from now on"; he added that with this new book he had entered a new "ring," one that would cause him to be regarded as mad, especially in Germany (B *6*, 321). He told Franz Overbeck that his new book was his "testament," a "poetic creation," as opposed to a collection of aphorisms; he informed his publisher that it was "a fifth gospel," and something for which there were as yet "no names" (B *6*, 326–27).

There was some delay in the printing and binding of *Thus Spoke Zarathustra,* Part One, a delay to which Nietzsche's sense of irony was equal. He informed Köselitz that Schmeitzner was overburdened with work of a religious nature—he had to print 500,000 hymnals before Easter and

Rapallo. The Hotel della Posta, where in January 1883 Nietzsche composed the first part of *Thus Spoke Zarathustra.*

distribute a whole range of anti-Semitic tracts. *Zarathustra* the godless would have to wait until the end of April, Nietzsche wryly observed, because of the good Christian competition (B *6*, 353; 388). Yet sometimes even his sense of irony failed him: Nietzsche had moments of despair about his *Zarathustra*. It was as though the Germans might for once be right. On March 22, 1883, he confided to Overbeck:

> My dear friend, I feel as though it has been ages since you wrote. Yet perhaps I deceive myself: the days are so long, I no longer know what I am supposed to do with them. All my "interests" have gone missing. In the deepest part of me an immovable, black melancholy holds sway. Otherwise, weariness. Mostly in bed. Also it's the most rational thing to do for my health. I've lost a great deal of weight; people are amazed. Now I've found a good trattoria and will fatten myself up once more. However, the worst thing is this: I can no longer seize on *any reason why* I should live even for another six months; everything is boring painful *dégoutant*. I am deprived, and I suffer too much. Further, I've begun to grasp the imperfections, the mistakes, and the genuine calamities of my entire *intellectual* past, which are inconceivably vast. It is too late to make up for them; I won't be doing anything good anymore. Why do anything at all!— (B *6*, 348)

No doubt, Zarathustra both as a figure and as a book "overcame" Nietzsche with such alacrity and intensity—though *Thus Spoke Zarathustra* followed upon *The Gay Science* with a relentless and even "impudent" internal logic (B *6*, 364)—that he did not know what to make of it. That was often the reaction he had to his creative work. Concerning his "Ermanarich Symphony," composed at age eighteen, Nietzsche had complained:

> All the world's pain *[Weltschmerz]* is introduced by strange harmonies that are doleful and bitter, harmonies that entirely displeased me at the beginning. Now they seem to me to be alleviated somewhat, or at least they can be excused in the light of the movement as a whole. The compulsions and pursuits of passion, with their sudden transitions and stormy eruptions, are bursting with harmonic monstrosities, concerning which I dare not make a decision. (J *2*, 104)

Yet the prevailing mood after the rush of *Zarathustra* was one of an exaltation trying to contain itself and remain cautious. The categories had not changed—it was still the philologist turned philosopher turned poet, though certainly not belletrist. He wrote, again to Overbeck, at the beginning of April 1883:

> In the end it is **possible** that with this past winter I have entered upon a new development. *Zarathustra* is something no human being alive apart from me can produce. Perhaps only now have I discovered my best powers. Even as a "philosopher" I still did not express my most essential thoughts (or "delusions"). Oh, I am so taciturn, so furtive! But now I write as a "poet"! My philology I have *forgotten;* I could have *studied* something better during my twenties! Oh, the things concerning which I am ignorant! (B *6*, 355)

With the final composition of Part Two of *Thus Spoke Zarathustra* in the summer of 1883 at Sils-Maria, and the initial thoughts toward Part Three, Nietzsche clearly felt the exaltation. To Heinrich Köselitz he sent the following breathless paragraphs on July 13:

> I have the second verse behind me—and now that it is finished I shudder at the difficulty I have overcome without really thinking about it.
>
> Since my last letter I am doing better and am more encouraged. The conception of this *second* part of *Zarathustra* came quite suddenly, as did the birth *after* the conception—all with the greatest vehemence.
>
> (In that regard the thought occurred to me that I will probably die of *that kind* of emotional expansion and explosion—devil take the hindmost!)

The printer's manuscript will be finished day after tomorrow; only the last five sections remain to be done, although my eyes set limits to my "diligence." . . .

My major task was to *use this second stage as a springboard*—to the third. (The title of the third part is "Midday and Eternity," did I tell you? But I beg you not to tell anyone about it! For the third part I shall give myself plenty of time, perhaps *years.*—) (B *6,* 397)

Part Three of *Thus Spoke Zarathustra,* at least as Nietzsche was planning it at the end of his Sils-Maria summer in 1883, would plunge into the "pessimistic" or, better, truly "tragic" character of existence. It was this third part that induced Nietzsche to link *Zarathustra* as a whole to his first major work, *The Birth of Tragedy.* He also associated it with a large-scale theoretical work that had as one of its titles *The Innocence of Becoming* (B *6,* 444–45). Initially, he conceived of the third part as a single episode, which split into two episodes in the finished book, namely, "On the Vision and the Riddle" and "The Convalescent." Here the idea of eternal recurrence received its most forceful—albeit enigmatic and uncanny—presentation. Once again the metaphor he used to describe the book was "explosion," along with the musical metaphor of the symphony, the architectural symbol of the tower, and the familial personification of paternity—he loved to call *Zarathustra* his "son." To Overbeck he enthused on February 6, 1884:

> In general the *whole* of Zarathustra is an explosion of forces that have been building up in me for decades: with such explosions the detonator can easily blow himself up. That is **precisely** the way I felt many times—I won't hide the fact from you. And I know ahead of time that when the finale tells you *what it is* that the entire symphony genuinely wants to say (—very artistically and step-by-step, as though one were building a tower), then you too, my old and faithful friend, will be unable to suppress a terrifying shudder. You have *an extremely hazardous* friend; and the worst thing about him is how **reticent** he can be. How happy I would be to *laugh* together with you and your dear and worthy wife (to *laugh myself to death* about myself!!!). (B *6,* 475)

Silsersee, Oberengadin. Looking west across Lake Sils to Grevasalvas and Piz Lagrev in the afternoon sun. *"A notion about the countryside.* — If a human being does not have firm, tranquil lines on the horizon of his or her life, lines formed by mountain and forest, as it were, then the innermost will itself grows restless, distracted, and covetous, after the manner of all city dwellers: they have no happiness, give no happiness" (MAM I, 290; *2,* 234).

Climbing up to the Moorish bastion at Èzé, where important sections of the third part of *Thus Spoke Zarathustra* were composed. "I draw circles and sacred boundaries about me; fewer and fewer climb with me up higher and higher mountains. — I am building a mountain chain out of ever-holier mountains" (ASZ, "Of Old and New Tablets," 19; *4*, 260).

Sometime during December 1884 Nietzsche ceased working on a prose text entitled "Midday and Eternity," no doubt related to Part Three of *Thus Spoke Zarathustra*. From January to April 1885 in Nice he worked on a *fourth* part to *Zarathustra*, projecting even a fifth, sixth, and *n*th part, inasmuch as he could not get Zarathustra to die.[4] In a sense, Nietzsche's treatment of "the superior human beings" in the fourth part of *Zarathustra* reflected his own frustration over the failure to find disciples for the thought of eternal return. The bitter irony and the tendency to caricature that earmarked this fourth and final part reflected Nietzsche's growing isolation. If one of the plans around this time bore the title *The Good Europeans,* it was nevertheless true that Nietzsche was consistently failing to find them.

Formally speaking, Nietzsche was able to construct a far more cohesive *dramatic* plot for the fourth part than for any earlier section of the work. The fourth part arched back to the dramatic Prologue that opened *Thus Spoke Zarathustra,* and thus lent a certain classical unity to the work, if only extrinsically so. On May 4, 1885, Nietzsche wrote to Overbeck concerning this fourth part, of which a small number of copies were printed privately during the spring of 1885, asserting that it was "intended as a finale" for the work. "Just read the Prologue of Part One," he added (B *7*, 46).

However, even before the fourth and final part of *Thus Spoke Zarathustra* was finished, Nietzsche began to call the entire work a "preface" or a "vestibule" to the major theoretical work he planned to compose (B *6*, 485). He wrote to Overbeck on April 7, 1884: "If I can go to Sils-Maria for the summer, I want to undertake a revision of my work on metaphysics and my epistemological views. I have to advance step-by-step through an entire range of disciplines, inasmuch as I am resolved to spend the next five years elaborating my 'philosophy,' for which, with my *Zarathustra,* I

4. On the relation of *Zarathustra* to the figure of Empedocles, and thus to death by suicide, see N *2*, 381, and Krell, *Postponements,* p. 112 n. 2.

have built a vestibule" (B *6, 496*). Yet the images of "preface" and "vestibule" were subtly altered by what followed: "As I was reading once again through *Daybreak* and *The Gay Science,* I found scarcely a sentence there that did not serve as an introduction, preparation, and commentary with respect to my *Zarathustra.* It is a *fact* that I wrote the commentary *before* the text.— —" At summer's end, after consuming many books of German metaphysics and epistemology, he pronounced himself satisfied and prepared:

> In general I am *finished* with the major task that I posed for myself this summer—the next six years will be devoted to the elaboration of a schematic outline of my "philosophy" that I have drawn up.[5] Things look auspicious in this regard. Meanwhile, *Zarathustra* has an altogether personal meaning: it is my "book of edification and encouragement," whereas to everyone else it is obscure and covert and ridiculous. (B *6,* 525; cf. 528)

The notes he began to sketch toward his "philosophical major work," notes of enormous range and power that did not dwindle until the spring or summer of 1888, were characterized by inner disquiet and, as Curt Paul Janz puts it, "daimonic drivenness" (N *2, 425*). At first they bore the title *The Will to Power.* Yet that was only one of the many titles he fashioned for them, and perhaps the least fortunate one. It was to be part of Nietzsche's terrible fate that his sister and Köselitz chose precisely that title for *their* version of Nietzsche's (unpublished) main work. If those hundreds and hundreds of scintillating notes, some of them never taken up into any published work, failed to constitute a main philosophical work, it was probably for the reason that Janz suggests: "If there is no truth that we can know; if there is no knowing subject who is capable of grasping truth; if there is no causality; if concepts never adequately match states of affairs, and are always incomplete;—how then under such circumstances is a systematic philosophical 'magnum opus' possible?" (N *2, 429*). Nietzsche's quandary was perhaps best expressed in his exclamation to Overbeck on February 12, 1887, "If only I had the courage to *think* everything I know" (B *8, 21*), along with his confession to Georg Brandes on December 2, 1887, "Only seldom do I have the courage for what I actually know" (B *8, 206*). Yet Nietzsche certainly devoted himself to the task of courageous thinking between the years 1885 and 1888. In December 1886 he told his publisher, "I now need, for many, many years, profound tranquillity: for what now confronts me is the elaboration of my entire system of thought" (B *7, 297*). Clearly, what Nietzsche now desired was *"a coherent structure of thought"* (B *8, 49*).

Beyond Good and Evil was published in August 1886. If *Zarathustra* consisted of several "explosions," Nietzsche's next book, as one reviewer wrote (much to Nietzsche's delight), was *dynamite.* Nietzsche relayed the following excerpts of his favorite review to Malwida von Meysenbug in Rome, mailing them from Sils-Maria on September 24, 1886:

> The supply of dynamite that was used in the construction of the Gotthard railway line bore the black flag that warned of mortal danger.—Entirely in this sense we may speak of the new book by the philosopher Nietzsche as a *dangerous* book. By calling it this, we do not cast a trace of aspersion on the author or his work, as little as those black flags were scolding the explosives. Still less is it our intention, when referring to the hazardous nature of his

---

5. The outline to which Nietzsche is referring cannot be identified. That spring he had been working on plans for a book entitled *Wisdom and Love of Wisdom: Prolegomena to a Philosophy of the Future* (see, for example, W *11,* 145; cf. 142 and 159). Two notes on truth and the problem of values seem to refer to "chapters" of such a book (162); another refers to the "Introduction" to the book (168). We also find here one of the early references to his next publication: *Beyond Good and Evil: Attempt at an Extra-Moral Observation of Moral Phenomena* (186). The most detailed schemata appear at 207-14, 284-85, and 291-96. In the midst of these notes is one very short one that is of particular interest to us: "NB live *outside of cities!*" (179).

Nietzsche's room in the house of Gian Durisch at Sils-Maria.

book, to turn over the reclusive author to the ravens of the chancellory and the crows of the altar. Intellectual explosives, like material ones, can serve a very useful purpose; they need not necessarily be misused for criminal ends. It is merely that one would do well, wherever such materials are deposited, to say quite explicitly, *"Here lies dynamite!"* (B 7, 258)

In a letter to a friend, Nietzsche called *Beyond Good and Evil* "a sort of commentary on my *Zarathustra"* (B 7, 270); he later urged Georg Brandes to begin the study of his philosophy as a whole with *Beyond,* since it was the "key" to all his work. In a letter to Köselitz he exulted, "It is a terrifying book that has flowed from my soul this time—very dark indeed, well-nigh inky squid" (B 7, 181). The notes that went into it, the bulk of them written during the labor-intensive period from 1884 to 1886, rejoined the themes first developed in Nietzsche's turning-point work, *Human, All-Too-Human.* For many months he called the projected new work the "second volume" of *Daybreak.* Yet by March 27, 1886, he had decided on the new title. He wrote to Köselitz (B 7, 166–67): "I have employed this past winter writing a book that is replete with difficulties, such that my courage, the courage needed to publish it, shakes and quakes from time to time. It is called:

Beyond Good and Evil:
Prelude to a
Philosophy of the Future."

Indeed, after the extraordinary detour of *Thus Spoke Zarathustra,* Nietzsche was looking for ways to continue his work, to rejoin his pre-*Zarathustra* works. Among the themes of *Beyond Good and Evil* were the prejudices of philosophers, especially their naive belief in clearly defined opposites; the origins of religious belief (especially in Christianity); a "natural history" of morality; the current state of the sciences and scholarly disciplines, along with the "virtues" of those who practice them; and, finally, the meaning of nobility. It is not too much to say that in this book Nietzsche took on the entire tradition of Western metaphysics and morals since Plato.

An important aspect of *Beyond Good and Evil* was Nietzsche's intensified preoccupation with "nations and fatherlands." In part, that intensification had to do with his brother-in-law, Bernhard Förster, whose book *German Colonies in the Upper La Plata Region, with Special Attention to Paraguay* Nietzsche had read in the fall of 1885. The chauvinism and imperialism of Förster's colonial plans— which were completely in line with the militarism and anti-Semitism of Adolf Stoecker, court chaplain in Berlin and head of the "Christian Socialist" party—stood for everything Nietzsche had come to despise. In Nietzsche's view, Germany had become "a genuine School for Stupefaction" (B 8, 31). The fact that his sister had married into the most offensive aspects of Bayreuth and Berlin was a source of rage and grief during the last years of Nietzsche's wakeful life. His final notes in 1888, on the verge of madness, called for the abolition of the House of Hohenzollern and the execution of Stoecker, Bismarck, and "all the anti-Semites."

Yet the reasoned arguments of *Beyond Good and Evil* remain the key to Nietzsche as the good European. In this regard, the book's subtitle is important: *Prelude to a Philosophy of the Future.* How long would Nietzsche have to wait for such a future? He offered two estimates. In one (B 7, 257), he declared that *Beyond Good and Evil* might well find its first audience "toward the year 2000"; in two others (B 8, 57, 70), he lowered his sights and suggested that 1901 (that is, as it turns out, only a few months following his own death) might be the year of its debut. The general lack of response to his work wounded Nietzsche deeply, however. In a letter dated June 17, 1887, to Overbeck, the friend on whom he relied more and more during the closing years of his life, Nietzsche lamented:

> To hold out over these past few years—perhaps that has been the very hardest thing my destiny has challenged me to do. After the sort of *call* that my *Zarathustra* was, a call from my inmost soul, not to hear a single peep by way of reply: nothing, nothing, only the soundless solitude multiplied a thousandfold—there is something terrible about that, beyond all comprehension; even the most robust person could perish on account of it— and, oh my! I am not among the "most robust"! Since that time it is as though I've been staggering about, mortally wounded; I'm astonished that I still live. However, there is no doubt about it: I am still alive. Who knows what life still has to show me! (B 8, 93–94)

Nietzsche completed the manuscript of *Beyond Good and Evil* by Easter, that is, by April 25, 1886, arranging for it to be privately printed by Constantin Gustav Naumann in Leipzig. It was with this book that the printer Naumann became an independent publisher. For the moment, however, Nietzsche was still caught up with publisher Ernst Fritsch's plans to release second editions of Nietzsche's earlier works, the rights to which Fritsch had purchased on August 5, 1886. These second editions, which Nietzsche prepared after the publication of *Beyond Good and Evil*, were not prompted by commercial considerations; rather, they were further evidence of Nietzsche's need to reassess his task and yet seek continuity. The prefaces he prepared over the next six months were in his own estimation (and also in ours) among the most powerful pieces of writing in his œuvre. He wrote more about them to his friends than about any other of his writings. To Overbeck he declared, "These five prefaces are perhaps the best prose I have written to date" (B 7, 282). Yet he did not always feel so positive about the actual books. On October 31 he wrote to Heinrich Köselitz:

> *Fritsch* has just sent my old books in their clean new clothes; they cut truly striking figures with the "Prefaces." In retrospect, it seems fortunate to me that I did not have either

Human, All-Too-Human or *The Birth of Tragedy* to hand when I wrote these prefaces: for, between us, I can no longer put up with any of that stuff. I hope my taste will grow and develop beyond Nietzsche "the author and thinker." Perhaps then I will be a bit more worthy of the presumptuous claim that lies in the words "free spirit." (B 7, 274)

By now he had given up the dream of traveling to Mexico or anywhere else outside of Europe. Bernhard and Elisabeth Förster's Paraguay project was enough to dispel such dreams. More positively, he conceded that he needed Europe because it was "the seat of science on Earth" (B 7, 278). He left Sils on September 25, 1886, and settled for a month—and for more prefaces to his earlier books—in Ruta Ligure, near Genoa. By October 20 he was in Nice, where he continued to elaborate plans for a philosophical "major work."

On April 3, 1887, he traveled to Cannóbio, on the western shore of Lago Maggiore, residing in the Pension Villa Badía, near the thermal springs of the Fonte Carlina. (The Villa Badía is today a heap of ivy-draped ruins in the rugged Val Cannóbio, about a kilometer west of the Fonte Carlina.) Nietzsche hoped that Cannóbio would be a solution to the problems of spring and autumn— the months that were too hot by the sea and too frigid in the Alps. Yet Val Cannóbio was unkind to his eyes, and Nietzsche moved on to the Pension Neptun in Zürich.

Once again we have the opportunity to note how strange it is that Nietzsche rejected Lago Maggiore in favor of the lakes at Sils—ostensibly on account of his eyes. However one may officially or scientifically measure *glare* the authors do not know, but there is no way that Lake Sils and Lake Silvaplana can be viewed as being gentle on the eyes! —But to resume the chronology of publications, the fruits of Nietzsche's mountain solitude.

On the Genealogy of Morals was published in November 1887. On May 6, 1887, Nietzsche went on to Chur, where he stayed at the Villa Rosenhügel for a month; then, by way of Lenzerheide, he arrived once again (on June 6) at Sils. It was here, during the week of July 10–17, that he composed his *Genealogy of Morals.* In its form, the work resembled the *Untimely Meditations* of the 1870s more than the aphoristic works of the early 1880s; each of its three treatises was a sustained, carefully

Cannóbio, Lago Maggiore, Italy. Ruins of a bench on the grounds of the now vanished Villa Badía. (Note at the center of the photograph the dark lines of a figure of the sun incised in the stone.)

constructed meditation, on (1) the oppositional pairs "good and evil," "good and bad"; (2) "guilt" and "bad conscience"; and (3) the significance of "the ascetic ideal" for Western religions, moral systems, science, and philosophy. Yet its style was considerably more trenchant, and even acerbic, than that of any prior text. On August 22, 1888, a full year after completing *On the Genealogy of Morals,* Nietzsche referred to its "extremely difficult problems," for which "no terminology lay to hand" (B *8,* 397). He continued: "Yet I must have been in a state of almost uninterrupted inspiration at the time, inasmuch as this writing flows along like the most natural thing in the world. Without being at all labored, its style is vehement and agitated, though at the same time full of *finesses;* it is malleable and colorful, more so than any prose I wrote prior to that point." It does not seem too far-fetched to claim that the crystalline, sharp-edged prose of Nietzsche's *Genealogy* matches the landscape of the Engadine during periods of *Föhn,* the peculiar atmospheric condition that induces brilliant clarity and piercing headache (N *2,* 526).

Although Nietzsche called the *Genealogy* an appendix or supplement to *Beyond Good and Evil,* its origins themselves go farther back: on October 15, 1885 (Nietzsche's forty-first birthday), he wrote to Baron Heinrich von Stein that he had recently read Paul Rée's book on "conscience." "How vacuous, how boring, how false!" he exclaimed. "One should talk only about things in which one has experienced something" (B *7,* 99). Among the most powerful passages of the *Genealogy of Morals* are those in which Nietzsche cited Tertullian on the delight experienced by the Christian saints at the prospect of watching the damned suffer in hell, and those in which Nietzsche portrayed the enormous range and variety of asceticisms in our culture—asceticism, for example, in our philosophies of beauty. Meta von Salis mentions the extended and repeated conversations she had with Nietzsche about Kant's concept of "disinterested delight" in beauty, and about Stendhal's contrasting idea—that beauty is *une promesse de bonheur,* in which "happiness" is essentially erotic (N *2,* 531). In the twentieth century, a number of thinkers—most notably Michel Foucault and Gilles Deleuze—have extended Nietzsche's project of a genealogy of morals; for them, Nietzsche's "polemic" was no doubt one of his most significant achievements.

When Nietzsche compared *On the Genealogy of Morals* with *Beyond Good and Evil,* he described the earlier writing as "neutral" in tone, and as slowly, even hesitantly advancing in its rhythm; by contrast, the *Genealogy* was written in the tempo *Allegro feroce,* with a "naked, raw, verdant passion" (B *8,* 245). When he compared the third and best-known treatise of the *Genealogy* to the first two, he found that it in turn was in a different "key" and "tempo," that it was more "finale" and "rondo," that is to say, "more daringly conceived" than they; only the preface to the entire book (the prefaces always meant most to Nietzsche!) exceeded it in strength and compactness (B *8,* 154). With the completion of his *Genealogy* in the summer of 1887, Nietzsche felt himself to be on a kind of plateau. He wrote to Overbeck on August 30: "With this book I feel that I am *at the end* of my labors to make my prior books 'comprehensible': from now on, at least for the next several years, I shall publish nothing—I have to fall back absolutely on my own resources, I have to wait until I shake the final fruits from my tree. *No* experiences; *nothing* from the *outside;* nothing *new*—these are now my only wishes for some time into the future" (B *8,* 140).

Finally, a vast number of unpublished notes toward a "philosophical magnum opus," along with the manuscripts of *The Antichrist, The Wagner Case, Twilight of the Idols, Ecce Homo, Nietzsche contra Wagner,* and *Dionysos Dithyrambs,* were written in 1888. For Nietzsche, the entire decade of the 1880s was incredibly productive. Yet the final active year of Nietzsche's life, 1888, soared beyond any usual

The view from Nietzsche's window in the Durisch house at Sils-Maria.

conception of productivity. The year became increasingly hectic, with four of the six works being composed in the autumn and early winter of the year.

During the autumn of 1887 Nietzsche had still been contemplating a return to the University of Leipzig to engage in studies that would contribute to the composition of his major philosophical work. Yet his health forbade such "dangerous experiments" (B *8*, 154). Nice and Venice were the sole possibilities. On September 19, 1887, Nietzsche departed Sils-Maria for what would be his final visit to Venice, the city of Vivaldi and Köselitz, or Pietro Gasti, as Nietzsche liked to call him, but also the city where Richard Wagner had died. While in Venice, residing at number 1263 Calle dei Preti, a minute's stroll from the Sotto San Geminian, the western portal of the Piazza San Marco, he sketched out a number of notes on Theseus (Richard) and Ariadne (Cosima), with himself cast in the role of Dionysos—if only for a "satyr play" that he hoped would cap "the perfect book."[6]

When he moved to Nice at the end of October, the feeling that an epoch had ended for him became all the more pronounced. On December 20, 1887, he wrote two long letters about this change of epoch, the first to Köselitz back in Venice:

> I am working energetically, but full of melancholy, and not yet liberated from the violent mood shifts that the last few years have induced in me. Not yet "sufficiently depersonal-ized."—Nevertheless, I know what has been done and what is *done for*: I have drawn a *line* under my entire prior existence—that is the meaning of the past few years. To be sure, my prior existence now stands in relief and shows itself for what it is—a mere *promise*. The passion of my most recent text *[On the Genealogy of Morals]* has something terrifying about it: I read it the day before yesterday with profound astonishment, as though I had never seen it before. (B *8*, 213)

6. See W *12*, 400-2; see also Krell, *Postponements,* pp. 81-82; 104-5.

The second letter that "draws a line" under Nietzsche's "prior existence" was to Carl von Gersdorff, with whom he had again struck up a cordial correspondence:

> In a significant sense my life stands now at *high noon*. One door is closing, another opening. Everything I've done in recent years was a settling of accounts, a coming to a conclusion, an adding up of things past: I've come to terms with people and things and have drawn a line under it all. *Who* and *what* will remain for me now, as I am compelled to proceed toward the proper and principal concern of my existence (*condemned* to proceed . . .), that is indeed a capital question. For, between you and me, the tension in which I live, the pressure of a great task and passion, is too great for me to allow still more human beings to approach me. The desert around me is vast indeed; I can bear only perfect strangers and passersby, or, on the contrary, those who have been close to me for a long, long time, since my childhood. Everyone else has drifted away, or has been *repulsed* (there was a lot of violence and pain in that—) (B *8*, 214)

And on January 3 of the new year, the final year of work, he wrote to his old friend Paul Deussen, "At bottom, everything with me now is epoch-making; my entire used-to-be is crumbling and falling away from me" (B *8*, 221).

He interrupted his notes and outlines for the magnum opus, notes that now focused on the history of *nihilism,* with plans for three further treatises (numbered 4–6) for a second *Genealogy of Morals,* number 4 on "the herd-instinct in morality," number 5 on "the history of morality" as "denaturalization," and number 6 on "moralists and moral philosophers."[7] That this proposed second *Genealogy* was interwoven with the larger project, the magnum opus, is suggested by the final line of the plan, underlined several times: **"Entry into the tragic age of Europe,"** an entry that Nietzsche always identified with the thought of eternal recurrence (W *12*, 388).

The bulk of *The Wagner Case* was composed after May 15; indeed, most of it was written in Sils, where Nietzsche spent his last Engadine summer, that of 1888, arriving on June 5. While many regard the work as an "occasional" writing, or a polemic against the Meister, it cost Nietzsche many months of hard work. The book may be viewed as an attack on German Romanticism as a whole, especially on German music from Schubert through Wagner, Liszt, and even Brahms: Nietzsche reiterated the association of Wagner's music not with Schopenhauer but with Hegel and the decadence of modernity.

The greater part of *The Antichrist* was likewise written during the spring and summer of 1888. Studies for it, as we noted in chapter 2, went all the way back to the winter of 1876–77 in Sorrento. Even earlier, Franz Overbeck's 1873 *On the Christian Character of Theology Today,* whose gestation he had witnessed first-hand in the "Poison Cottage" in Basel, surely influenced Nietzsche's attack on Christendom. In Turin, early in May 1888, Nietzsche stumbled across a French translation of the ancient Sanskrit moral codex of the Brahman priests, *The Laws of Manu;* this codex, based on the Vedas, became for him an important integrating figure for his study of the ancient Hindu, Buddhist, Judaic, and Christian religions. No doubt many of the notes intended for the major work wound up in *The Antichrist,* which received its final spur from Nietzsche's conversations with the dogmatic theologian Julius Kaftan, who visited Sils for three weeks in August 1888. Nietzsche began to work intensely on *The Antichrist* (which could also be translated as *The Antichristian* and bore the subtitle *A Curse on Christendom*), as soon as Kaftan left Sils. Kaftan was to take his revenge after Nietzsche's collapse by interpreting the philosopher's works as symptoms of irreligion and madness, divine retribution at its merciless best.

---

7. See W *12*, 377-78; cf. 344, 357, 407; see also the discussion in Janz, N *2*, 562-63.

During this intense summer, Nietzsche sometimes began to write at two o'clock in the morning. In a letter to Meta von Salis, dated September 7, he reported that he could often hear his landlord, Gian Durisch, slipping off to hunt chamois in the predawn hours. "Who knows," he mused, "maybe I myself was on a chamois hunt." He continued:

> The *third* of September was a remarkable day. Early in the morning I wrote the preface to my *Transvaluation of All Values* [that is, *The Antichrist*], perhaps the proudest preface that has ever been written. Afterwards I went outside, and behold! the most beautiful day I have ever seen in the Engadine—all its colors aglow, a blue sheen on the lakes and in the sky, the air pristine, altogether unheard-of. . . . And I *wasn't the only one* to say so. The mountains dusted in white far down into the valley—for we had had some serious winter days— at all events enhanced the intensity of the light. (B *8,* 410)

The Antichrist(ian) was more interested in the intensity of the dark, however. It was directed principally against Paul and Pauline Christianity, that is, against the Church. Nevertheless, it also contained a genealogical analysis (in sections 28–30) of the "redeemer type," which as a type was closer to Dostoevsky's *Idiot* than to Renan's heroic Jesus; in retrospect, Nietzsche's redeemer type perhaps most closely resembles the Jesus of Kazantzakis's *The Last Temptation of Christ*. Nietzsche's focus, to repeat, was on Paul, inasmuch as his was the nefarious betrayal: Paul saw to it that "the 'good news' *died* on the cross" (W *8,* 211). Nietzsche did not expect his book to be popular. Its preface began: "This book belongs to the very few. Perhaps none of them are even alive yet. They may well be those who will understand my *Zarathustra.* . . . For only the day after tomorrow will be mine. Some are born posthumously" (W *6,* 167). Yet he fully expected that *The Antichrist* would cleave history in twain: when the task of transvaluation was finally understood, it would "split the history of humankind into two halves" (B *8,* 426, 447). If prior history, at least for Christian Europeans, had been marked by the eras B.C. or A.D., it would, as of September 30, 1888, be marked exclusively as A.N., *anno nietzschensis.*

The Nietzsche-Haus at Sils-Maria. Nietzsche's room was located on the second floor at the rear of the building. Bottom photo: Stiftung Weimarer Klassik. GSA 101/604.

Twilight of the Idols originally bore the title *A Psychologist's Leisure*. Nietzsche changed the title upon the urging of Köselitz, altering it quite late in the process, when the proofs were being corrected in Turin (B *8*, 442–43). C. G. Naumann had encouraged Nietzsche to publish several smaller works in order to boost interest in his forthcoming magnum opus. Nietzsche himself came to regard *Twilight* as an excellent introduction to his thought, one that flowed fairly effortlessly from his hand: "It is a perfect collective introduction to my philosophy" (B *8*, 414). The book's preface was dated *"Turin*, on the 30ᵗʰ of September, 1888, on the day that the first book of my *Transvaluation of All Values* [that is, *The Antichrist*] was finished" (W *6*, 58). Indeed, Nietzsche conceived of *Twilight of the Idols* as a particularly apt introduction to *The Antichrist*. He wrote to Heinrich Köselitz on September 12, 1888, concerning this "bold and precisely formulated summary" of his "most essential philosophical *heterodoxies,"* noting that the new book was to "initiate" readers and "awaken their appetites" for *The Antichrist* (B *8*, 417). To Overbeck he enthused, "It seems to me as though I had quite suddenly learned how to *write"* (B *8*, 434).

Indeed, learning how to write is what the book is all about. *Twilight of the Idols* contains ten sections along with a preface and an epilogue; some of the sections are in Nietzsche's succinct aphoristic style, others in the form of extended essays, after the manner of the *Untimely Meditations.* Among the most famous sections are those on "The Problem of Socrates" and "How the 'True World' Finally Became a Fable." Among the most biting are those on "What the Germans Lack," which includes the following advice about learning how to see, think, speak, and write:

> One must learn how to *see,* one must learn how to *think,* one must learn how to *speak* and *write:* the goal in all three is a noble cultivation. To learn how to *see:* to get the eye accustomed to calm, patience, and letting things approach on their own, postponing judgment, learning how to circumambulate the particular case, examining it from all sides. . . . To learn how to *see,* as I understand it, is well-nigh what the unphilosophical manner of speech calls a strong will: what is essential about a strong will is precisely *not* to "will," but to be *able* to suspend decision. . . . Thinking has to be learned, just as dancing does, thinking *as* a kind of dancing . . . with the feet, with concepts, with words. Need I add that one must also be able to dance with the *pen,* that one must learn how to *write?* (W *6*, 108–10)

The first copies of *Twilight of the Idols: Or, How One Philosophizes with a Hammer* reached him on November 25 in Turin. It was also in Turin that the final works—*Ecce Homo, Nietzsche contra Wagner,* and *Dionysos Dithyrambs*—were completed. We shall turn to them in chapter 4, paying special attention to *Ecce Homo,* Nietzsche's fascinating auto-hetero-biography, but not before we engage in some reflections on Nietzsche's life in Sils-Maria and on his solitude in high mountains.

Nietzsche knew what the mountains of Sils-Maria would mean to him before he ever saw them. At the end of June 1878 he wrote from Basel to Carl Fuchs, who had just read the first volume of his *Human, All-Too-Human:*

> Do you not in retrospect feel something of the air of heights? It is a little chillier around us, yet how much freer and purer than in the mist of the valleys! I at least feel more robust and more resolved for all the good things in life than ever before—also ten times *more gentle* toward human beings than in the period of my earlier writings. In sum, and with regard to the smallest particulars: I will now dare to pursue wisdom itself, will now dare *to be* a philosopher. (B *5*, 334–35)

Yet it was the sky of Sils as much as the mountains that liberated Nietzsche. He wrote to Franz Overbeck from Sils-Maria on September 14, 1884: "An Italian recently said to me, 'In con-

View of the mountains of the Fextal across the Silsersee, Oberengadin, taken from Chastè. "Whoever knows how to breathe the air of my writings knows that it is an air of the heights, a *strong* air. One has to be made for it, otherwise there is no little danger that one will catch cold in it. Ice is close by, and the loneliness is vast—yet how tranquilly all things repose in the light! how freely one breathes! how many things one feels to be *beneath* one! — Philosophy as I have understood and lived it till now is a voluntary life in ice and high mountains— . . ." (EH, Preface, 3; *6, 258*).

trast to what we Italians call *cielo,* that is, *sky,* your German *Himmel* is *una caricatura'*" (B *6, 532*). Mountain and sky, forest and lake: on June 14, 1888, after a decade of experience in the Engadine, he wrote to Heinrich Köselitz in Venice: "Sils is truly beautiful. In a rather daring Latin, I would say that it is *perla perlissima.* An abundance of *colors,* a hundred times more southern in this regard than Turin" (B *8, 331*).

When traveling to Sils from Basel, or from anywhere in the north of Europe, he would go by train to Chur, the final railway station, on the very threshold of the mountains of Canton Graubünden. As he changed trains in Zürich, he would no doubt be thinking of his circle of friends there,

An old photograph of Sils-Maria, looking east. The large turreted building in the left foreground is the Hotel Alpenrose; the house of Gian Durisch is the second-to-last house to the right in the central cluster of buildings making up the village. Nietzsche's window on the second floor of the house has been marked by a faint "x." On the far side of the Nietzsche-Haus stands the Hotel Edelweiss. Photo: Stiftung Weimarer Klassik. GSA 101/294.

the first women to earn the doctorate in Switzerland, the women whom he publicly scolded and privately prized—above all, Meta von Salis and Resa von Schirnhofer. From Chur he would travel by horse-drawn coach, passing through Lenzerheide and Tiefenkastel, then either eastward to the Albula Pass or due south to the Julia Pass, climbing toward the final station at St. Moritz in the Oberengadin. When traveling from the south—from Nice, Genoa, Venice, or Turin—he would make his way by train to Milan, then north to Como, and thence by coach through Chiavenna and the Maloja Pass to his beloved Sils.

To be sure, he was never certain whether the mountains of the Engadine would restore his health, although health was always one incentive for his voyages of discovery. There was something desperate about his letter to Heinrich Köselitz, written from Recoaro in the Dolomites on June 23, 1881, but with the Oberengadin very much in mind:

> Well, it is still the Engadine—because among my many attempts in Switzerland (perhaps 20–30 different places) the Engadine is the only one that barely scrapes through. It is *hard* for my nature to find the correct spot with regard to heights and depths; at bottom it involves a *groping,* there are factors that cannot be rigorously circumscribed (for example, the electrical patterns in the cloud cover and the effects of the wind: I am convinced that 80% of my suffering results from *these* influences.) Where is the countryside with lots of shadow, eternally clear sky, a *steadily* forceful wind off the sea from morning till night, without reversals in the weather pattern? *There, there* is where I long to go! Even if it means leaving Europe! (B *6,* 95–96)

The same hope and the same desperation reappeared two years later in another letter he wrote to Köselitz from Sils: "Once again I am in possession of my Sils-Maria in the Engadine, the place where I would like to die some day. Meanwhile, it gives me the best motivation to live on. *As a whole* I am oddly oscillating, shattered, full of question-marks—: it is cold up here, and that is what holds me together and strengthens me.—I want to stay here for three months: but what then? Oh, the future! — — —" (B *6,* 388–89).

Nietzsche seemed to find something of the sea in these high mountains and deep lakes. Indeed, he seemed to find even the most remote places and climes to be somehow represented

Silsersee, Oberengadin. Taken from the tip of the Chastè Peninsula, looking southwest toward the Maloja Pass.

there. In his famous letter to Heinrich Köselitz, dated August 14, 1881, the letter that told of his inspiration concerning eternal recurrence, Nietzsche wrote:

> I take it as a kind of reward that this year has shown me two things that belong to me and are intensely intimate to me—namely, *your music* and *this landscape.* This isn't Switzerland, isn't Recoaro; it is something *altogether different,* at all events something far more south-ern—I would have to travel to the highlands of Mexico, near the Pacific, in order to find something similar (for example, Oaxaca), and even then it would have to be with tropical vegetation. Now, I shall try to retain this Sils-Maria in my life.[8]

The thought of leaving Europe, or perhaps traveling to lesser-known cities on the periphery of Europe, such as Barcelona (B *6,* 346), was common in his letters during the early 1880s. On August 18, 1881 he wrote to Elisabeth, trying to explain this obsession with solitude: "A human being caught in the midst of a web, the web of my thoughts, shooting up around me on all sides—that is a frightening thing. And if I cannot guarantee my solitude from now on, I shall leave Europe for many years, I swear it! I have no more time to lose, have already lost much too much time. Whenever I am not *miserly* with my good quarter-hours I have a wretched conscience" (B *6,* 115). Evidence of Nietzsche's fascination with meteorology was also common in these letters, a fascina-tion we have only now heard him confessing to Köselitz: he was convinced that the electrical fields produced by thunderstorms were ruining his health, and was on the search for a sky that was clear, open, and discharged of all insalubrious force fields.[9] At summer's end, on September 22, 1881, he told Köselitz: "These were dangerous times, *death* was peering over my shoulder, I suffered terribly

8. B *6,* 113. Nietzsche clearly learned about Oaxaca from a group of Swiss colonists who were on vacation in Sils. He reported on Oaxaca's splendidly stable climate to Elisabeth—who herself would soon be interested in colonies—in August 1883 (B *6,* 431).

9. See also the letter written in Latin to Franz Overbeck dated September 18, 1881 (B *6,* 128-29).

all summer long: where can I turn!" (B *6*, 131). The next winter he reported to his mother and sister that he was almost blind, knocking things off the table in his room, stumbling as he walked down the street. The broad, generous valley of the Oberengadin offered him the best walking paths and the most generous skies. At the end of June 1883 he wrote to Carl von Gersdorff:

> I'd like to have enough money to build myself a kind of idealized doghouse here: I mean a wooden house with two rooms; I'd locate it on a peninsula that juts out into Lake Sils, on which a Roman bastion once stood. For it is impossible for me to reside permanently in these farmhouses, as I've done up to now: the ceilings are too low and oppressive, and there is always some sort of noise going on. Otherwise the people of Sils-Maria are very pleasant to me, and I like them. I eat at the Hotel Edelweiss, an excellent restaurant; I eat there alone, of course, and at a price that is not altogether beyond my meager means. I brought a large case of books with me: once again I am of a mind to stay for three months. Here is where *my* Muses live: as far back as "The Wanderer and His Shadow" I wrote that this region is "related to me by blood, and by more than blood."— (B *6*, 386–87)

The reference to Sils as a blood relative appeared in one of the most striking passages of "The Wanderer and His Shadow." Here Nietzsche invoked nature's *Doppelgäng erei*, that is to say, its uncanny pull on us at different times in different places—a pull that is somehow both human and alien, hence *double* in its effects.

The peninsula that he mentioned in his letter to von Gersdorff, the peninsula that exerted an uncanny pull on Nietzsche, was Chastè, a long finger of land beckoning out into Lake Sils *(Silsersee)*. Chastè offered the most spectacular views of the lake and the surrounding mountains; it was also host to dozens of varieties of wildflower and grass. Chastè and the Fex Valley *(Fextal, Val Fex)* to the south, proved to be Nietzsche's favorite haunts in the Engadine, the places where he filled his pocket notebooks with indecipherable scratch.

Solitude was what Nietzsche prized above all about the Oberengadin. Solitude began with isolation from the tourists. He defined them in a note from the second part of *Human, All-Too-Human: "Tourists.*—They clamber up the mountain like animals, silent and sweaty; someone forgot to tell them that there were fine views along the way" (W *2*, 641). Yet it also involved isolation from his own family and friends, or, more accurately, isolation with intermittent and carefully

NATURE'S DOUBLES

In many of nature's regions we rediscover ourselves, with a pleasing sense of dread; it is the loveliest way to traffic in doubles.—How happy must that one be who experiences such a thing precisely here—in this perpetually sunny October air, in this jocular and happy play of the winds from dawn to dusk, in this purest brilliance of light and most moderate coolness of temperature, in the entire, charmingly earnest character of this plateau, with its hills, lakes, and forests, a plateau that has imperturbably nestled quite close to the terrors of the eternal snows—here, where Italy and Finland unite, here in the homeland of all the silvery hues of nature. How happy must that one be who can say: "There are surely many things in nature that are more grand and more beautiful, but *this* is intimate and familiar to me, related to me by blood, and by more than blood." (MAM II, 338; *2*, 699)

Silsersee, at the tip of Chastè, in
the late morning sun of July.

orchestrated human contacts. For Nietzsche tried to perch on that notoriously fine line—or to
dwell within that no man's land—between solitude and loneliness.

If we take the summer of 1884 as an example of Nietzsche's solitude in high mountains, we
note that his seclusion was always punctuated by significant human contacts, without which Nietzsche could scarcely have survived. The summer of 1884 set the seal on his friendships with his Swiss
acquaintances, Meta von Salis and Resa von Schirnhofer, his two English friends, Emily Fynn and
Helen Zimmern, and the young Baron Heinrich von Stein. Since Meta von Salis was the last living
scion of an ancient Graubünden family located at Marschlins, not far from Maloja, Nietzsche felt
that she somehow "legitimated" his presence in the Engadine. Along with Helen Zimmern, Meta
von Salis best understood and appreciated his ideas. It was as though she authorized his residence
there—in the way King Friedrich Wilhelm had granted his father the pastorate in Röcken and himself the scholarship to Pforta—and blessed his thought. The Engadine itself was a privileged place,
perhaps the most glorious watershed between the north and south of Europe, where the melting
snows of the dramatic Err Mountains to the north and the craggy Bernina group to the south
replenished the most beautiful lakes and the most fertile pastures of the high Alps.

In Sils-Maria, perhaps during that same summer of 1884, Nietzsche came into contact with
one of the most famous mountaineers of his time, Christian Klucker. Klucker was associated with
the Hotel Alpenrose, where Nietzsche's friends stayed, and where by the mid-1880s Nietzsche

Hotel Alpenrose, Sils-Maria,
today in ruins.

Three views of Nietzsche's room in Sils-Maria.

regularly ate his noonday meal. Though Klucker could never have invited the half-blind philosopher to be his climbing companion across the Biancograt of Piz Bernina, or along the massive glacier-ridden sides of Piz Scerscen, or up the steep pyramid of Piz Roseg, he could certainly have fascinated Nietzsche with his stories. He might well have told Nietzsche how the snow atop Roseg or Piz Bernina, apparently pure white, is stained brown by granulated rock, and how the air on the peak of Corvatsch tastes of cinder and ash, supporting no life. Klucker, born in the lush Val Fex, would have known a thousand tales about the hazards and the near-escapes of solitary wanderers in high mountains.

Nietzsche was staying not in a hotel but in a room he had rented from Gian Durisch, who knew Klucker quite well. We do not know who first guided Nietzsche to Durisch. His simple country house was quite large. There were pigs and chickens around the back, but Durisch himself was a coffee, tea, and spice retailer in addition to being a farmer. Nietzsche's room on the second floor was well lit by the late afternoon sun, which was the sun he preferred. At some point Durisch papered one wall of the room with the green wallpaper that Nietzsche always craved. The philosopher also designed his own green silk tablecloth: two bands of light green silk ran the length of its dark, textured surface, and a gay folk-motif graced its edge. Green, forever green, as though moving the outdoors indoors. The unfinished pinewood floors and walls of the Durisch house were much to his liking; only the low ceiling oppressed him. No doubt he dreamed in Sils of the high ceilings of Genoa and Nice.

Front door of the Nietzsche-Haus, Sils-Maria.

Throughout that summer of 1884 Nietzsche read his own "literature," that is, all his books, from *The Birth of Tragedy* through *Thus Spoke Zarathustra,* Part Three. He was approaching his fortieth birthday, taking stock of his thirties, full of plans for his forties. Now that the vestibule to his philosophy was finished, or three-quarters finished, he was working on plans for the main structure. To Overbeck he wrote on July 23, "I am firmly positioned in the midst of my problems: my doctrine, that the world of good and evil is merely an apparent and perspectival world, is such a novelty that sometimes I lose the powers of hearing and sight" (B *6,* 514). Even though the fourth and final part of *Zarathustra* was not yet written, Nietzsche was working on his theoretical "problems," beyond good and evil, dreaming of a more comprehensive and systematic presentation of his views. He read a number of "bad books" on German metaphysics, and, several times over, a very good book by Adalbert Stifter, *Late Summer.* Yet it was his own "task" that absorbed his energies. During moments of respite he rowed a boat on the lakes with his friends, or hiked northeast along the southern shore of Silvaplana to Surlej and its magnificent waterfall, Ova da Surlej, or trekked southwest along the southern shore of Lake Sils to the village of Isola, or farther on to the town of Maloja, or due south into the Fex Valley. Isola, like the other Bergell dairy centers, was famous for its ancient stone-roofed houses and barns; of all the villages, Isola, on a low-lying delta formed by the Fedozbach, was (and still is) the most famous for its cheeses. No doubt Nietzsche often stopped there on his seven- or eight-hour hikes to Maloja. Lake Silvaplana, to the east of Lake Sils, was guarded by the massive

Tools of the art, at Isola, on the Silsersee.

Piz Corvatsch, which he could see clearly from the Chastè peninsula; Lake Sils was guarded by the towering Piz da la Margna. Even his dim eyes were drawn south and west again and again by the peaks of Piz Badile and the other Kletterbergen of the Bergell and the Maloja Pass, toward which the lakes themselves seemed to be stretching, as though remembering the late Ice Age in which they had been formed. To the north he could see the mountains of the Suvretta, Albula, and Julia Passes, which themselves seemed impassable.

The accord between this mountain landscape and the work Nietzsche did there can be viewed in two contradictory but equally valid ways. From one point of view, the mountains, valleys, lakes, forests, and halcyon skies of the Oberengadin provided both a multiplicity of angles and perspectives and a clarity of focus, which we find reflected in the work. From another, the Oberengadin, for all its sublimity, seems somehow "contained," or at least well defined, whereas the work—reaching out into the cosmos of a nature become chill and lifeless, a morality grown malignant, and a history gone voracious—seems to lack any bounds or limits. It is difficult to decide, or to know if such a thing can be decided, whether the work site helped to open up the work or, on the contrary, to protect the worker from his uncontainable work; difficult to know whether it further exposed the thinker to his dire thoughts or graciously enfolded him, shielding him from them. In either case, it is impossible to remove those thoughts from the site. Meta von Salis observes:

> For me, Nietzsche is as bound up with Sils as Heraclitus of Ephesus was with the sacred precincts of the goddess. In the northerly countries, it was his optimum. . . . In the silent, mountainous world of the Oberengadin, in the pristine environment of Sils-Maria, so replete with colors and shapes, where the fragrances of the nearby south seem to hover over the two peaks of the Piz Badile like a promise, the loneliest, proudest, and tenderest man of our century entered into his inherited kingdom, like a prince born in exile. (N 2, 480)

The most accessible goal for Nietzsche's peregrinations in the vicinity of Sils was the Chastè peninsula, where travelers today come upon the gigantic "Nietzsche Stone," inscribed with a verse from *Thus Spoke Zarathustra*. Nietzsche easily managed to reach the tip of Chastè after a half-hour's walk from the Durisch house. There he enjoyed the variety of splendid wildflowers whose very names are vivid and fragrant, and sometimes even palpable: *rhododendron hirsutum, pulsatilla alpina, sempervivum montanum, campanula barbala, viola calcarata, lilium martagon, ranunculus glacialis,* not to forget the humble daisies and forget-me-nots. Nietzsche had to be careful not to trip over the many tree roots that crisscross the pathways, or to stumble over the creeping juniper and blueberry hedges. His eyes were shaded from the glare of the sun off the lake by gigantic pines—the *Arve,* or stone-pine, is the rugged pine of these parts—and towering larches. The fallen needles of the larch, which loses its needles each autumn and sprouts new ones each spring, softened his footfall everywhere on the rocky peninsula. The fragrance that rose from the fallen larch needles, sweeter than the pungent odor of the stone-pines, along with the wafting perfumes of the flowers and grasses, produced an air that inspired Nietzsche. To be hyperoxygenated with such air was perhaps the secret of a certain kind of writing and thinking. And if the hyperoxygenation and the writing became too intense, there was an immediate possibility of escape: from July through August, Lake Sils, milky green near the shore and deep aquamarine farther out, is chilly but by no means frigid. Whether Nietzsche, the lover of both saltwater and Alpine freshwater, availed himself of this bracing opportunity we do not know.

The Latin names of the flowers were not the only linguistic delights of the Engadine. An old philologist like Nietzsche must have been fascinated by the three dialects of Rhaeto-Romance, or Romanish, spoken in the region—Ladin, Surmiran, and Sursilvan, the first being the primary

Larch and stone-pine *(Arve),* on Chastè, looking southeast across the Silsersee toward Piz Tremoggia.

dialect of the Oberengadin.[10] As we have heard, Nietzsche once described the landscape of the Engadine as Finland meeting Italy—and the dialects must have made the same impression on him. East of St. Moritz were two villages called Cho d' Punt and Chamues-ch; across the valley lay hills called Munt da la Bês-cha and Muottas Muragl. Except that when the local children said these names they made music.

Meta von Salis records the following recollection concerning Chastè in the Silsersee:

> When Nietzsche came to meet me on the morning of September 9, 1886, our first walk was devoted to the peninsula. . . . Soon we were standing on the first rise of the peninsula. Here Nietzsche had composed [the second] part of his *Zarathustra,* hiking up to it before there were any paths leading there, and lying in the sun-dried moss and brush. . . . He had hoped at the time that one day they would bury him on that spot. . . . He spoke of the surprising affinity in the characters of the Riviera di Levante [southeast of Genoa] and this peninsula. . . . Then Nietzsche cast a look back at the long convalescence he had experienced during his years at Sils-Maria. The hike around Lake Silvaplana [some twelve kilometers] was at first so strenuous for him that he used to recline in a fold in the "Zarathustra Stone" until he felt recovered enough to head back through the woods to Sils. (N 2, 481)

Helen Zimmern, a German Jew from Hamburg who had moved to England as a child, and who was to become one of Nietzsche's first English translators, relates that after their lunch at the Hotel Alpenrose she and Nietzsche would walk along the shore of Lake Silvaplana, that is, eastward, in the opposite direction from Chastè. He would take her to that large pyramidal boulder and its fold, which he identified as the birthplace of the thought of eternal recurrence. "He often told me about what he had been writing during the morning. I understood very little of all that; but I felt that it made it easier for him to be able to speak about it to another human being. The man seemed so lonely, so terribly lonely! If I made any kind of objection, and that didn't happen very often, he would reply, 'Yes, of course, but as Zarathustra says . . . ,' and then he would cite a passage from his major work, which had been largely completed by that time" (N 2, 320).

Resa von Schirnhofer recalls:

> He took me too, as he did other visitors before and after me, to that large boulder on the shore of Lake Silvaplana against which the waves were breaking, the Zarathustra stone, that wonderful place where nature is so earnest and so beautiful, where the dark green lake, the encroaching forest, the high mountains, and the solemn stillness wove their magic. After I sat down on the stone, which was a "sacred stone" to him, as he had asked me to do, Zarathustra began to speak from him, from the world of his high-strung spirit and emotions, and began to release a flood of thoughts and images clothed in dithyrambic words. He then told me of the astonishing alacrity with which each part of this work had come to be, emphasizing the phenomenal nature of this productivity, this inspiration, with which the writing could scarcely keep pace. . . . As we walked on along the lakeshore, leaving the zone of Zarathustran magic behind us, the mysterious vibrations also vanished from Nietzsche's person, a natural relaxation supervened, supported by the lovely freshness and purity of the air on this clear summer day, with the horizon undisturbed by even a speck of "electrical cloud," which was something Nietzsche greatly feared. (N 2, 320–21)

Resa von Schirnhofer also records a walk in the other direction, westward beyond Chastè, along the southern shore of Lake Sils toward Isola, then beyond Isola toward Maloja:

10. Students of language will want to refer to Richard Scarry, *Mieu prüm dicziunari* (Munich and Zürich: Delphin Verlag, 1973), available in the Cultural Center of Bergün, in the Albula Pass. And readers of Expressionist literature, along with hikers, will want to consult Paul Raabe, *Spaziergänge durch Nietzsches Sils-Maria* (Zürich: Arche, 1994), especially for Raabe's account of the procession of poets and writers who followed Nietzsche's footsteps through Sils and its environs.

I also remember a walk we took one morning along the shore of the Silsersee to the point where we could see the newly built hotel of Maloja [the "Kursaal"] in the distance. It was quite picturesque. Nietzsche said it had been built "for the Catholic aristocracy." Then we retraced our steps, ascending a small promontory, where we found a stretch of luxuriant green grass. Scattered throughout it were mossy boulders, and the whole area was bordered by thick bushes. It was Nietzsche's hidden resting place, where the poet and thinker could conduct his dialogues of self and soul undisturbed. (N *2,* 321)

Curt Paul Janz notes that these landscapes—of forest, lake, and mountain—served as Nietzsche's *narcotica.* They were all he needed to step beyond the everyday, the customary and habitual, into a land of unaccustomed thoughts and insights (N *2,* 322). It was as though the macrorhythm of the sun's passage across the blazing cerulean sky of Sils-Maria, along with the microrhythms of wave and wind, was all he needed to release the music in him. Those rhythms did not cure his illness. They did not relieve him of painful memories, such as those occasioned by Wagner's recent death. They did not assume any of the burdens associated with his task. Yet when everything else conspired to make the work impossible, Sils-Maria and the Oberengadin worked in scarcely describable ways to ease its realization. Janz also argues that Nietzsche's notes from 1884 onward show evidence of his *perspectivism*—in more than one sense. In addition to the epistemological perspectivism or radical relativism, Janz sees in Nietzsche's notes and plans for a philosophical magnum opus evidence of an influence of landscape: it was as though Nietzsche now surveyed his entire philosophy from one of the mountain slopes above Sils, with the entire landscape of his thought laid out *in perspective,* as it were, in the valley below (N *2,* 375).

In August 1884 the young Baron Heinrich von Stein paid his respects to the author of "Richard Wagner in Bayreuth." Concerning his days in Sils he commented:

> In the narrow parlor of a farmhouse in Sils I found a man whose appearance first aroused feelings of pity. . . . Yet would you believe that there were moments during those days when I admired that man with all my heart and soul? Of course, he dare not talk about himself. And because he does not, one is oneself driven to ponder all the things he has to put up with, and to conclude that a potent feeling of life has rescued him from it all. I experienced such a day of his suffering. That night he did not sleep. But then a bright, sunny day greeted us. During this day we walked together for about eight hours, talking constantly about the big things in life, about our collective memories, historical materials, and eternal matters. That evening he was as fresh as a daisy and utterly clear of eye, the way I had always imagined he would be. The mountain meadows of the Oberengadin and the snowcaps that illuminated them set these days in sharp profile for me, one that will not fade. . . . A fatality hangs upon him, and I could tell from even the apparently most remote matters we discussed that he will never be happy again in this life. Not because he has grown hard, but because he is in earnest. (N *2,* 331–32)

Baron von Stein admired the "energy of thought" that Nietzsche expended over the notion of eternal recurrence. That energy caused von Stein to greet Nietzsche as a brother, one of the few in the "chaos" of modern times. For the times were "too proud of their nonphilosophy" to devote energy to a thought that was simply that and no more—a thought (N *2,* 332). Yet von Stein did not underestimate the antiquity and longevity of the thought: "The tranquil sublimity of a beautiful day up there in Sils . . . enabled us to breathe the air of the most profound feeling of cosmic tragedy, the air of Aeschylus and Heraclitus" (N *2,* 333). Baron von Stein's death on June 20, 1887, only three years after their days together in Sils, left Nietzsche with one brother less and one regret more in a universe of tragedy.

One of the most detailed literary portraits of Nietzsche in Sils comes from Adolf Ruthardt, a

View of Isola and the Piz da la
Margna from Chastè, Silsersee.

composer who visited the Engadine in the summer of 1885. Many years later he recorded these impressions of Nietzsche:

> Nietzsche's external appearance made a supremely sympathetic impression on me. Above average in height, thin, nicely built and with good carriage, though not stiff, his occasional gestures were harmonious and calm; in lively contrast to his almost black hair and the thick Vercingetorix mustache, his light-colored, well-tailored suit made him seem quite different from the usual type of the German scholar; he reminded one rather of a nobleman from southern France or a high-ranking Italian or Spanish officer in civilian dress. From his aristocratic facial features, well tanned because of his many hours in the fresh air and sun, and from his large, dark eyes, one gained the impression of profound seriousness; yet there was nothing of the forbidding, angular, and demonic expression that sculptors and painters love to invent in their portraits and busts of him. (N *2, 394*)

A similar literary portrait was sketched by Julius Kaftan, the theologian who visited Nietzsche in August 1888, during his last summer in Sils. He used (or abused) that portrait in order to justify his thesis that the works of the atheist Nietzsche were unmitigatedly mad; yet we can ignore the thesis for the sake of some details of the sketch. Kaftan observed that Nietzsche was "quite different" from the author who so often spoke with a strident voice, that he always talked quietly and with *Gelassenheit* ("releasement," "sublime calm") about the matters that interested him most. There was never a trace of "mask," Kaftan adds, "but in all things one sensed the amiability that was his by nature" (N *2*, 620). Kaftan recounted an excursion in Nietzsche's company: "We hiked up the Fextal toward the glacier. Our talk turned to his illness, and to all that he had experienced in this regard, all that he owed it. Near a small bridge . . . he stopped on the narrow path and spoke in a quiet voice about the great metamorphosis that had occurred in him. . . . What he meant was his transition from 'no' to 'yes': that was the root of all his teachings and doctrines" (N *2*, 621). Kaftan also reported a noteworthy shift in their conversation after a walk to the neighboring village, Sils-Baselgia: "Then Nietzsche earnestly expounded upon a recipe for some dish. . . . I laughed and said, '. . . Here we are, two professors walking along, talking about recipes.' He then became truly angry, and gave me a good lecture about what blasphemy it was to neglect proper care of the body" (N *2*, 621–22). Recipes were among those "closest things" that Nietzsche had always preferred to the eschatological four last things: let Kaftan and his crew preach death, judgment, heaven, and hell; Nietzsche would teach life, suspend judgment, promote clear skies, and concoct dietetic delights.

As for those delights, by 1886 the staples of Nietzsche's diet in Sils-Maria were goat's-milk cheese and fresh cow's milk, along with whole-wheat bread or crackers. From the mid–1880s on, Nietzsche's mother sent him packages of hams, sausages, and crackers. When Meta von Salis lunched at the Alpenrose Hotel, she tried to sit next to him to make certain he ate well. He had no objection to the mothering. In fact, Nietzsche both needed and liked to eat well, but complained that his income was equal to neither his needs nor his likes (B *7*, 233).

None of the companions and interlocutors we have heard from thus far penetrated the growing isolation and hyperbolic reclusion of the thinker. It was not merely a question of isolation from tourists, family, and friends. Nietzsche experienced isolation as a burden of his *thought,* his heaviest burden in a life beset with burdens. In effect, he never was and never could be among equals. Among the notes he was sketching for the book that would bear the title *Beyond Good and Evil,* we find the following reflection on the cost of such being "beyond":

> *Inter pares* [among equals]: an expression that intoxicates me—it embraces so much happiness and misery for one who all his life was alone, one who encountered no one who was one of his own, even though he searched down many a path; a man who, when in society, always kept himself concealed behind a benign and cheerful disguise, always having to seek (and often finding) ways of appearing just like everyone else, knowing from long experience what it means to put on a happy face—what people call "affability"—in the midst of someone else's nasty games; of course, from time to time a person of this kind is also the victim of dangerous, heart-rending eruptions of suppressed misery, of whatever cravings one has not managed to suffocate, of all the streams of love that have been dammed up and grown turbulent—the sudden madness of those hours when the recluse wraps his arms around someone or other, greeting him as a friend, a costly gift, and as manna from heaven, then casting that very person from himself an hour later with feelings of revulsion—disgust with himself, as though he himself had been besmirched, debased, and estranged from himself, sick on account of his own society—. (W *12*, 71)

In the summer of 1885, Nietzsche declared to Franz Overbeck that his philosophy was *"no longer* communicable, at least not through the printed word" (B *7*, 62). Indeed, he experienced the strongest sort of resistance toward his own insights: "My life consists now in the *wish* that all matters stand *otherwise* than the way I conceive them, and that someone can *make me incredulous* about my 'truths'" (B 7, 63). When Overbeck sent him a birthday card on his forty-first birthday, Nietzsche replied:

> It was the only birthday greeting that anyone put to paper for me this year:—I thought about this fact of a forty-first birthday long and hard. It is also a kind of *result,* perhaps not in every respect a sad one, at least if one may grant oneself the right to say that the meaning of one's life has been staked on knowledge. To that pertains estrangement, isolation, and perhaps a congelation. You will have had many occasions to observe that the scale of "frosty feelings" is practically a specialty of mine by now: that comes of having lived so long "in the heights," "on mountaintops," or also, like the outlaw, as free as a bird "in the air." One becomes sensitized to the smallest sensation of warmth, increasingly so as time goes by—and oh, one is so *grateful* for friendship, my dear old friend! (B 7, 101)

A year later he noted that the woman who sat next to him at the hotel restaurant in Nice (another auxiliary mother, perhaps?) complained that she had caught a cold from the chill he exuded (B 7, 290).

During Nietzsche's final summer in Sils, in 1888, everyone was catching colds. The first six weeks of his stay were cold and rainy. There were serious floods, and by June 17 it was snowing! On June 14 he wrote to Heinrich Köselitz in Venice: "All about us lie the remains of twenty-six landslides, some of them quite severe ones. Entire forests broke away and slid down the hillsides. By this mechanism a man who lives in Bevers received a handsome little gift of about 5,000 francs' worth of wood. Well into May there was about six feet of snow here in Sils. Then it melted with an inconceivable alacrity and was gone" (B 8, 331). Nietzsche responded to the horrendous weather with intense focus on matters meteorological. He wrote to Meta von Salis on that blustery June 17:

> It is snowing to beat the band! I am sitting in my cave reflecting in a melancholy mood about whether the weather (or the weatherman) has lost its (or his) mind. When I got here it was humid and pleasant, with a heat of 24 degrees centigrade. It almost caused me to rue having left Turin, where it was thirty-one every day, but with its *aria limpida elastica,* and that famous Zephyr. . . . I'm writing this mainly to invite you to make the trip up here. I do not doubt that you will bring me better weather—and the rationality that the weather has misplaced.
>
> There are fourteen people staying in the "Alpenrose," almost all of them ladies and gentlemen from Hamburg. They *all* fled the tropical heat of the summer—and now they are sitting in the snow.
>
> I've just now fastened upon the following truth, a *truth that sounds most improbable,* with the help of certain meteorological tables.

"January in Italy"

	Sunny days	Rainy	Degree of cloud cover
Turin	10.3	2	4.9
Florence	9.1	9.7	5.7
Rome	8.2	10	5.8
Naples	7.7	10.8	5.2
Palermo	3.2	13.5	6.5

> This means that the farther south one goes in winter, the worse the weather gets (—fewer bright days, more rainy days, and an increasingly overcast sky). And we all instinctively believe the exact opposite!! (B 8, 335–36)

Nietzsche-Haus, Sils-Maria, as it may have appeared in June 1888. Photo: Stiftung Weimarer Klassik. GSA 101/604.

The weather—and the mood—took a turn for the better in August. Nietzsche wrote to his mother on August 13:

> For the past four days we have had incomparably wonderful weather, and we are all breath-ing a sigh of relief. Before that we were buried deep in winter, so that my landlady laid a double set of blankets on the bed and I put on all the winter clothes I had with me. But suddenly the most wondrous summer mood is upon us; the loveliest colors I have ever seen up here, and the sky as clear as in Nice. This morning I went rowing around the lake with Fräulein von Salis; yesterday an excellent musician [Carl von Holten] gave me a private recital, during which he played a number of pieces by Köselitz that he had rehearsed in order to play them especially for me. In my hotel [i.e., the Alpenrose, where he takes his noonday meal] there are now sixty guests. I've been very busy these days; once again we are caught up in the work of setting things in print [i.e., *The Wagner Case*]. . . . Sils has got-ten some new bells, with a very soft and full tone. (B *8,* 392)

At summer's end, the end of all his summer residences in the Engadine, Nietzsche wrote to Over-beck:

> I believe that in the end the astonishing malevolence of meteorological conditions may be blamed for every kind of exhaustion that I have suffered this year—I speak from experi-ence. One is never isolated from the whole life of nature: if the wine does not develop because of a lack of sun, then we too go *sour.* . . . It is odd that the final test of our patience was saved till last: conditions here all last week would have made you positively *shiver:* I lay in bed for an entire day as though sedated. The amount of rain that fell in only four days was 220 millimeters, whereas the normal quantum for an *entire month* in Sils is usually 80 millimeters. Nevertheless, Sils was the only place in the region that survived the catastro-

phe (unheard-of in the entire history of the Engadine!) without damage. My hotel, the "Alpenrose," where I spend a good bit of time, but eating alone, had the privilege this summer of housing Herr and Frau Baedeker of Leipzig [author of the famous series of touring books] for a couple of months: Sils too will now have to earn its stars!— (B *8,* 433)

However cheerful Nietzsche might have been from time to time, as he was here with Overbeck, his thoughts were constantly on his ill-health, in spite of the extraordinarily active and work-filled summer he was having. On July 4 he wrote once again to Overbeck in Basel:

> Eternal headache, eternal vomiting; a recrudescence of my old symptoms veiling a profound nervous exhaustion, as a result of which the whole machine just won't work. It's all I can do to defend myself against the most mournful thoughts. Or rather, I'm thinking quite clearly about my position as a whole, but in a way that doesn't do it any good. It isn't health that's gone missing, it's the prerequisites for becoming healthy—the life-force is no longer intact. The forfeiting of at least ten years can no longer be made good: I've been living off the principal, the "capital," and have garnered no interest. But that spells *poverty*. . . . You don't make up losses *in physiologicis;* every bad day *counts.* . . . At bottom, there is *nothing* wrong with my head, *nothing* wrong with my stomach: but under the pressure of nervous exhaustion (which is partly *hereditary*—from my father, who died only because of the *after*effects of a general lack of life-force—and partly earned, as it were), the consequences eventuate in all their sundry forms. . . . Forgive, dear friend, this miserable letter, which has turned into a medical chronicle! (B *8,* 347–48)

A large part of the story of Nietzsche's agonizing convalescence, however, is a story of the sea, which he could hardly hope to find up in the mountains. Like his "son," Zarathustra, Nietzsche knew that he too had to go down to its shores, to swim, even if he would also have loved to fly. In a petulant letter to his mother and sister dated March 14, 1885, he wrote:

> One is punished severely for one's ignorance: if only I had occupied myself *at the right time* with medical, climatological, and such kinds of problems, instead of with Suidas and Diogenes Laertius, I would not be a human being who has perished by half.— —
>
> Thus I *need* the sea. Etc. Pardon me, I'm boring you with these old stories.
>
> And so one loses one's youth and is now over forty years old, still caught up in the very first experiments concerning what one has needed all along, what one *should have had* for at least twenty years.— (B *7,* 22)

It is therefore to the cities of the sea, to the need for intimate converse with the sea, that we must now turn. For during the last active decade of his life, Nietzsche himself turned that way every autumn. On October 2, 1886, he told Emily Fynn that whenever he prepared to leave Sils in order to move to the warmer climes of the sea, his landlord would cry out in dismay, "Now the winter is going to start!" (B *7,* 259). Yet Durisch had to suffer so that the overman might live: "Behold, what abundance surrounds us! And from such abundance it is lovely to gaze upon the distant sea" (ASZ II; *4,* 109).

THE SOLITUDE
OF
HIGH MOUNTAINS

Riva del Garda

Stresa

Recoaro

Cannóbio

Airolo, St. Gotthard Pass

Pennine and Lèpontine Alps

Albula and Julia Passes

Sils-Maria, Upper Engadine

Riva del Garda, in the Trentino-Alto Adige region of the Italian Dolomites; the boardwalk at evening.

I observe that all the landscapes that consistently agree with me, no matter how variegated they are, possess a simple geometric line-scheme. Without such a mathematical substrate, no region will offer anything that is conducive to the artist. And it may well be that this rule permits of a similar application to human beings.

MAM II. 116: 2. 602

*P*hysiognomy of nature. The blueness of the atmosphere, the quality of light, the fragrances that remain remote, the form of the animals, the juiciness of the plant life, the glossy leaves, the outline of the mountains: these determine the total impression of a region.

Journal entry at Pforta, written at age eighteen: J 2. 259

Stresa, on the western shore of Lago Maggiore, a work site for *Daybreak* in the autumn of 1880.

165

To Heinrich Köselitz in Venice; from Recoaro, June 23, 1881; B 6, 96

As far as landscape is concerned, Recoaro is one of my most beautiful experiences. I literally chased after its beauty, and expended a great deal of energy and enthusiasm on it. The beauty of nature, like every other kind of beauty, is quite jealous; it demands that one serve it alone.

Recoaro Terme, in the South Tyrol. Views of the Fonti Centrali and of the dining-room of the Albergo Tre Garofani ("Three Carnations"), where Nietzsche and Köselitz stayed.

In a tiny mountain resort not far from Vicenza, called Recoaro, where I spent the spring of 1881 with my friend Peter Gast, likewise one who has been "born again," I discovered that the Phoenix called *music* was flying over our heads on lighter and more luminous pinions than it had ever before sprouted.

EH. "Why I Write Such Good Books." on ASZ. 1: 6, 335

The gorge of the Cannobino
River, west of Lago Maggiore,
is several hundred feet deep;
below, the Fonte Carlina, Val
Cannóbio, where the Villa
Badía was once located.

W*ater* suffices. I prefer loca-
tions where one everywhere has
the opportunity to drink from
flowing fountains (Nice, Turin,
Sils). A little glass of it pursues
me everywhere like a puppydog.
In vino veritas: it seems that
here too, with regard to the concept "truth," I am once again out
of kilter with the rest of the
world: — in my case, the spirit
hovers over the *water....*

EH. "Why I Am So Clever." 1: 6, 281

The wanderer in the mountains to himself. — There are sure signs that you have traveled farther and higher: it is now more open, richer in prospects about you, than before. The air blows cooler, but also more gently, over you—maybe because you have gotten over the foolishness of confusing gentleness with warmth. Your footfall is livelier and firmer, courage and perspicacity have intertwined. — For all these reasons your path will have to become more solitary; in any case it will become more treacherous than your earlier paths, though not by any means as hazardous as it is believed to be by those people who watch the wanderer— those people down in the misty valley who see you, wanderer, striding upon the mountain.

MAM II. 237: 2. 486

Views of Airolo, near the St. Gotthard Pass, and the Lepontine and Pennine Alps.

Views of the Albula Valley, looking north toward Bergün.

To his sister in St. Romay; from Bergün, Hotel Piz Aela, July 22, 1874: B 4, 245

The region is beautiful beyond measure, and much more impressive than Flims. All we miss is the chance to go swimming. Of course, a couple of hours' hike up the mountain we have a lake, but when we went swimming there recently it was so cold that I looked like a crab when I came out, and my skin swelled up a bit.

At the waterfall. — When we look at a waterfall, its countless twists and turns, the braidings and beadings of its waves of water, we believe that we can descry in it a freedom of will, a kind of autonomy. However, everything about it is necessary; every motion can be calculated mathematically. So it is with human actions: if

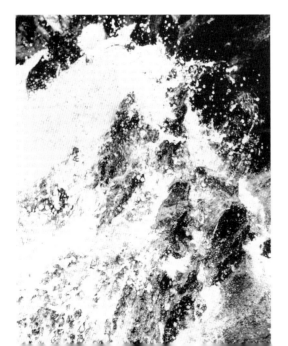

one were omniscient, one would be able to calculate every action ahead of time, including all progress of knowledge, every error, every piece of malice. To be sure, the one who acts is himself stuck in the illusion of autonomy. Yet if the cosmic wheel stood still for a moment, and if an omniscient, calculative intellect were on hand to take advantage of this moment, that intellect could tell the future of every creature into the most remote of times, marking every track on which the wheel would roll. The actor's self-deception, the supposition of free will, is itself attributable to this utterly calculable mechanism.

MAM I, 106; 2, 103

The tragedy begins. — When Zarathustra was thirty years old he left his home on Lake Urmi and went into the mountains. There he enjoyed the fruits of his spirit and his loneliness, and for ten years he did not weary of them. Yet in the end his heart turned—and one morning he rose at daybreak, stepped before the sun, and spoke to it thus: "You great star! What would become of your happiness if you did not have those you shine upon! For ten years now you have been coming up to my cave: without me, my eagle, and my serpent, you would have had enough of your light and this path; but every morning we waited for you, relieved you of your superfluity, and blessed you for it. Behold! My wisdom has become irksome to me; I am like a bee that has gathered too much honey; I need outstretched hands; I want to give it away, distributing it until the wise among human beings are happy with their folly and the poor with their abundance. Thus I must descend into the depths, as you do evenings, when you disappear behind the sea, bringing light to the very underworld, you superabundant star! — Like you, I must *go down*, as human beings call it: I must go down to those to whom I would descend. So, then, bless me, you tranquil eye, eye that can look without envy upon a boundless happiness! Bless the cup that wants to overflow so that its waters spill golden from it, bearing the reflection of its delight to all parts! Behold, this cup wants to become empty again, and Zarathustra wants to become a human being again." — Thus began Zarathustra's downgoing.

FW, 342; 3, 571

Oberengadin. The "Zarathustra Stone" on the southern shore of Lake Silvaplana, near Surlej; the Ova da Surlej waterfall above the lake.

Oberengadin. Lake Sils and the Chastè Peninsula still in morning shadow, with Grevasalvas and
Piz Lagrev in the background; *below,* standing on the threshold of Chastè in the afternoon sun, looking
southeast up the Val Fex toward Mount Chapütschin and Piz Tremoggia.

Et in Arcadia ego. — I looked down, over waves of hills, through white
and red pines hoary with age, to a milky green lake. Assorted fragments of
rock surrounded me, the ground was alive with flowers and grasses. A herd
of cows ambled, stretched, and lazed before me.... On my left, cliffs and
snowfields hovering over broad bands of forest; on my right, high over my
head, two vast icy peaks, swimming in a veil of sunny mist. Everything
grand, silent, and brilliant. The collective beauty of the place caused me to
tremble and mutely to adore the moment of its revelation: unwittingly, as
though nothing could be more natural, one transposed ancient Greek
heroes into this pure, sharply defined, luminous world (which had nothing
about it of yearning, anticipating, looking fore and aft); one had to experience it as Poussin or one of his pupils would have experienced it, that is,
as both heroic and idyllic.

MAM II. 295; 2. 686-87

Silsersee, Oberengadin. A barn in the village of Isola; the Isola
delta, created by the stream of Val Fedoz.

W*here one must travel.* — Direct self-observation does not by any means suffice for self-knowledge. We need history, inasmuch as the past wells up in us in hundreds of ways. Indeed, we ourselves are nothing other than what we sense at each instant of that onward flow. For even when we wish to go down to the stream of our apparently ownmost, most personal essence, Heraclitus's statement holds true: one does not step twice into the same river. — The maxim has by now grown stale; yet it is as nourishing and energizing as ever. So too is the maxim that in order to understand history one must search for the living remnants of historical epochs—and do so by *traveling,* as the venerable Herodotus traveled to sundry nations. . . . It is quite probable that the last three centuries, in all the hues and refracted colors of their civilization, live on, *quite close to us:* they only have to be *discovered. . . .* Most assuredly, in remote places, in rarely penetrated mountain valleys, self-contained communities manifesting a much older sensibility can be more readily preserved. That is where we have to go looking for them. . . . Whoever after long practice has become a hundred-eyed Argos in this art of traveling will finally rejoin *his Io*—I mean his *ego*—everywhere, and will rediscover the travel-adventure of this transformative and evolving ego in Egypt and Greece, Byzantium and Rome, France and Germany, in the periods of the migratory or the sedentary peoples, in the Renaissance and Reformation, in one's own homeland and abroad, and indeed in the sea, the forest, the vegetation, and the mountains.

MAM II, 223; 2, 477-78

Now, my dear and good friend! The August sun shines over our heads, the year is fugitive, it grows quieter and more peaceful on the mountains and in the woods. Thoughts have been looming on my horizon the like of which I have never seen—I don't want to say a word about them, I want to preserve an unruffled calm in myself. It seems I shall have to live *several* years longer. Oh, my friend, sometimes the realization runs through my head that I am actually living a supremely dangerous life; for I belong among those machines that can *explode!* The intensities of my feeling make me shudder and laugh aloud— already on several occasions I was unable to leave my room for the ridiculous reason that my eyes were inflamed—from what? On each occasion I had been weeping excessively during my hikes the day before; no, not sentimental tears, but tears of exultation; during which I sang and muttered nonsense, filled to the brim with my new vision, which I am the first of all human beings to have.

Opposite: The "Little Island," Isoletta, in Lake Sils, looking west toward Grevasalvas, Piz Lagrev and the Maloja Pass.

On the capacity to be little. — One must be as close to flowers, grasses, and butterflies as a child, who does not tower over them. By contrast, we adults have grown too big for these things; we must descend and condescend to them. I think that all the while we are declaring our love to the grasses they must be *hating* us. — Whoever wants to partake of *everything* that is good must at the given hour know how to be little.

MAM II, 51: 2, 575-76

Sempervivum montanum, Chastè Peninsula, Oberengadin.

FOUR

INTIMATE CONVERSE
WITH THE SEA

At bottom, I am not at all
made for solitude.
Nietzsche to Elisabeth

One can perish
by being "immortal."
Nietzsche to Malwida von Meysenbug

When a terrified Pip leapt from the whaling boat a second time, Stubb and the others pursued the White Whale and left him to bob in the horizonless Pacific. The sea was so vast, and Pip's solitude so intense, that even though his body remained buoyant his soul foundered in infinity. By some inexplicable chance, the *Pequod* happened upon the abandoned Pip and fished him out of the brine. Yet poor Pip never recovered his wits. Having sounded the sea, he could only play the ship's fool, until, along with all the others, in the end he too drowned.

For his part, Nietzsche never quit the sea willingly. The sea was not a place that one abandoned. In mid-March 1882, when Genoa had become too warm, Nietzsche knew that he had to return to the mountains; yet he hated to leave the seaside, even if his health there had been abysmal. He lamented to Overbeck, "Spring is behind us: we have the warmth and the brightness of summer. It is the season of my desperation. Where can I go? Where? Where? I am so unhappy to leave the sea. I fear the mountains and everything inland, but I have to go. What attacks I've been through once again! The vast quantities of gall that I am vomiting forth these days arouse my interest" (B *6,* 180). On March 23 he complained to Paul Rée, "Should I really be so crazy as to go back into the *mountains* again? Things go best for my health when I'm at the seaside. Yet where is there a place on the sea that has enough *shade* for me? *è una miseria!*" (B *6,* 187). As though in heedless flight, Nietzsche booked passage on a freighter bound for Messina, Sicily. Not even the boiling heat on the island of Empedocles could discourage him from thinking that at long last he had found the right place.[1]

Genoa had been an important "discovery" to Nietzsche. For him it was always the city of Columbus, Mazzini, and Paganini—the city of explorers, founders, and innovators. On March 24, 1881, he wrote to Erwin Rohde, "Even now there are moments when I pace the heights sur-

---

1. Of course, Richard Wagner's—and Cosima's—presence in Palermo may have been the magnet that both drew him to Sicily and repelled him from it. During the early years of his nomadic life, while Wagner was still alive, the Meister's whereabouts were never far from Nietzsche's mind. Usually it was a matter of avoidance; yet sometimes the temptation seemed to pull him into the greatest possible proximity. As Wagner was finishing *Parsifal* in Sicily, however, Nietzsche was composing *The Gay Science.*

Opposite: Nice. View from the Parc du Château.

rounding Genoa, filled with visions and sensations that the august Columbus himself may have enjoyed, gazing out over the sea and into the distant future" (B 6, 75). He communicated to Overbeck something of his enthusiasm for Genoa early on in several letters, including one from November 1880 and another from January 1881. In the first he wrote:

> All my creative labors and struggles now aim to realize my ideal roof-top solitude here, in such a way that all the necessary and extremely simple demands of my nature receive their due. Many, many pains have taught me how important this is. And perhaps I will succeed! . . . I've just recovered from a nasty bout of illness, and scarcely did I shake off the calamity of these past two days, when my folly once again went chasing after impossible things, from the moment I woke up. I don't think there is another roof-top dweller for whom the daybreak has illuminated more lovely and more desirable things. Help me to preserve my concealment here, don't tell anybody about my being in Genoa. For a good stretch of time I must live in the midst of an anonymous city, a city whose language I do not know—I repeat, I *have to* do this. Fear not for my sake! I live as though the centuries meant nothing, pursuing my thoughts without a nod to the date or the daily newspapers. (B 6, 49–50)

On January 8, 1881, Nietzsche once again enthused about Genoa to Overbeck: "I think so often about you, especially in the afternoon when almost every day I sit or lie on my lonely cliffs along the coast, resting like a lizard in the sun, while my thoughts set sail on some adventure of the spirit. My diet and my day should eventually do me good! Sea air and clear skies: now I see that these are indispensable to me! The new year is chillier than the old, and I have no stove—but who down here has a stove!" (B 6, 57). On the same day, and in the same vein, he wrote to his mother and sister in Naumburg, "Whenever the sun shines I climb onto a lonely boulder on the coast. I lie there quietly under my umbrella like a lizard. That has helped my headaches several times. The sea and the clear sky!" (B 6, 56–57).

No doubt he came to know his adoptive family in Genoa rather well—at least after he had finally located a room to his liking at the end of October 1881—as he would get to know the families of Gian Durisch in Sils throughout the 1880s and Davide Fino in Turin at the end of the decade. At Christmas time in 1881 he reported to his mother and sister that he had delivered a *pane dolce*, what the German bakers called a *Stollen*, to his landlady's son (presumably the landlady named "Carlotta"), who was confined to an insane asylum (B 6, 151, 153). During his winter sojourns in Genoa, Nietzsche occupied various rooms in the house at number 8, Salita delle Battistine. The steeply rising street of red brick and cobblestone was closed to all but pedestrian traffic. It bordered

Nietzsche's landlady, Carlotta, in Genoa, presumably at Salita delle Battistine, 8. Photo: Stiftung Weimarer Klassik. GSA 101/529.

November 6, 1881, to Heinrich Köselitz (B 6, 138): "This month is *very beautiful* here. In the evening I sit in a vineyard, with mountains, villas, and the sea below me; and, yes, I take a swim in the sea, in my grotto, at *Daybreak*."

Genoa. Salita delle Battistine, number 8, with the park of the Villetta di Negro off to the right.

the shady baroque gardens of the Villetta di Negro, where Nietzsche often spent his evenings. From the vantage point of the gardens, Nietzsche could survey the old city and the port of Genoa, watching the laden ships quit the harbor and sail west toward new seas.

Genoa was the home port for some of Nietzsche's own boldest explorations. Concerning his two "most personal" books, *Daybreak* and *The Gay Science,* both composed principally in Genoa, Nietzsche told the French historian Hippolyte Adolphe Taine:

> These two books are dear to me. The first, *Daybreak,* I wrote in Genoa during a period of the most severe and painful degeneration, given up for dead by the doctors, in the midst of incredible renunciation and isolation: but I did not want things any different at that time, and in spite of it all I was at peace with myself, sure of myself. The second, *The Gay Science,* I owe to the first rays of sunlight—my health being on the mend. It originated a

Zoagli, looking southeast toward Chiavari and Sestri Levante;
a view on Nietzsche's morning walk along the Via Aurelia.

The Castrum Venagi, in the Bay of Rapallo.

year later (1882), likewise in Genoa, during a couple of sublimely clear and sunny weeks
in January. The problems with which these two books grapple make one lonely. (B *8,* 107)

In the backward glance provided by his autobiography, *Ecce Homo,* in the section entitled "Why
I Write Such Good Books," Nietzsche remembered the gestation of *Daybreak.* He pictured the
book as lying in the sun, "round, happy, like a sea animal sunning itself between the rocks." Ultimately, he said, he himself was this sea animal: "Almost every sentence in the book was thought,
hatched, in that chaos of rock near Genoa, where I was alone and held intimate converse with the
sea" (W *6,* 329). Perhaps the most scintillating secret of that intimate conversation was expressed in
a passage from *Daybreak* entitled "In the great silence." Here the vast stillness of the sea invaded
Nietzsche's heart:

> *In the great silence.*—Here is the sea; here we can forget the city. True, the bells are still nois-
> ily tolling their *Ave Maria*—it is that lugubrious and foolish yet sweet sound at the cross-
> roads of day and night—but it lasts only a moment! Now all is silent! The sea lies there,
> pale and shimmering, and cannot speak. The sky puts on its evening mime, forever mute,
> with red, yellow, and green colors, and cannot speak. The low-lying cliffs and the rows of
> boulders that march into the sea as though in order to find the place that is loneliest, none
> of them can speak. The vast taciturnity that suddenly befalls us is beautiful and terrifying,
> our hearts swell with it.—Oh, the deception of this taciturn beauty! How well it could
> talk, and how wickedly too, if only it wanted to! The happy misery on its tongue-tied face
> is a deceit, it is there to mock the compassion you feel for it!—But let that be! I am not
> ashamed to be mocked by such powers. Indeed, I feel compassion for you, nature, because
> you must remain silent, even if it is only your malice that binds your tongue: yes, I feel
> compassion for you on account of your malice!—Ah, it grows even quieter, and once again
> my heart swells: it is terrified by a new truth, *for it too cannot speak,* it mocks me too when-
> ever my mouth cries something out into this beauty; my heart too enjoys the sweet mal-
> ice of its silence. Speech, and even thought, are despicable to me: Do I not hear behind

every word of mine the raucous laughter of error, hallucination, and the spirit of delusion? Must I not mock my compassion? Mock my mockery?—Oh, sea! Oh, eventide! You are treacherous mentors! You instruct human beings to *cease being human!* Should they give in to you? Should they become as you are now, pale, shimmering, mute, monstrous, resting contentedly upon themselves? Elevated sublimely beyond themselves? (M, 423; *3*, 259–60)

Like Genoa itself, the cities and towns of the Riviera to the south were vital to Nietzsche and his work. On July 20, 1886, in the retrospect that three years had granted him, Nietzsche recommended to his friend Köselitz a "tiny, cheap albergo" in Rapallo, the "Albergo della Posta, directly on the sea, the place where I wrote the first part of *Thus Spoke Zarathustra."* He hoped Köselitz would be his guest in that old haunt of his, in full view of the Castrum Venagi, the medieval fortress that dominated the harbor. As he reminisced—now also about his old haunts in and about Genoa—he waxed lyrical: "And we would clamber about the gloomy bastions of my Belvedere in Sampierdarena, where we would drink a glass of Monteferrato! Truly, there is nothing I could look forward to more; it is a part of my past, the Genovese part, for which I have *respect. . . .* It was terribly lonely and demanding" (B *7*, 213).

What would have tempted Nietzsche's eyes on the Genovese and Ligurian coast? The intense blue of the sea at midday, flashing gold like the serpent's belly in the afternoon, undulating beneath its thick skin of molten lead in the evening; the angles of the many rocky inlets from Portofino east to Santa Margherita, Rapallo, and Zoagli, and from Portofino west and north to San Fruttuoso, Ruta, and Camogli; the twisted ribs of mountains and the ubiquitous wash of the sea making it hard to orient oneself except by the sun. What would have tempted his highly developed sense of smell? The fig tree, fragrant in every season, the rosemary and boxwood, the jasmine and rose. What would have tempted his feet? The terraces, winding paths, and beautifully engineered steps of the Via Aurelia, articulating the hillsides of pine and olive throughout the region.

The sea, an essential part of Nietzsche's life, was not merely a place of rest and recuperation. He never worked harder than he did in Ruta, for example, perched atop the richly forested mountains at the southern end of the Gulf of Genoa. Residing there in the stately Albergo Italia during the winter of 1886–87, he prepared several of the prefaces for the second editions of his works: the prefaces to *Daybreak* and *The Gay Science* were both signed *"Ruta* near Genoa, in the autumn of 1886."* The first begged its readers to proceed slowly, in *tempo lento,* for the sake of an old philologist, that is, a lover of *logos* and "a teacher of slow reading" (W *3*, 17). The second announced itself in terms of *pleasure,* that is, "jubilation in the face of recurrent force, the newly awakened belief in a tomorrow and a day after tomorrow, the sudden feeling and premonition of a future, of adventures close by, of seas that once again lie open" (W *3*, 346). On October 2, 1886, he wrote to Emily Fynn back in St. Moritz:

> To my left, the Gulf of Genoa up to the lighthouse. Below my window, in the direction of the mountains, everything green, dark, refreshing to the eye. The Albergo Italia is clean and pleasantly furnished. The cuisine is *awful:* I haven't yet seen a decent piece of meat. All the more praiseworthy is the pure and always bracing air, the paths that take me high over two different coves of the sea, a pine forest with almost tropical luxuriance. Three times we lit a fire; there is nothing more beautiful than looking at flames leaping into the clear sky. Solitude as on an island of the Greek archipelago; numberless mountain chains surround us. (B *7*, 259)

A week later he offered Köselitz some more details about this wayward Greek archipelago. His letter said nothing about the execrable cuisine (the hotel cooks, however, no doubt remembered a

A balcony of the today abandoned Albergo Italia, in Ruta, looking toward San Rocco, on the Ligurian coast.

man who was always finicky about food, finicky to mythic proportions), but a great deal about the exotic beauty of his surroundings:

> About four hundred meters above sea level, on the
> road that takes you over the saddle of Portofino.

Ruta Ligure, October 10, 1886

My dear friend,

A word from this wonderful corner of the world, where I wish you could be, instead of in Munich. Imagine an island of the Greek archipelago uprooted, drifting off, and accidentally washing up on shore one day, never to find its way back home. No doubt about it, there is something *Greek* about this place, but also something for buccaneers, something precipitous, hidden, hazardous. Finally, at one lonely turn of the road one comes across a piece of *tropical* pine forest, which takes you right out of Europe—there is something Brazilian about it, as a table companion of mine says, one who has traveled the world over several times. Never have I loafed about so much, in true Crusoe-like insularity and forgottenness. Several times I lit a bonfire, whose pure, restless flames lifted their pale gray bellies to the cloudless sky. Surrounded by heather and by that blessed October light that knows how to produce a hundred yellows—oh, my dear friend, such late summer happiness would be something for you as much as it is for me, and perhaps even more! (B 7, 261)

Tower of the Albergo Italia in Ruta, overlooking the Gulf of Genoa at evening.

Perhaps it was the food at the Albergo Italia that drove him back to Nice, to which he had first moved in November 1883 and which had been in his plans years before (B *6, 133*). Yet Genoa and the Ligurian coast retained a special place among the cities and sites of the sea. One of the poems that Nietzsche appended to his second edition of *The Gay Science* was called "Toward New Seas" (W *3, 649*):

> I *will* go there, and will rely
> On myself and my steady grip.
> Open lies the sea; into the tide
> Plunges my Genovese ship.
>
> All shines new before the mast!
> Space and time sleep at midday.
> Only *your* eye—unutterably vast
> Gazes on me, O infinity!

The eventual move from Genoa to Nice, via Menton and Villefranche, did not so much interrupt Nietzsche's conversation with the sea as shift its location and alter its dialect. Nietzsche described the period of transition in a draft of a letter to Franz Overbeck dated Nice, early December 1883:

> Genoa was an excellent school for me; it taught me the hard and simple life—I now know that I *can* live like a worker and a monk. In the end I became *too well known* there—and so I could no longer live the way I wanted to.
> Nice is big enough; it can hide me.
>
> 1. I *sensed* that the moment my ideal showed itself to me I would be all alone. Now I *know* it. Up to the end I suffered from the most stubborn illusion.
> 2. Germany, and the hope that I might have an impact through the university, now pertain to a standpoint I have overcome—in general, that of living and achieving some sort of impact in the north. . . .
>
> The month in Genoa was critical: I suffered states that spoke to me of utter desperation—I didn't know what to do. *Now* I believe that many things are clear again, and I am *content* with the past two years—precisely on account of this clarity.
> Further, for me Genoa was from the outset the city of a single man, Columbus. Now I myself have *discovered* a new land—in all my good hours I have faith in this. It only remains for me now—**to conquer it**[.] (B *8, 600*)

Nietzsche recounted his decision to abandon Genoa for Nice in a letter to Köselitz, dated Nice, December 4, 1883:

> I left Genoa the day before yesterday, and, after considerable doubts, have determined to spend the winter here in *Nice!* What ultimately decided me was the fact that 220 days of the year have perfectly clear skies: the impact of such a splendid cornucopia of light on this tortured mortal (who so often desires to realize his mortality) borders on the miraculous. Over a six-month period here I shall have as many sunny days as I did in Genoa for a whole year. With that, I said farewell to the beloved city of Columbus—it was *never* anything else to me—and at the end it was so touchingly beautiful to me, with all its October colors.
>
> Nice, as a *French* city, is unbearable to me, almost a stain on this splendid southern landscape. Yet it is also an Italian city—here in the older part of the city, where I have rented rooms [at number 38, rue Cathérine Ségurane]—and whenever I have to talk I speak *Italian.* Then it seems that I am in a village on the outskirts of Genoa. (B *6,* 456–57)

Both Rapallo and Nice, that is, both the Italian and French Rivieras, were principal work sites for *Thus Spoke Zarathustra.* Although we often think of Zarathustra as a man of the mountains, we forget that he comes down to human beings in order to teach his ideas about the overman and eternal recurrence, and that when he comes down, he most often finds himself at the sea.

As Nietzsche was planning the third part of *Zarathustra,* still living in Genoa, he wrote on April 6, 1883, to Köselitz in Venice that his new book was a direct descendant of "Sanctus Januarius," the fourth and final book of *The Gay Science* in its first edition. He recalled the verse that opens that book, and the words, "You who with your flaming spear cut the ice of my soul, so that it **hurries** its flow to the sea of its supreme hope" (B *6,* 358). On December 3, 1882, still on the hither side of the first part of *Thus Spoke Zarathustra,* somewhere between ice and thaw, Nietzsche wrote from Rapallo to Köselitz in Leipzig:

> I froze as never before in my life. Finally I fled to an albergo directly on the sea, and my room has a fireplace. My realm now stretches from Portofino to Zoagli; I dwell midway between the two, namely, in Rapallo; but my walks take me daily to these boundaries of my kingdom. The main hill of the region, starting just outside my lodgings, is called "Mount Gleeful," *Monte Allegro:* a good omen—I hope. . . . The world is round and has to spin: let us make music, "good music," for it! Every now and then one becomes convinced that one should dance with it a while, but nobody else wants to dance with us organ grinders—no one is there *for that! Addio,* long live the god of Italy! (B *6,* 288–89)

In the retrospect offered by *Ecce Homo,* Nietzsche described the winter in Rapallo during which the first part of *Zarathustra* came to the light of day. He also emphasized that the work sometimes had to struggle against the work site and the climate in order to be born:

> The following winter [1882–83] I lived near that charming, quiet bay that intervenes between Chiavari and the foothills of Portofino, the Bay of Rapallo [Tigullio], not far from Genoa. My health was not the best; the winter was cold and excessively rainy; a small albergo, fronting directly on the sea, a happenstance that made sleep impossible during the nights when the sea was high, in all respects offered the very opposite of everything my heart desired. Nevertheless, and well-nigh as evidence for my statement that everything decisive originates "despite all," it was during this winter and under these unfavorable circumstances that my *Zarathustra* came to be. In the morning I would ascend in a southerly direction along the splendid road that leads high up to Zoagli, a road that passes through pines and offers a view far out over the sea. In the afternoon, whenever my health permitted, I would walk around the entire Bay of Santa Margherita and over the hills all the way to the tip of Portofino. . . . On these two paths, the entire first part of *Zarathustra,* and

(12) RAPALLO.

Rapallo - Il lungomare V. Veneto (1900)

A view of Rapallo; postcard from about 1900. Nietzsche's hotel is the square building on a line with the two church steeples above; farther to the right is the Castrum Venagi.

above all the figure of Zarathustra himself as a type, came to me. Or, rather, he *overcame me.* . . . (W *6,* 335–37)

Nietzsche would have been the first to notice that his two Rapallo paths, the forenoon and the afternoon paths, were in fact one. The view over Portofino recurs eternally as one walks the Via Aurelia about the Bay of Tigullio; one cannot turn one's back on Portofino forever, not even when one crosses the crest of the hill that separates Zoagli from Rapallo; it is as though Portofino were the narrow gateway to eternity, the eternity that may be found in the blink of an eye. Nietzsche would have been pleased by the thought that just as Zarathustra haunted that stretch of road beneath Monte Allegro between San Pantaleo and San Ambrogio, so he, Nietzsche, would haunt that space of seascape and pine for countless others in the future—others such as Ezra Pound, who lived there, and William Butler Yeats, who followed Nietzsche's footsteps there under all the phases of the moon.[2]

After Part Two of *Thus Spoke Zarathustra* was composed (some episodes had come to life on the Piazza Barberini in Rome, but most were written on Chastè, near Sils), Nietzsche wrote Part Three while residing in a Swiss pension in Nice, the Pension de Genève, on the petite rue St. Étienne. Once again he was near the Mediterranean shore. Some episodes of Part Three—he mentions "Of Old and New Tablets" specifically—he composed while climbing the steep path at Èzé (or Eza), east of Nice. He took the train from Nice for about twenty minutes along the coastline, beyond St. Jean/Cap Ferrat and Villefranche, alighted at Èzé-Gare, then clambered upward to the Moorish bastion on top of the mountain. The sky burned a deeper blue than even the sea below could muster. Solitary pines jutted from granite rock. Yellow and pink wildflowers blossomed early in the spring, flouting the wind and chill. Nietzsche had to grope his way along the rocky, meandering path: the sun was blinding, the silvery stone slippery; the lush vegetation bordering the path covered gaping holes in the rock, and this was not a convenient place to fall. His only companions, but constant ones, were his shadow against the rock and the sounding sea far below.

2. See Laurence Lampert, "Yeats's Nietzschean Dialogue," in *Yeats: An Annual of Critical and Textual Studies* 11 (1993), 129-58.

View of Portofino, taken from a point between San Ambrogio and San Pantaleo. Nietzsche passed this spot on his trek along the Via Aurelia from Portofino through Santa Margherita and Rapallo to Zoagli. (Photo by Erika Schopp, used by permission.)

Èzé, between Nice and Monte Carlo, on the "Chemin Nietzsche."

Coastline at Nice,
late afternoon.

On January 4, 1884, he described the entire *Zarathustra* project—which he regarded now as complete—as a maritime adventure. He wrote Franz Overbeck: "Forgive, old friend, this scrap of paper—but I wanted to write you some *good* news. Since last Friday my *Thus Spoke Zarathustra* is completely *finished*—and I am now in the midst of recopying. The whole thus came to be in the course of *one year,* strictly speaking in three two-week periods. The last two weeks were the happiest of my life: **never** have I voyaged across such seas under such sails; and the incredible boldness of this *entire* seafarer's story, which has been going on for as long as you have known me, since 1870, has now reached its zenith" (B *6,* 466–67). Nietzsche was able to experience the sea in all its moods, whether it was sleeping peacefully or shooting brine through clefts in the rocks at the Cap de Nice, along the St. Jean Peninsula, or farther east toward Èzé. He could hear Poseidon crashing onto the pebble shores of Old Nice herself, the waves receding to the regular rhythm of horses' hooves—the rounded gray stones rolling down to the sea in the undertow. He strode westward along the Promenade des Anglais, seeking out the times when no one else was likely to be there, then turned back as the late afternoon sun illuminated the seastrand, the windows on the facades of the old city, and the bastion atop the Parc du Château, today known as the "Terrasse Frédéric Nietzsche."

As we have seen, by the mid–1880s Nietzsche had developed a regular routine: Sils-Maria in the summer, the Italian or French Riviera in the winter, with the transitional months of the spring and fall still a problem. To Malwida von Meysenbug, on December 13, 1886, he wrote from his Pension de Genève on the petite rue St. Étienne in Nice: "Nice and the Engadine: this old horse will never be able to escape from that circle dance" (B *7,* 290). Nice became Nietzsche's winter "residence" for the years from 1883–84 to 1887–88; only in the final weeks of his active working life did the "old horse" decide to abandon it for Turin. He composed a birthday letter in Nice to his mother in Naumburg on January 29, 1885, telling her about his hopes to settle permanently in Nice, hopes that were now bound up with plans for a philosophical magnum opus:

> I have already found a place in which I would later like to live: the St. Jean Peninsula, not far from Nice. But there is a lot to be done, and done well, before I will be able to settle in over there. In the same way, my summer existence in the Engadine has to be set up on an entirely new basis. I now understand that in every respect the past is past, that I now have to create the *definitive* conditions for my work over at least the next ten years; I shall not act in haste, for now it is a question of getting a grip on my life's work, and doing so with the most perfect equanimity. An environment that *suits* me, I mean, suits *my work!* October to May in St. Jean; July and August in the Engadine; with the transitional months perhaps in Zürich: at the moment, that's how the program looks.— —
>
> In St. Jean about a week ago we found the most beautiful hedges of geranium, full of red blossoms; I thought of you and of your sad and snowy world. —
>
> In the evenings I always drink a strong grog—today I shall drink to your health! (B 7, 8–9)

During the first days of his sojourns in Nice, Nietzsche always stayed in the Pension de Genève—today but a memory, the building having been damaged by earthquake and obliterated by an expanding railway station and a modern superhighway. He described the pension to his mother and sister in a letter dated November 11, 1885:

> Do not be amazed, my dears, if today this Hamlet's mole is making noises from Nice and *not* from Vallombrosa ("Valley of Shadows"). It was *very worthwhile* for me to experiment almost simultaneously with the atmospheres of Leipzig, Munich, Florence, Genoa, and Nice. You wouldn't believe *how handily* Nice took the prize in this competition. My lodgings are as usual in the Pension de Genève, petite rue St. Etienne; since I was last here it has been altogether renovated, repainted, and supplied with completely new upholstery, all of it in very good taste. My neighbor at table is a bishop, a monsignor, who speaks German. (B 7, 108)

In a letter to Franz Overbeck written on the next day, Nietzsche recounted a "zigzag" voyage across Europe—he was seeking the place and the people that would improve his health. He concluded, "It seems that Nice and Sils-Maria cannot be outbid and *are not to be replaced*" (B 7, 109). In a similar vein, reaffirming all the virtues of Nice, he wrote to Heinrich Köselitz in Vienna on November 24, 1885, the day after he had moved into more permanent lodgings:

> A few days ago I was delighted to learn that this city, which I can no longer exchange for any other, has something of *victory* in its name. ["Nice" being derived from the Greek goddess of victory, Νίκη.] And when you hear what the square onto which my window opens is called, namely, "The Square of the Phoceans" (there are beautiful trees there, and, in the distance, large red buildings, with the sea beyond called "The Bay of Angels"), you will perhaps laugh as I do at the truly vast cosmopolitan implications suggested by these words. And it is true that the Phoceans once settled here. Yet something victorious, something ultra-European resounds in these names, something very consoling, which says to me, *"Here you are in your proper place."*
>
> Meanwhile I've tested Munich, Florence, Genoa—but nothing suits my old head like this Nice, minus a couple of months in Sils-Maria. At all events, I am told that the summer here is more refreshing than at any place in the interior of Germany (the evenings with sea breeze, the nights cool). The air is incomparable, the strength it gives one (and also the light that fills the sky) not to be found anywhere else in Europe. Finally, I should mention that one can live here cheaply, *very cheaply,* and that the place is large enough in scope to permit every degree of concealment to a hermit. The altogether select things of nature,

Nice. 38, rue Cathérine Ségurane, viewed from the eastern side of the Parc du Château, near the old port. Nietzsche resided here during the winter of 1883–84.

Nikaia, the ancient Greek ruins atop the Parc du Château, Nice.

Two views of the Gallo-Roman ruins at Cimiez, in the northern part of Nice.

such as the forest paths on the closest hill, or on the St. Jean Peninsula, I have all to myself. Similarly, the entire Promenade (about a forty-five minute walk) is splendidly free, inasmuch as people visit it for only a few hours during the day. . . . One is so "un-German" here: I can't emphasize that strongly enough. (B 7, 114–15)

No doubt the erstwhile classical philologist wandered through the ruins of the ancient Nikaia (founded in the sixth century B.C.) on the summit of the Parc du Château; no doubt he took time to explore the extensive Gallo-Roman ruins of Cimiez to the north. If his earlier lodgings on the rue Cathérine Ségurane had placed the Parc and its Nikaia at his disposal for morning and evening walks, his new room, at "rue St. François de Paule 26, 2e étage, à gauche," gave him—as we have heard in

Nice. The fountain on the
Place des Phocéens.

his letter to Köselitz—the Place des Phocéens, the Promenade, and the Baie des Anges. His new room, located at the rear of a building that fronted on the sea, looked out onto the splendid Place and its fountain of Bacchants. The late afternoon sun, filtering through the lofty umbrella pines and eucalyptus of the Place, warmed his room, which he further described in a letter to Franziska Nietzsche in Naumburg on December 10, 1885:

> I myself have settled in for the next four months, and have signed a contract to that effect. The room I am now occupying is the first room *in all my life* in which I can live without revulsion and self-overcoming—it corresponds to the principal demands of my health and taste. It is twenty feet long, fourteen feet wide, and fourteen feet high; the window is eight feet high and three feet wide; the wallpaper is dark yellow, the rug a dark color, my bed three times the size of my bed in Naumburg. Nothing in the room is reminiscent of elegance, luxury, bric-a-brac, or other womanly appurtenances; everything in here is necessary, such as a very large working table and a "Voltaire" (a comfortable scholar's chair, of a kind I have never seen in Germany). My view encompasses splendid trees (eucalyptus trees of the largest kind), the blue sea, and the mountains—but above all the *glowing* sky. The sun enters my room in the afternoon, which is the only time it is allowed to enter, on account of my eyes.— (B 7, 125)

In letters from Nice during the spring of 1885 we get a more detailed sense of Nietzsche's eye trouble. He was complaining of excessive tear flow, of a "veiling" of his vision (as if with cataracts, though there is no medical confirmation of this), and of "blind spots," as if there had been damage to the retinas.[3] When a Christmas package arrived from his mother and sister, he opened it out on the street; he never saw the money they had carefully wrapped in it—he hoped now that some poor old woman would recover it and celebrate Christmas properly (B 7, 128). At the beginning of the year 1886 he expressed to Overbeck the irony of his beleaguered eyes: "That a thinker such as I, who can never deposit his best in books but only in select souls, is compelled 'to make literature' with these half-blind, painful eyes—that is so completely crazy! so hard!" (B 7, 136). Yet it was not only the physical trouble with his eyes and the migraine they induced that caused Nietzsche so much suffering: he was also haunted by the fear of blindness—further shades of the father—during the entire decade of his nomadic life, the fear that at some point the mountains would vanish in the night and the seas founder in gloom.

Even so, he wrote. And even so, he read. In addition to all the scientific books, works on metaphysics, on the theory of knowledge, and on the history of religion and morality, he read poetry and fiction. Dostoevsky's *Notes from Underground,* which, because he was in Nice, he read in French translation, captivated him. He insisted that, after Stendhal, Dostoevsky was the only psychologist who shared his own gifts and insights.[4]

Nice is particularly glorious in the winter months, with halcyon skies from December through February. Yet it can also be bitter cold. So it was during the winter of 1886–87 while Nietzsche was working on plans and sketches for his philosophical magnum opus. On Christmas day he reported to Overbeck from the Pension de Genève that Nice's skies were as brilliant as ever:

> But for all that it is cold—in my particular case *very* cold. A room with northern exposure and no stove: habitually blue fingers. How I have frozen during the seven winters of my existence in the south! At bottom, my means are not sufficient for me to live here: the prices for pension rooms with a southern exposure are much too high for me, as are the private apartments that are well situated. If I calculate into the equation my Engadine summers, with their average temperature of 10, 11, and 7 degrees Celsius (in September it was 7 degrees), the result is a frosty existence that one constructs for oneself in this life. (B 7, 294–95)

On January 3, 1887, he managed to rent a room with a southern exposure on the first floor of number 29, rue des Ponchettes, with the sea before him and the open marketplace behind him. In his new quarters he escaped unscathed a severe earthquake that inflicted heavy damage on central Nice during the early morning hours of February 23, 1887. The fourth floor of the Pension de Genève, normally Nietzsche's first port of call when he arrived in Nice, was destroyed.[5] Nietzsche's bemused reaction to the earthquake indicated how deeply he was absorbed in his work. To Reinhart von Seydlitz in Munich he wrote on February 24:

> Nice has just had its long international Carnival (with Spanish ladies at the forefront, incidentally), and hard on its heels, six hours after its final Girandola, still rarer and more novel existential excitements. For we are now living in the interesting expectation of *perishing*—thanks to a well-meaning earthquake that has everyone here baying at the moon, and not just the hounds. What a pleasure it is when these ancient houses rattle over our heads like

3. There is *some* medical confirmation of this: see B 7, 33, 42-43.

4. On Nietzsche's psychology in general, see Graham Parkes, *Composing the Soul: Reaches of Nietzsche's Psychology* (Chicago: University of Chicago Press, 1994), esp. chap. 7.

5. It was presumably to the Pension de Genève that Nietzsche was referring when he wrote Emily Fynn in St. Moritz (B 8, 38) that the "advantage" or "positive side" of the Nice earthquake was that posterity—to which the authors and readers of the present text appear to belong—would have one less "pilgrimage site" to visit!

Nice. Parc
du Château.

coffee grinders! when the inkwell suddenly becomes independent! when the streets fill
with horrified half-clothed figures and shattered nervous systems! That very night,
between 2 and 3 A.M., like the *gaillard* I am, I made my inspection tour throughout the various quarters of the city, in order to see where the consternation was greatest—for the
population was camping out-of-doors day and night: there was something refreshingly
military about it. And then the hotels! where a great deal had simply collapsed, and full-
scale panic prevailed as a consequence. I located all my acquaintances, male and female,
found them huddled miserably under green trees; they were wearing their flannels, for it
was bitter cold, and with even the slightest tremor they were brooding on The End. I

don't doubt that this will bring the season to a precipitate close! Everyone is thinking of *departure* (provided one can get away, and that the railroad lines were not the very first things to be all "torn up.") Yesterday evening the guests at the hotel where I eat could not be coaxed to take their *table d'hôte* inside the building—they ate and drank outside; and apart from an elderly and very pious woman who was convinced that Our Dear Lord **dare** not do her any harm, mine was the only *cheerful* countenance among the tragic masks and "heaving bosoms." (B *8*, 31–32)

The unresolved dilemma that plagued Nietzsche's own life in the 1880s, whether on the sea-coast or in high mountains, was the need for solitude *and* human intercourse. Especially in Nice during the mid–1880s Nietzsche felt the pressure of his old pedagogical drive—he needed to teach, to communicate his ideas. Yet those who were disposed to learn from him often turned out to be "mediocre enthusiasts," and absolute isolation seemed preferable to a compromising companionship. Thus in Nietzsche's letters we find side by side the contradictory complaints of too much and too lit-

Nice. A neighboring house
on the rue des Ponchettes.

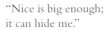

"Nice is big enough;
it can hide me."

tle solitude, insufficient companionship and excessive company. Several days before his sister's wedding, which he did not attend, Nietzsche wrote to her (on May 20, 1885) of his extreme loneliness:

> From childhood on, and up to the present, I have found *no one* who felt the same need in the heart and conscience. *This* compels me even today, as in all earlier periods, to present myself as well as I can to the types of human being that are permissible and comprehensible today; often enough I've had to do it in the worst possible frame of mind. Yet my principal article of faith is that one can actually *flourish* only among people who share the *identical ideas* and the identical will (such flourishing extends all the way down to the nourishment and general enhancement of the body). I have no one; that is my *malheur.* My university existence was the protracted effort to *adapt myself* to a false milieu; my becoming close to the Wagners was the same, albeit in the opposite direction. Almost all my relations with people originated from attacks of a sense of isolation: Overbeck as well as Rée, Malwida as well as Köselitz—I was *ridiculously* happy whenever I could share, or thought I could share, a common piece of turf with someone. My memory is replete with a thousand shameful recollections of such moments of weakness in which I *absolutely* couldn't bear the loneliness any longer. I include my being ill, for illness always disheartens me in the most onerous way. Not in vain have I been so ill, and, on the average, I am still quite ill—as I said, because I don't inhabit the proper milieu and always have to put on some sort of comedy instead of finding my recuperation in people.—I by no means regard myself as a reclusive or furtive or distrustful human being on that account. On the contrary! If I *were,* I wouldn't *suffer so much!* However, to communicate is not something you can have altogether in hand, even if you are one who loves to communicate; rather, you have to find someone with whom you *can* communicate. The feeling that there is something utterly remote and foreign about me, that my words take on different *tones* in the mouths of others, that there is a great deal of colorful foreground in me that *deceives*—precisely this feeling, corroborated recently on various fronts, is really the very sharpest degree of "understanding" I have found until now. Everything I have written prior to this is foreground; for me it all starts with the hiatuses. I am dealing with the most dangerous sorts of things. If, in between times, adopting a popular manner, I recommend Schopenhauer or Wagner to the Germans, or conjure up Zarathustras, these are my recuperations; above all else, they are hiding places where I can sequester myself for a time. (B 7, 52–53)

Even though Nietzsche was a man of solitude, and even though his isolation intensified with each Engadine summer and Riviera winter, he remained a gregarious human being, a born teacher who, without his pupils, was forlorn. The hermit remained human. Meta von Salis reports that he was an excellent listener, that "he never despised the simple things that lay on his path" (N *2,* 529–30). She cites, by way of example, the genuine concern Nietzsche showed over Gian Durisch's worry that his oxen might be coming down with hoof and mouth disease on the eve of harvest time. However subversive his task, Nietzsche needed a community in which some shared his passions even if most had no idea what he could be thinking. Von Salis observes: "He himself was tender, vulnerable, ready for reconciliation, shy about offending others," whereas "his task demanded hardness, forbade compromise, and brought himself and others pain and bitterness" (N *2,* 530). These gentle qualities remind her of Nietzsche's much-admired Emerson, though Emerson's task never cracked the ice—admittedly, the *thin* ice—of his optimism. Nietzsche's letters to friends and family, urging many of them *not* to read his books, were not disingenuous. When he fought with friends about ideas, he insisted that it simply did not matter whether he was in the right. From Marienbad, on August 20, 1880, he conceded to Heinrich Köselitz in Venice:

> You are made of sterner stuff than I am, and may be able to achieve higher ideals for yourself. For my part, I suffer miserably when I have to renounce sympathy. For example, nothing can compensate for the fact that during the past several years I have been deprived of

Nice. *La vielle ville.*

Wagner's sympathy. How often I dream of him, and the scene always involves our intimate togetherness back in the old days! An angry word never passed between us, not even in my dreams; yet there were many encouraging and cheerful words, and perhaps I have never laughed with anyone as much as I did with him. That's all gone now—and what good is it to be *right* when I *oppose* him in this or that respect! As if that could erase from my memory the sympathy I have lost!—And I've experienced similar situations before; presumably I shall do so again. They are the hardest sacrifices that my paths through life and thought have demanded of me. Even now my entire philosophy teeters after an hour's sympathetic conversation with a total stranger. It seems to me so foolish to insist on being right at the cost of love, so foolish that one is *unable to communicate* the most valuable things because they might well disperse the sympathy. *Hinc meae lacrimae.*— (B 6, 36–37)

"Hence my tears." Not much changed in this respect throughout the 1880s. Meta von Salis depicts the lighter hours of the summer of 1887, but also the melancholy hour of her departure from Sils-Maria:

Nice. *La vielle ville,* with a reminiscence of Gian Durisch's tea-and-spice shop in Sils.

> At times during the summer of 1887 Nietzsche was quite cheerful and ready for harmless jokes. He enjoyed accompanying my friend [Hedwig Kym] and me to the lakes: he had been initiated into the fine art of rowing, and he enjoyed the mild *frisson* of danger that our trips took on whenever the wind was up. One day when he was to meet me the sky was heavy with storm clouds. I was standing in the boat, waiting for him impatiently, and he cried out: "You are a real adventuress!" . . . My departure in September I will never forget. The day before my departure was a Sunday. We walked along the shore of Lake Silvaplana at the foot of Mount Corvatsch. The air had that silvery autumnal hue that Nietzsche liked to call *jenseitig* ["from beyond"]. The lake stirred only slightly, and the little waves, tinted by the red clouds of evening, gurgled onto the sandy shore and then glided back. "It's as though they all wanted to touch your hand to say good-bye," said our companion in his melodious voice. Then, as we made our way back home, walking across the barren strip of meadow that stretches between the lake and the part of Sils that fronts it, he observed with something of a sigh, "Well, here I am again, a widower and an orphan." (N *2,* 532–33)

What most delighted Nietzsche about Sils was its proximity to Italy; what most delighted him about Nice was its proximity to things Italian *and* French—its *Provençal* character. For *gai saber* had been important to him since the early 1880s. In *Beyond Good and Evil* he opined:

> In the essence of the French we find a halfway successful synthesis of north and south. This makes them able to understand and do many things that an Englishman will never comprehend. The temperament of the French periodically turns toward and then away from the south; from time to time the Provençal and Ligurian elements overflow in that temperament. This protects them from the wretched northerly gray-on-gray, from conjuring spectral conceptualities, and from the poverty of blood that characterizes the sunless north—it protects them from the *German* malady in matters of taste, an illness against whose excesses stiff doses of Blood and Iron are currently being prescribed (in accord with a very dangerous homeopathy, which has taught me how to wait and wait, but not yet how to hope—). Even now there exists in France a predisposition and susceptibility to those rarer and more rarely satisfied human beings who are too broad in scope to find satisfaction in any sort of traffic with fatherlands, human beings who know how to love the south in the north and the north in the south—these native midland folk, the "good Europeans." (JGB, 254; *5,* 199–200)

When Nietzsche eventually had to confront the possibility of having to surrender both Sils and Nice, he could hardly bear the thought; in both cases, his despair had to do with insufficient isolation—that old dilemma of the need for both companionship and solitude. From the Villa Badía in

Rome. Nietzsche's view of the Coliseum from the Via Polveriera.

Rome. Fountain on the Piazza Barberini, where Nietzsche composed the "Night Song" of *Thus Spoke Zarathustra*.

Cannóbio, near Lago Maggiore, where he was taking the waters and sketching notes for his planned major philosophical work, he wrote to Overbeck on April 14, 1887:

> I still do not know exactly how I will spend the summer. I hate to admit that I have to close the books on my old Sils-Maria, likewise on Nice: what I miss in both places is the primary and most essential condition for my work, to wit, solitude, profound equanimity, isolation, remoteness, without which I cannot *get down to* my problems. (For, between us, I am to a terrifying degree a human being of the *depths;* and without this subterranean work of mine, I can no longer bear life.) My most recent winter in Nice amounted to a martyrdom. Likewise my last sojourn in Sils: the tranquil concealment that is the very condition of my existence, the only way I can make my existence *healthy,* managed to slip away from me. My health gets continually worse from year to year, and it is a dependable standard for measuring whether I am going *my* way or somebody else's. The problems that oppress me, problems I can no longer evade (how I have had to pay retribution for all those evasions! for example, my study of philology!), problems in the face of which I literally have no peace day or night—these problems take terrible revenge on me for every mistake I make with regard to human beings, places, or books. (B *8,* 56)

Neither Rome nor Venice had solved the problem of always insufficient yet relentlessly oppressive isolation. Neither his memories of Malwida von Meysenbug in the past nor the undying devotion of Heinrich Köselitz in the present had supplied a truly nurturing companionship. Not even memories of the recent "Night Song," composed for Part Two of *Zarathustra,* could endear the city of Rome to him. He stayed at first on the Via Polveriera, with its spectacular view upon the Coliseum and the Roman Forum, several blocks from San Pietro in Vincoli and Michelangelo's *Moses.* He then moved farther north in the city to the Piazza Barberini, with its "leaping fountain" and the fountain's slippery, night-singing dolphins.[6] To no avail. On May 20, 1883, he wrote to Overbeck:

6. He listed his address as number 56, but the numbers of the Piazza Barberini stop at 54. One may presume that he resided on the top floor of the building at the bottom of the Square that faces onto the Via delle Quattro Fontane. His first Roman residence, Via Polveriera 4, no longer stands.

Bernini Colonnade, St. Peter's Square, Vatican.

With regard to convalescence and the secure restoration of body and mind, Rome was a good thought, and till now it has acquitted itself well. . . . To be sure, Rome has not enhanced my health in the literal sense. A *large* city is actually quite *opposed* to my needs. I am too little prepared for everything that Rome has to offer; or rather, I am too overloaded with preparations of another kind to have enough free will to devote to so many novel and strange things. The antique bust of Epicurus, and that of Brutus, gave me food for thought, as did three landscapes of Claude Lorrain. But at bottom I have found *nothing* in which I might recognize the words of a friend and brother—and yesterday I caught sight of people climbing the stairs of St. Peter's on their knees! . . . My address is Piazza Barberini 56, ultimo piano, Rome, and I shall remain here until sometime in June. (B *6*, 378–79)

Nietzsche resided many more months in Venice than in Rome. Yet even though he declared his love for the city of canals, especially its grand Piazza San Marco, Venice too failed to become an enduring work site for Nietzsche. To be sure, he had spent many work-filled weeks in the city, usually in the Cannaregio district where Köselitz lived during the 1880s. On September 19, 1887, quite late in the season, he left Sils for what would be his last visit to Venice. He traveled down the Maloja Pass, through the Bergell to Chiavenna, then down the western shore of Lake Como. He stopped in the village of Menaggio on the shores of the lake, visiting his friends Emily Fynn and Zina von Mansuroff. He then traveled on to Venice, taking lodgings at number 1263 Calle dei Preti, a gloomy, narrow passage one block west of San Marco. He wrote his mother from there on October 18, 1887. His missive betrayed the effects of protracted solitude, and it included the following barbed words: "The fact that ever since my childhood I never heard a profound and understanding word—such is my *lot,* and I do not remember ever having complained about it" (B *8,* 170). On October 22 he departed Venice for Nice, where, however, the sense of isolation only increased. His final, desperate effort to salvage his friendship with Erwin Rohde, in a letter written on November 11, 1887, ended with the words, "I now have forty-three years behind me, and I am every bit as alone now as I was when a child" (B *8,* 195). The next day he wrote Overbeck:

> It seems to me that a kind of epoch is coming to a close for me; a retrospective is now more than ever in order. Ten years of illness, more than ten years; and not the straightforward sort of illness for which there are medicines and physicians. Does anyone really know *what* made me ill? what held me fast in proximity to death, yearning for death? I do not believe so. When I exclude Richard Wagner, there is no one who ever came to me with a thousandth part of passion and pain in order to reach "an understanding" with me. I was alone in this respect even as a child, and am still so today, in my forty-fourth year of life. The terrifying decade I have now put behind me gave me a generous taste of what it means to be alone, of reclusion to an extreme degree: the isolation and defenselessness of

Venice. Calle dei Preti (number 1263 is on the right).

Venice. The window of Köselitz's apartment on the Calle Nuova, San Canciano.

an infirm man who has no means of protecting himself, or even "defending himself." . . . The best thing I can say about it is that it made me more independent; but perhaps also harder and more contemptuous toward my fellows than I would like to have been. Fortunately, I have enough of the *esprit gaillard* in me to laugh at myself concerning these reminiscences, as I laugh at everything that touches only *me;* further, I have a task that does not *allow* me to worry much about myself (a task or a destiny, call it what you will). This task made me ill, and it will make me healthy again; not only healthy but also friendlier toward my fellows, and whatever else pertains to that.— (B *8,* 196)

Once again, during the winter of 1887–88, Nice was bitter cold. Yet Nietzsche was now prepared. For the first time in his many sojourns in the wintry south he had a stove in his room at the Pension de Genève. He could scarcely conceal his glee to Heinrich Köselitz in a letter dated November 24, 1887: "This morning I am enjoying an *enormous* benefit: for the first time a 'fire idol' stands in my room—a tiny stove—and I confess that I have already performed a few heathenish hops around it. Up to now it's been frosty blue fingers, and even my philosophy failed to be on its best footing" (B *8,* 202). Once again he was enjoying the "cheerful worldly elegance" of Nice and the "exotic, somewhat African" vegetation of the hilly coastline nearby (B *8*, 176). He distributed his recently published "Hymn to Life" to every European conductor he knew, in the (vain) hope of having it performed, for the south and the sea were *musical* entities to him.

Nietzsche left Nice for Turin on April 2, 1888, hoping to find a solution to the climatological "problem" of the spring and summer months. Later in the year, on September 14, he expatiated to his sister on the geographical and meteorological reasons for his choice of Turin: "The chains of high mountains that enclose Turin on three sides preserve the very same kind of *dry* and *thin* air that Sils and Nice have, and for the very same reason. Now that I am caught up in the decisive labor of my life, the very first condition is a perfect *rule* by which the next few years can be regulated. *Winters,* Nice; *spring,* Turin; *summers,* Sils; *the two autumnal months,* Turin—that is the plan" (*8*, 428). Traveling by train from Nice to Genoa, then changing trains for Turin, he got desperately lost in Savona, where he had to change again. Because he could not see, and because of the general nervousness and state of upset that travel increasingly induced in him, he boarded a train that was returning to Genoa. After spending two days in Sampierdarena, a former haunt on the outskirts of the old city of Genoa, he finally made his way north to Turin, where he arrived on April 5. The initial impression was overwhelming:

> This is the city I can use *now!* That is crystal clear to me, and it was so from the very first moment. . . . What a worthy and serious city! Not at all a metropolis, not at all modern, as I had feared: rather, it is a city of seventeenth-century royalty, which has but one commanding taste in all things, that of the court and the nobles. Aristocratic *tranquillity* in everything has been preserved. There is no wretched *faubourg*. There is a unity of taste, down to the colors (the whole city is yellow or reddish brown). And for the feet as well as the eyes it is a classic spot! What safety, what sidewalks, not to mention the omnibus and the trams, which are miraculously arranged here! . . . What earnest and solemn piazzas! And the palaces are built without pretension, the streets clean and well made—everything far more dignified than I expected! The most beautiful cafés I've ever seen. These arcades are necessary here, given the changeable weather: yet they are spacious, not at all oppressive. Evenings on the bridge over the Po: splendid! Beyond good and evil!! (B *8*, 285–86)

Nietzsche secured lodgings at number 6, Piazza Via Carlo Alberto, on the third (the top) floor, in the apartment of Davide Fino. Fino's apartment was located above an exhibition and concert hall, the splendid iron-and-glass Galleria Subalpina, built in the mid-nineteenth century; from his room, Nietzsche could hear *The Barber of Seville* as often as he liked, and even when he would have preferred something else. From his window he looked out onto the northeast corner of the grand Palazzo Carignano and the generously spaced, uncluttered piazza below—where an equestrian Carlo Alberto rode his stately bronze horse into eternity.

Among Nietzsche's many preoccupations during the final winter in Nice and spring in Turin was the fear—which we have already seen expressed in a letter to Overbeck—that he was becoming too hard-of-heart, too harsh in his judgments. Even though Zarathustra had counseled, "Become hard!" Nietzsche feared the excess of hardness, the advance of brittleness, that he sensed in himself. On February 1 he confided to Köselitz:

> To lack health, money, reputation, love, protection—and for all that *not* to become a tragic growly bear: this is the paradox of my current situation, its *problem*. A state of *chronic vulnerability* has come over me, on which, in my good moments, I take my revenge in a way that is not really very flattering, namely, through an excess of *hardness*. Witness my last book *[On the Genealogy of Morals]*. Even so, I take all this with the cleverness of an astute psychologist, without the slightest moral prejudice: oh, how *instructive* it is to live in so extreme a state as mine! Only now do I understand *history;* I've never had such profound eyes as in the past few months. (B *8*, 239–40; cf. 363)

Turin, near the Via Carlo Alberto. "What safety, what sidewalks!"

Turin, Via Carlo Alberto, 6. Nietzsche's room, in the apartment of Davide Fino, was on the top floor behind the balcony on the left. His room looked out upon the Palazzo Carignano, which is out of view on the left. At lower left in the photo is the entrance to the Galleria Subalpina, the building's atrium.

Turin. Palazzo Carignano,
on the Piazza Carlo Alberto,
toward midnight.

In another letter to Overbeck from about the same time, he called himself a "troglodyte," a cave dweller so accustomed to the blackness of darkness that he no longer trusted the light he craved. He noted the terrible discrepancy between his "mode of thought," which was one of affirmation and great health, as even the theologian Julius Kaftan had recognized, and the "human *décrépitude*" that so exasperated him (B *8*, 267). To his sister in Paraguay he expressed impatience with his prior "literature," and confessed, "One does not write masterly works in a state of *décadence:* that would conflict with natural history!" (B *8*, 282).

However delighted he may have been with his discovery of aristocratic Turin, his mood in the spring of 1888 was dour, even dire, in contrast to the euphoria that Turin was to induce in the fall. To Carl Fuchs he exclaimed, "How everything slips away! How everything scatters! How silent life is becoming! No human being in sight who knows me. My sister in South America. Letters increasingly rare. And I'm not even old!!! *Merely* a philosopher! *Merely* apart! *Merely* compromisingly apart!" (B *8*, 294). Nietzsche's grim mood did not prevent his producing an enormous amount of work, however, especially on a wide range of notes for his planned magnum opus. On May 4, 1888, he informed Georg Brandes about the general scheme of that never-completed opus:

Turin. Galleria Subalpina, midnight.

These weeks in Turin . . . have gone better for me than any during the past few years—above all, better philosophically. Almost every day I have attained one or two hours of that energy-level I need in order to see my general conception from *top to bottom,* whereby the vast multiplicity of problems lies spread out beneath me as a relief with clearly defined lines. For that I require a maximum of force, which I had scarcely dared hope for. It all hangs together; everything has been coming along smoothly for the past several years now; one constructs one's philosophy as a beaver does his dam; one is a piece of necessity, but does not know it: one has to *see* it all in order to believe it, as I have seen it now. (B *8,* 310)

Nietzsche's final departure from Sils-Maria for Turin, on September 20, 1888, was a dramatic one. Rainstorms had caused severe flooding throughout the Fex Valley and indeed all the way down through the Maloja Pass to the Bergell, Chiavenna, and the Lake Como region. Nietzsche arrived in Milan at midnight. The next day, exhausted, he was in Turin.

Once again he was thrilled by the architecture of the city—both its seventeenth-century residences and the recently completed Antonelli Tower, monuments to the past and to the future. With his arrival in Turin an extraordinary change took place in him. The headaches and nausea were suddenly gone. Nietzsche exulted. He was euphoric. His appetite was more vigorous than it had ever been. He felt no pain, never slept better. He did not seem to heed the intermittent disturbances in his thought patterns, disturbances whose rhythm was becoming increasingly insistent. He spent his days working furiously: "On and on it goes, in a *tempo fortissimo* of hard work *and* good mood" (B *8,* 469). He took his recreation down by the Po: he would walk down the Via Po, cross the bridge that led to the church of Gran Madre di Dio, and turn either left or right, ambling along the banks of the Po, enjoying its island parks and the poplars that lined the river. He was cheerfully elaborating the final detail of his plans for travel, residence, and writing, having finally found the solution to his spring and autumn puzzle. The only change in the old plan was that, even though Nietzsche still announced his intention to head for Nice at the end of November, Turin would now be his winter residence as well, through a January that never ended. *"Turin* is not a place that one abandons," he confided to Meta von Salis on November 14 (B *8,* 472); months later, in the Basel and Jena clinics, he would often speak to the personnel as though he were still in Turin.

In spite of the euphoria, his letters betrayed some sense of the changes taking place within him. On October 30, 1888, he confessed to Heinrich Köselitz in Berlin that the face in the mirror surprised and delighted him: "Dear Friend, I just looked at myself in the mirror—I have never looked like this. In an exemplary mood, well nourished, and looking ten years younger than ought to be allowed" (B *8,* 460). Again to Köselitz, on November 25, 1888, Nietzsche described the alterations that were becoming less and less subtle in him, ending his letter with an appeal that Köselitz would neither comprehend nor obey:

> I pull so many silly stunts with myself and have such private Till Eulenspiegel brainstorms that occasionally all I can do is stand in the public thoroughfares for half-an-hour *grinning,* I don't know what else to call it. . . . For the past four days I have been unable to give my face a serious demeanor—
>
> I think that anyone who has achieved such a state must be ripe to become "Savior of the World"? . . .
>
> Come. . . . (B *8,* 489)

He mailed a copy of *The Wagner Case* to Malwida von Meysenbug, knowing that her loyalty to Wagner would force her to reject it as offensive. He then used her reply as an excuse to lambast her "idealism" as "dishonesty become instinctual" and "intellectual sordidness" (B *8,* 458). One month later he broke off relations with his publisher Ernst Fritsch in a letter with the valediction "In forthright contempt." The break with Fritsch left his works entirely in the hands of Fritsch's printer, C. G. Naumann of Leipzig, who would publish the first collected editions of Nietzsche's works—under Elisabeth's direction, not Nietzsche's own.

Turin. The Mole Antonelliana, which Nietz-sche came to identify with his *Ecce Homo.*

The Po River, Turin.

Gran Madre di Dio church, across the
Po from the town center of Turin.

On October 15, his forty-fourth birthday, Nietzsche began to compose his extraordinary autobiography. The account was both acute and inflated, trenchant and beyond the pale. On November 6, 1888, he reported the following to C. G. Naumann: "Between October 15 and November 4, I carried out an extremely difficult task: I recounted my self, my books, my views, all in fragmentary form, presenting only what was called for. I believe that *this* will be heard, perhaps heard too much. . . . And then all would be in order. . . . The new text is called:

Ecce Homo
How One Becomes What One Is" (B 8, 464).

On November 13, 1888, he wrote to Franz Overbeck: "The manuscript of *Ecce Homo: How One Becomes What One Is* is already at the printer's. This work, of absolute importance, provides some psychological and even biographical materials about me and my literature: they [the readers] will *behold* me all at one go. The tone of the text is cheerful and fateful, as with everything I write" (B 8, 470). Finally, to Meta von Salis he confessed, "For I myself am this *homo,* including the *ecce;* the attempt to spread a bit of light *and fright* about me seems to me to have succeeded almost too well" (B 8, 471). He sensed that his harvest season had commenced, as he told Overbeck three days after his birthday:

> Yesterday, with your letter in hand, I took my usual afternoon walk outside Turin. Everywhere the purest October light. A splendid tree-lined path that led me for about an hour right along the Po; the trees were scarcely touched yet by autumn. I am now the most grateful man in the world—*attuned to autumn* in every good sense of the words: it is now my magnificent *harvest time.* Everything has become easy for me, everything is turning out well for me, although it is hardly possible that anyone has ever had such tremendous things as objects of their labor. The fact that the *first* book of my *Transvaluation of All Values* [that is, *The Antichrist*] is finished, *ready to go into print,* is something that I announce to you with a feeling for which I have no words.[7] There will be *four* books in all, appearing as separate volumes. This time I am bringing out my big guns, as an old artillery soldier: I fear that I will shoot the history of humanity in two, separating it into two halves. . . . My plan is to hold out here until November 20 (it is a somewhat *frosty* plan, since winter is coming early!). Then I want to go to *Nice.* There, breaking with all my past usages, I will establish the kind of existence that I need. (B 8, 452–53)

Nietzsche never made it back to Nice. Yet the work on his autobiography proceeded apace. The spirit of harvest time dominated the opening exergue of the book, standing alone and without a title on a page that separated the table of contents from the first part, "Why I Am So Wise."

The flavor of the rest of the book, which recounted a life to the selfsame one who had lived it, was reflected by the titles of its sections: after "Why I Am So Wise" came "Why I Am So Clever," "Why I Write Such Good Books," and "Why I Am a Destiny." The manuscript itself passed through several stages of revision: Nietzsche mailed the manuscript to Naumann on November 6 but demanded it back and worked on it during the first week of December, mailing it once again on December 7. On December 29 he sent a packet of final corrections to the publisher. To Georg Brandes in Copenhagen he described the book *Ecce Homo,* the first version of which was finished by the time he wrote, on November 20, 1888. Once again the metaphors of the old artillery man prevailed, and it seemed as though Nietzsche was conflating his autobiography with *The Antichrist,* to which, he said, *Ecce Homo* served as a prelude:

7. In fact, Nietzsche did not prepare the final printer's manuscript for this book, but left it in the form of a rough draft. The book did not appear until 1895, and even then only after intense debates between Overbeck and Nietzsche's family. (Nietzsche's mother adjudged it a "terrible book.")

ECCE HOMO

On this perfect day, when everything is ripening, and not only the grapes are turning russet, a ray of sunlight fell across my life: I looked back, I looked ahead, and never did I see so many things, and such good things, at once. Not in vain did I bury today my forty-fourth year: I was *allowed* to bury it—whatever was of life in it has been rescued, is immortal. The first book of the *Transvaluation of All Values*, the *Dionysos Dithyrambs*, and, for recuperation, the *Twilight of the Idols*, are all gifts of this year, even of its last quarter. *How should I not be grateful to my entire life?*—And so I shall narrate my life to myself. (W *6*, 263)

> With a cynicism that will become world-historical, I have now recounted myself: the book is called *Ecce Homo*, and it is an *assassination of the Crucified*, carried out without the least compunction. It ends with thunder and lightning-bolts against everything that is Christian, or *infected* with Christianity, so much so that one will lose one's powers of hearing and sight. In the end I am the first psychologist of Christianity, and I can, as an old artillery soldier, draw out my heavy guns, which no opponent of Christianity has ever dreamed existed.—The whole is a prelude to my *Transvaluation of All Values,* the work that *lies finished before me:* I swear to you that after the next two years we shall have the entire Earth in convulsions. I am a fatality. . . . Turin *shall remain* my residence. (Signed) Your Nietzsche, now *Beast.* . . . (B *8,* 482–83)

One of the most famous sections of the book is the opening of Part One, "Why I Am So Wise," in which Nietzsche analyzes the "fortune" and the "riddle" of his existence in terms of his parentage:

> The fortune of my existence, perhaps its very singularity, lies in its fatality: I have—to put it in the form of a riddle—as my father already died; as my mother I am still alive and am growing old. This double provenance, from the highest and the lowest rungs on the ladder of life, as it were, simultaneously a *décadent* and a *commencement*—this, if anything, accounts for that neutrality, that freedom from all bias with respect to the entire problem of life, which perhaps distinguishes me. . . . I know both, I am both. (W *6,* 264)

Among the most contested sections is the third of Part One, in which Nietzsche goes into greater detail concerning his mother and father. In the packet of replacement pages that Nietzsche sent to Naumann during the final days of December, there were pages designated to replace section three of the first part of *Ecce Homo*. Naumann was reluctant to print them. For whereas the version from the autumn treated both the maternal and paternal sides of the family with the same gentle irony, the replacement pages excoriated Nietzsche's mother and sister in the most derisory terms. Only a stroke of fate saved these replacement pages from the mother's and sister's efforts to annihilate them.[8]

By mid-December Nietzsche completed plans for the publication of a kind of polemical anthology of his writings on Wagner, in order to shore up what he had hoped to accomplish in *The*

---

8. On the strange fate of these replacement pages, discussed above in chap. 1, see Mazzino Montinari's commentary (W *14,* 460-62); see also Tracy B. Strong, "Oedipus as Hero: Family and Family Metaphors in Nietzsche," in *Why Nietzsche Now?* ed. Daniel T. O'Hara (Bloomington: Indiana University Press, 1985), pp. 311-35, esp. pp. 322-28; see also chap. 11 of Krell, *Infectious Nietzsche.*

Galleria Subalpina, Turin. Davide Fino's apartment was adjacent to the Galleria's highest porticoes, near the iron-and-glass roof, on the right.

Wagner Case. The new book, *Nietzsche contra Wagner,* contained Nietzsche's aphorisms on Wagner and the Wagnerites from *Human, All-Too-Human, The Gay Science, Beyond Good and Evil,* and *On the Genealogy of Morals.* Finally, by the end of the month he was revising and arranging a number of his earlier poems for inclusion in a volume entitled *Dionysos Dithyrambs.* Nietzsche devoted his final labors during the first days of January 1889 to these poems.

Nietzsche was growing increasingly nervous about the possible confiscation of *Ecce Homo* and his other texts in Germany. Already his books had been banned in Russia. That perhaps provided the context for his remark to Köselitz on December 16, which had an ominous ring: "I now see no reason why I should accelerate too quickly the *tragic* catastrophe of my life, which begins with *Ecce*" (B *8,* 528). If autumn was harvest time, the approaching winter announced itself quite clearly as tragic downfall. Nietzsche wrote to Anna Dmitrievna Tenischev in St. Petersburg on December 8: "At this moment, a monstrous task drives me away from all human relationships, and my loneliness steals upon me with the footfall of every voice" (B *8,* 510). He warned Helen Zimmern, "My life is now coming to its long-prepared, monstrous *éclat*" (B *8,* 511). He tried to postpone the publication of *Nietzsche contra Wagner* in favor of *Ecce Homo,* but the printing process had already begun. When Overbeck arrived in Turin in order to bring Nietzsche back to the Basel sanitarium, he found his friend hunched over the proofs of *Nietzsche contra Wagner,* proofs Nietzsche examined assiduously for typos but no longer seemed to understand.

Even before the famous letters of his madness were written, January 3–6, Nietzsche's missives toward the end of his active life became increasingly incoherent. He signed his penultimate letter to Malwida von Meysenbug, which he said he hoped would offer proof "that Nietzsche is always *despicable,*" as "The 'Immoralist,'" one of the many adopted names to come (B *8,* 463). Yet as the coherence waned, Nietzsche sensed that something providential—a Dionysian providence—was guiding

"Not to mention the omnibus and the trams, which are miraculously arranged here!"

him unerringly. "There are no longer any accidents in my life," he repeatedly told Overbeck (B *8,* 547, 550). He drafted the following letter, more hilarious than cheerful, at least up to the chilling close, to Heinrich Köselitz in Berlin on December 30, 1888:

> The municipal orchestra of Turin is playing at full steam directly below my window, as though I were already the *princeps Taurinorum, Caesar Caesarum,* and suchlike. They are play-ing, among other things, a Hungarian rhapsody, and I recognize the grandiose Cleopatra piece by Mancinelli. Earlier I walked by the *mole Antonelliana,* perhaps the most ingenious building ever constructed—odd that it still doesn't have a name—the result of an absolute drive for elevation—reminds me of nothing so much as my *Zarathustra.* I have baptized the tower *Ecce Homo,* and in spirit have opened an enormous free space around it.—Then I walked to my palace, which is now the Palazzo Madama—we'll have to supply the *madama* ourselves—: it can *remain* precisely the way it is, by far it is the most picturesque type of grandly conceived palace—namely, a stairwell. Then I received a letter of homage from August Strindberg, my poet, a veritable genius, in honor of my "grandiosissime *Généalogie de la morale,*" with yet another expression *de sa profonde admiration.* Then I wrote—in hero-ic-Aristophanic audacity—a proclamation to the European courts, calling for an *annihilation* of the House of Hohenzollern: this race of flaming idiots and criminals has controlled the throne of France and also Alsace; meanwhile I appointed Victor Buonaparte, the brother of our Laetitia, Kaiser, and named my excellent Monsieur Bourdeau, Editor-in-Chief of the *Journal des débats* and the *Revue des deux mondes,* ambassador to my court—afterwards I ate my noonday meal at my cook's (not for nothing is he named *de la Pace*—), and now I am writing my friend and supremely perfect maestro a letter. . . . [P.S.:] I was also present at the funeral of the ancient Antonelli this past November.—He lived just long enough for the book *Ecce Homo* to be finished.—The book and the *human being* as well . . . (B *8,* 565)

One of Turin's countless equestrian statues.

Palazzo Madama, named after the "Madama Reale," Marie-Christine of France.

Köselitz took this and all the final letters to be pieces of high comedy. Overbeck and Burckhardt were not fooled by the euphoria. When they received such epistles from Nietzsche in the early days of January, they decided that Overbeck would have to travel to Turin in order to assume custody over their friend.

Perhaps the last influence of place on Nietzsche's labors was that of aristocratic Turin on his final obsession with the coming wars and with the political intrigues of the House of Hohenzollern. In the ambiance of the impressive Baroque palazzi and granite piazze of seventeenth-century Turin, and perhaps under the wild gaze of the bronze horses that dominate so many of the city's squares, Nietzsche remembered his days near Metz when the good Europeans were dying like flies. He informed Overbeck on December 26 of his "Promemoria" to all the courts of Europe, which invited them to form an "anti-German league" (B *8,* 551). The "final considerations" of his philosophical notebooks included the following passage: "If we could dissuade from wars, so much the better. I would know how to find better use of the twelve billion that it costs Europe each year to preserve its armed peace; there are other means of honoring physiology than through army hospitals. . . . To put it briefly and well, *quite* well, in fact: now that the old God has been done away with, I am prepared *to rule the world* . . ." (W *13,* 646).

In an earlier draft of these "final conclusions," Nietzsche had indicated how his reign would differ from the preceding one: "We *others* would go to work without reluctance on the grandiose and elevated labor of life—we still have everything to organize" (W *13,* 644). The only thing that remained clear to the good European was that wars should not destroy the best: "To take such a select crop of youth and energy and power and then to put it in front of cannons—that is *madness*" (W *13,* 645). He condemned the priests and rulers of Europe to perdition, and concluded, "By annihilating you, Hohenzollern, I annihilate the lie" (W *13,* 647). If the final days in Turin were marked by a certain euphoria, they were not without pain and nightmare—visions of the horror that would constitute the larger part of the twentieth century.

A view of the Lepontine Alps north of Turin, on the way to Basel.

What, then, at the final beginning of his ends, high and dry in Turin, became of Nietzsche's intimate converse with the sea? Perhaps, to repeat, and to close, his was the fate of Herman Melville's Pip. When Pip was abandoned to "the awful lonesomeness" of the sea, his body floated but his soul sank,

> carried down alive to wondrous depths, where strange shapes of the unwarped primal world glided to and fro before his passive eyes; and the miser-merman, Wisdom, revealed his hoarded heaps; and among the joyous, heartless, ever-juvenile eternities, Pip saw the multitudinous, God-omnipresent, coral insects, that out of the firmament of waters heaved the colossal orbs. He saw God's foot upon the treadle of the loom, and spoke it; and therefore his shipmates called him mad.[9]

9. Herman Melville, *Moby-Dick, or, The Whale* (Boston: Houghton Mifflin, 1956), chap. 93, pp. 321–22.

INTIMATE CONVERSE
WITH THE SEA

Genoa

Rapallo

Portofino

Ruta

Rome

Venice

Nice

Èzé

Turin

Genoa. The entrance to Nietzsche's favorite residence in the city, Salita delle Battistine, 8; *below,* a Genovese "Telamon," in the old city of Genoa, not far from Nietzsche's rooms.

Genoa. — I have surveyed this city for some time now, its villas and secluded gardens, including the broad sweep of its populated hills and slopes. In the end I have to say that I see the *visages* of past generations—this region is sown to the bursting point with vestiges of bold and confident human beings. They *lived,* and they wanted to live *longer*—that is what their houses say to me, houses that were built and adorned for the centuries, not the fleeting hour. They were eminently well disposed toward life, no matter how often they were ill disposed toward themselves. Always I see the builder, as he gazes about him at everything near and far that has been built in the past; he also scrutinizes the city, the sea, and the surrounding mountains. His gaze exercises dominion, and is a kind of conquest: he wants to integrate all these things into *his* plans, ultimately making them his *property,* as each element becomes a piece of his plan. This entire region is surfeited with the splendid, insatiable egotism of the one who takes pleasure in booty and possession. And just as these people acknowledged no boundaries abroad, in their thirst for something novel erecting a New World alongside the Old, so everyone who stayed at home raged against his neighbors and invented a way to express his superiority, planting between himself and his neighbor his personal version of infinity. Everyone conquered the homeland one more time for himself by overpowering it with his architectonic thoughts, transforming his surroundings into a feast for the eyes, a feast of his House. When one sees the way in which cities are built in the north, one is impressed by the regularity, the universal desire for lawfulness and obedience. One thereby discerns the internal sense of approximation to the same, of getting into line, that must have dominated the souls of all builders there.

Every time you turn a corner here, however, you find a human being standing alone, one who knows the sea, adventure, and the Orient, a human being who is averse to the law and to his neighbor, as though they were the ultimate boredom, a human being who casts envious glances at everything hoary and established. Through a wonderful quirk of imagination, he would like to found all these things anew, at least in his thoughts, setting his hand to them and implanting his notions in them—if only for an instant, on a sunny afternoon, when his insatiable and melancholy soul is fed up, when his eye will suffer only those things that belong to him, with no alien element intruding.

FW, 291; 3, 531-32

Portofino cape and harbor; *below,* the view from Ruta, looking west across the Gulf of Genoa.

*K*nowing how to find the end. — Masters of the very first order can be recognized by the following characteristic: in all matters great and small they know with perfect assurance how to find the end, whether it be the end of a melody or of a thought, whether it be the fifth act of a tragedy, or the end of a political action. The very best of the second-in-rank grow restive toward the end. They do not plunge into the sea with a proud and measured tranquillity, as do, for example, the mountains near Portofino—where the Gulf of Genoa sings its melody to the end.

FW, 281; 3, 525

*O*n the horizon of the infinite. — We have left the land and boarded the ship! We have left all the bridges behind us; indeed, we have severed all our relations with the land. Now, little ship, look ahead! Beside you lies the ocean. It does not always roar, that is true, and every now and then it lies there like silk and gold and sweet dreams. Yet the hour is coming when you will know that the sea is infinite, and that there is nothing more terrifying than infinity. Oh, the poor bird that has felt what it means to be free and that now crashes against the walls of its cage! Woe, if homesickness for the land befalls you, as though there would have been more *freedom* for you there—for, at all events, there is no more "land."

FW, 124; 3, 480

The fountain of Piazza Barberini, Rome.

For several weeks [in March 1883] I lay ill in Genoa. Thereupon followed a depressing spring in Rome, where I took life as it came—and it did not come easy. At bottom, this most indecent locale on Earth for the poet of *Zarathustra*, a locale I had not freely chosen, revolted me beyond measure. . . . At last I made my peace with the Piazza Barberini. . . . In a loggia high above the Piazza, from which one could look out over all Rome and overhear the fountains gurgling far below, the loneliest of songs was composed, "The Night Song." . . .

It is night: now all leaping fountains speak more clearly. And my soul too is a leaping fountain.

It is night: only now do the songs of lovers awaken. And my soul too is the song of a lover.

A thing unstilled and unstillable is in me; it wants to speak. A craving for love is in me; it speaks the very language of love.

I am light. Oh, that I were night! Yet this is my loneliness, that I am girded by light.

Oh, that I were dark, nocturnal! How I would suck at breasts of light!

. . . Thus sang Zarathustra.

EH, "Why I Write Such Good Books," on ASZ, 4; 6, 340-41; and ASZ II; 4, 136

Right now I am thinking of my most beautiful writing room, the Piazza di San Marco, provided it is a morning in springtime between the hours of ten and twelve....

ZGM III. 8: 5. 353

To his mother in Naumburg; from Venice. March 13. 1880: B 6. 12

Here I have good lodgings, it is quiet, and I have a warm stove. The Piazza of St. Mark's is quite close. Yesterday it was beautiful, but cold; even so, I had coffee in an outdoor café. Music was playing, banners were flying everywhere, and the doves of St. Mark's fluttered about at peace. Nothing but tiny shadowy streets, with hard and perfectly smooth pavements.

Venice, St. Mark's Square. A portico of the Procuratorie Vecchie on the north side of the Piazza; *below*, a column adjacent to the entrance of St. Mark's (note the incised script, which would have piqued Nietzsche's interest); *left*, the interior of St. Mark's.

It is reported that the madman also broke into several churches that day and began to intone his "Eternal rest grant unto God." Dragged outside and forced to explain himself, he always replied in this way: "What, then, are these churches now, if not the crypts and tombstones of God?"

FW. 125: 3. 480-82

219

To Franz Overbeck in Basel; from Nice, March 24, 1887; B 8, 47

Venice.... The only place on Earth that I love.

Venice. *Left,* house wall above the canal of San Canciano, the district where Heinrich Köselitz lived; *above,* Calle Nuova, Köselitz's street in San Canciano; *below,* the island cemetery of San Michele.

To Franz Overbeck in Basel; from Venice, March 27, 1880; B 6, 14

Today I am moving into an apartment I've found here. It suits my needs because it is *not* located alongside the *narrow* lagoons, but stands free, as though on the open sea, with a view to the Island of the Dead.

It is my *fourth* winter in this place, my *seventh* on this coast: that is the way my health wants it, for it is as stupid as it is demanding, ready to make mischief as soon as the occasioning circumstances pile up. Nice and the Engadine: that is the circle dance this old nag cannot escape. . . . To be sure, there can be no more beautiful season in Nice than the current one: the sky blindingly white, the sea tropical blue, and in the night a moonlight that makes the gas lanterns feel ashamed, for they flush red. And here once again I perambulate, as so many times before, thinking my kinds of thoughts, *ebon* thoughts.

Nice. The beach near the Promenade des Anglais; Nietzsche's residence at "rue St. François de Paule, 26, third floor, to the left," which places him on the shadow side of the building. Photograph taken from the Place des Phocéens.

The following winter [1883-84], under the halcyon skies of Nice, which glistened above me for the first time in my life, I discovered the third part of *Zarathustra*—and the book was finished. Scarcely a year for the composition of the whole. Many concealed spots and many heights in the landscape of Nice have become sacrosanct to me because of unforgettable moments there. That decisive part of the third book, "Of Old and New Tablets," was composed on the difficult and steep ascent from the railway station at Èzé to the marvelous Moorish eagle's nest overhead. — My muscle tone was always greatest when my creative energies flowed most abundantly. *The body* is spirited— let us leave the "soul" out of play. . . . One could often have spotted me dancing: at that time I could wander through the mountains for seven or eight hours at a time without tiring. I slept well, I laughed a lot—I was as fit as I could be, and I was patient.

EH. "Why I Write Such Good Books,"
on ASZ. 4: 6, 341

Views in the vicinity of Èzé, east of Nice. Looking down through broom and scrub to the sea at Èzé-Gare; the St. Jean Peninsula and Cap Ferrat seen from the path that leads up to Èzé-Ville.

Willing and welling. — How hungrily this wave approaches, as though there were something to achieve! How it slithers with terrifying haste into the innermost corners of the rocky cliffs! It seems to be in a race to get there; something valuable, extremely valuable, seems to be hiding there. — And now it comes back, somewhat more slowly, but still white with excitement. Is it disappointed? Has it found what it was looking for? Does it wear a frustrated look? — However that may be, yet another wave approaches, hungrier and wilder than the first, and its soul too seems full of secrets, full of the pleasures of treasure hunters. That is the way the welling waves live—and that is the way we who are always willing live! I won't say more. — So? You don't trust me? You are angry with me, you pretty monsters? Are you afraid that I am baldly betraying your secret? Well, then! Be angry with me! Raise your green and menacing bodies as high as you can, build a wall to cut me off from the sun—yes, like that! Truly, nothing is left of the world but green twilight and green lightning bolts. Carry on as you will, you obstreperous creatures, roar with lust and malevo-

lence—or dive down again and scatter your emeralds into the deepest depths, undo your endless hoary shaggy locks of foam and spray—it's perfectly all right with me, because it all becomes you so, and I am well disposed to you for everything you've done for me: how could I betray you! For—listen carefully!—I know you and your secret, I know you in a familial way! You and I, we are members of one big happy family! — You and I, we have but one secret!

FW. 310: 3, 546

Turin, city of clandestine courtyards
and porticoed *loggie*.

To Reinhart von Seydlitz in Munich: from Turin, May 13, 1888: B 8, 313

I have discovered *Turin*.... Turin is not a well-known city, is it? The educated German travels right on by it. Granted my gratuitous hardness of heart in the face of everything that education commends, I have established Turin as my *third* residence, with Sils-Maria as the first and Nice as the second. Four months at each place; in the case of Turin it is two months in the spring and two in the fall. Odd! What convinces me is the air, the dry air, which is the same in all three places, and for the same meteorological reasons: snow-capped mountains to the north and west. That is the calculation that brought me here, and I am enchanted! Even on very warm days—we have had such already—that famous Zephyr blows, of which I had heard only the poets speak (without believing them: pack of liars!). The nights are cool. From the middle of the city you can see the snow.

In addition, the theater here is excellent, whether Italian or French; *Carmen*, as is meet and just, in honor of my presence (*piramidale successo*—if you can forgive the allusion to Egypt!). An earnest, well-nigh magnificent world of quiet streets lined with palaces from the eighteenth century, very aristocratic. (I myself dwell across the street from the Palazzo Carignano, in the old Palace of Justice.) An elevated coffeehouse culture, with *gelati* and *cioccolato Torinese*. Bookstores in three languages. University, good library, seat of the general staff. The city has splendid boulevards; incomparably landscaped banks along the Po. By far the the most pleasant, *cleanest*, most generously laid out city in Italy, with the luxury of porticoed sidewalks—10,020 meters' worth of them. —

Turin, with its pavements and sidewalks of smooth black granite, which Nietzsche so admired—and needed.

To Heinrich Köselitz in Berlin: from Turin, December 16, 1888: B 8, 528-29

Ⅰn the evening I sit in a splendid high-ceilinged room: a brief but *quite decent* concert (piano, four stringed instruments, two horns) wends it way up to me in as muffled a form as I could desire—there are three concert halls next to one another. I am brought *my* newspaper to read, the *Journal des débats*, and I eat a portion of excellent ice cream.... In the Galleria Subalpina (down into which I gaze whenever I step out of my room), the loveliest, most elegant space of its kind I know of, they play *The Barber of Seville* evening after evening, and they play it *excellently*.... And how *good* the city looks when the weather is gloomy! Recently I said to myself: Earlier I would have thought it impossible—to have a place *one does not want to leave*, not even to go out into the countryside; a place where one is happy to walk *out in the streets!*

To Unknown: from Turin, November 27, 1888: B 8, 495

Ⅰ emerge from a hundred abysses no gaze dares penetrate. I know heights no bird has climbed. I have lived on ice—I have been burned by a hundred snows: it seems to me that both warm and cold are altogether different concepts in my mouth[.]

Reflections of the river Po, seen from the bridge that leads us back from the Gran Madre di Dio church, back to the city no one ever wants to leave.

A CHRONOLOGY OF NIETZSCHE'S WORKS AND TRAVELS

1844   *October 15:* N is born as the first child of Franziska Oehler and Karl Ludwig Nietzsche in the tiny village of Röcken, near Lützen, in Saxony. He spends his infancy and early childhood in the parsonage at Röcken.

1849   *July 30:* N's father dies in Röcken of "liquefaction"—perhaps tuberculosis—of the brain.

1850   *Early March:* the death in Röcken of N's infant brother, Ludwig Joseph, at two years of age.
      Early April: the widow Nietzsche moves with her two surviving children, Friedrich Wilhelm and Elisabeth, along with her husband's mother and sisters, to the town of Naumburg an der Saale. They live first on the corner of Neugasse, then in the rooms of another pastor's widow, until in 1858 they move to Weingarten 18. October: N begins to study in the public elementary school in Naumburg, where he remains for only one year.
      Early June, once again in October, and many times over the years: N spends the summer and the autumn vacations at his maternal grandparents' home in Pobles, a small village back in the direction of Röcken.

1851   *Spring:* N begins to attend the private academic institute of Professor Weber, remaining there until the autumn of 1854, when he begins to study at the Cathedral School.

1858   *Summer:* Widow N moves with her children to the house at Weingarten 18 in Naumburg, which remains her home—and that of her son—until her death in 1897. For the next several years, N spends his summer vacations with relatives in the nearby villages and towns of Pobles, Plauen, Naumburg, Bad Kösen, and Gorenzen.
      Early October: N begins his secondary school education proper at Schulpforta, about an hour's walk southwest of Naumburg. He will live and study there for six years.

1859   *August:* N spends his vacation in Jena with an uncle who is Bürgermeister there.

1860   *Summer:* N journeys with Wilhelm Pinder to Gorenzen in the Harz region of Germany, where his uncle Edmund Oehler is pastor.
      July 25: having returned to Naumburg, Pinder and N, joined now by Gustav Krug, climb the Schönburg and there ceremoniously found their literary and musical club, "Germania."

1864   *September 7:* graduation and departure from Schulpforta. A holiday on the Rhine with Pforta schoolmate Paul Deussen during the remaining weeks of September.
      Early October: N is on vacation at Oberdreis with Paul Deussen's family.
      Mid-October: he begins his studies at Bonn, joins the fraternity "Franconia."

1865   *August 9:* leaves Bonn for Leipzig University, first making a two-month visit to Naumburg. By October 19 he is in Leipzig.

1866   *January-July:* N attends the University of Leipzig. He is there for most of the year, with the exception of the vacation months, mid-March to mid-April, and again at the end of August, when he is in Naumburg. He studies classical philology under the direction of Professor Friedrich Ritschl.

   Mid-September to mid-October: N is in Bad Kösen, escaping the cholera epidemic that is raging in Naumburg.

   Christmas and New Year's: N is back in Naumburg.

1867   *January-July:* N is at Leipzig for the first half of the year, with the exception of the month of April, when he is in Naumburg.

   August 8: he begins a walking trip with Erwin Rohde through the Bohemian and Thuringian Forests to Meiningen and Wartburg, where they arrive on August 28.

   September-December, and on through the end of June, 1868: after his plan to serve in Berlin falls through, N is in Naumburg for military service (in the 2d Cavalry Battalion, 4ᵗʰ Field Artillery Regiment).

1868   *Early March:* N breaks his breastbone and ruptures his pectoral muscles in a riding accident during his military service. The wound becomes infected, refuses to heal.

   June 30: N arrives in Wittekind, at the baths, in order to seek a cure for his wound.

   Early August: N returns to Naumburg, his health restored after five months of suffering.

   Mid-October: he returns to Leipzig to take up his studies once again. Already he is working on themes that will be fully developed in his first major work, *The Birth of Tragedy from the Spirit of Music.*

   Early November: first meeting with Richard Wagner at the Leipzig home of the Brockhaus family.

1869   *January-March:* invitation from the University of Basel to assume a professorship of classical philology.

   Mid-March: N returns to Naumburg, preparing for the move to Basel.

   April 12: N leaves Naumburg for Basel.

   April 19: he takes up residence in Basel at Spalentorweg 2.

   Early May: he begins to teach his secondary school classes (the Pädagogium) at the Mentelinhof, and to hold his seminars and give his lecture courses at the University of Basel; he continues to work on "Greek pessimism" and the rebirth of musical art through Wagner.

   May 15: N's first (unannounced) visit to Tribschen, Wagner's villa in Lucerne.

   May 28: N holds his inaugural lecture in Basel, "Homer and Classical Philology."

   End of July-first week of August: on holiday in Interlaken, near the Jungfrau, and then on the Pilatus, "6,000 feet above sea-level."

   July 31: N's first recorded invited visit with the Wagners in Tribschen.

   August 14–15: his first excursion to Badenweiler/Schwarzwald, where he stayed at the Hotel Römerbad.

   October 6–18: N's autumn holiday; he visits Naumburg.

   October 18: N returns to Basel. From mid-October through December the first explicit notes toward *The Birth of Tragedy* are jotted down.

   Christmas-New Year's: N visits the Wagners at Tribschen.

1870   *January-July:* N is principally in Basel, teaching.

   January 18: N delivers his public lecture, "The Greek Music Drama."

   February 1: the public lecture "Socrates and Tragedy" delivered to a largely hostile audience. By this time he is living at Schützengraben 45 (today no. 47), the future "Poison Cottage" he shares with Romundt and Overbeck.

Latter half of April: in the Pension Ketterer in Basset, Clarens, Lake Geneva, on spring break.

July 19: war is declared between Germany and France.

July 20: on vacation in Axenstein near Brunnen.

July 28 [Janz has July 30]: N and his sister Elisabeth arrive at the Maderanertal and register at the Hotel Alpenclub.

Around August 9: N leaves the Maderanertal, where he has been working on texts surrounding his forthcoming book, *The Birth of Tragedy,* especially "The Dionysian Worldview," in which the oppositional pair Apollo and Dionysos first come to dominate his analysis of tragedy. He returns to Basel in order to arrange his trip back to Germany, in preparation for his participation in the war as a medic. By August 13 he is in Erlangen, Bavaria, receiving training as a medic in the *Felddiakonie,* a prototype of the Red Cross.

August 23: N sets off for the front at Wörth, passing through Stuttgart and Karlsruhe, and then through the recent battlefields of Weissenberg, Sulz, Gersdorf, Langensulzbach, Hagenau, and Bischweiler near Strasbourg.

September 2: having arrived at Nancy on the first, N moves on to the war front, now at Ars-sur-Moselle, near Metz. For two nights he treats six seriously wounded men who are being transported by train back to Karlsruhe; N himself is infected with dysentery and diphtheria, and is hospitalized for a week after his return to Erlangen.

September 14-October 21: he recuperates at his mother's house in Naumburg. He takes brief trips to Oelsnitz and Leipzig, the latter in order to visit Professor Ritschl; he works on a new theory of prosody and meter in ancient Greek poetry.

November-December: he returns to his teaching in Basel and continues to work on *The Birth of Tragedy.*

New Year's: N is once again in Tribschen.

1871   *January:* N is teaching in Basel.

Mid-February: N and Elisabeth cross the St. Gotthard Pass and settle for six weeks (until the end of March) in Lugano, at the Hotel du Parc. He continues to work intensely on the text of *The Birth of Tragedy.*

April to mid-July: teaching in Basel.

Mid-July to the beginning of August: N vacations with Elisabeth at Gimmelwald in the Lauterbrunnen Valley, staying in the Hotel Schilthorn.

August-December: N is teaching in Basel, with a brief visit to Naumburg in mid-October. He works on the final printer's manuscript of *The Birth of Tragedy.*

Mid-December: he rides with Cosima as her "cavalier" to a concert conducted by Wagner in Mannheim for the benefit of the Bayreuth project.

New Year's: Cosima performs N's "Echoes of a New Year's Eve" at Tribschen; N has sent the piece, but, fearing Wagner's judgment of it, he remains in Basel for the holidays.

1872   *January: The Birth of Tragedy* is published by E. W. Fritsch, Leipzig. N is teaching in Basel for the greater part of the year.

January-March: five public lectures on "The Future of Our Educational Institutes," delivered in the Aula of the Museum, Basel.

March-April: N is invited by Karl Mendelssohn-Bartholdy (the composer's son) to travel to Greece; N declines, fearing to offend Wagner. N never travels to Greece. He refines his five public lectures for possible (but not actualized) publication.

Second half of April: N visits Montreux on the northeastern shore of Lake Geneva.

April 25–27: N's last visit to Tribschen; the Wagners take up residence in Bayreuth.

May 18: N arrives in Bayreuth, Erwin Rohde arrives a day later; the Wagners are in residence in the Hotel Fantaisie from April to August.

May 24: by this date N is back in Basel. He composes his first sketches toward the unpublished essay "On Truth and Lie in a Nonmoral Sense."

June 27–30: he is in Munich together with Carl von Gersdorff for two *Tristan* performances.

End of September: brief holiday in Splügen and Chiavenna, via Chur, Bad Passugg, and the Via Mala. N returns to Basel before his birthday, remains there until a brief Christmas visit to Naumburg. He is back in Basel by January 6.

1873   *January-June:* N is teaching in Basel.

Early March: he escapes "Fasnet" (the Basel carnival) by traveling to Gersau on Lake Lucerne.

Early April: N travels to Bayreuth, taking with him the manuscript of *Philosophy in the Tragic Age of the Greeks.* There are discussions with Rohde and the Wagners on the subject of what will become the first *Untimely Meditation,* namely, David Friedrich Strauss.

April 15: N returns to Basel and begins work on the polemic against Strauss, which is completed by early May.

End of July to mid-August: N is on a working vacation at Flims-Waldhaus and the Caumasee with von Gersdorff and Romundt.

August 8: the first *Untimely Meditation* is published by E. W. Fritsch, Leipzig, and is celebrated by the friends at Flims. During this same summer N dictates to Gersdorff "On Truth and Lie in a Nonmoral Sense," based on notes jotted down the previous summer.

Mid-August to December: N is in Basel, teaching from October through December. He is also writing the second of his *Untimely Meditations,* "On the Use and Disadvantage of History for Life."

Christmas and New Year's: N goes once again to Naumburg, and is back in Basel on January 4.

1874   *January-mid-July:* N is in Basel teaching.

January-February: he is working on the proofs of the second *Untimely,* which appears in print at the end of February, published by E. W. Fritsch; until mid-July he is in Basel working on notes that will become the third of his *Untimely Meditations,* "Schopenhauer as Educator." He is also correcting the proofs of the second *Untimely Meditation.*

Second half of July: N travels to Chur and on to Bergün, staying at the Hotel Piz Aela. He continues to work on the third *Untimely,* the revision of which he finds difficult.

August 4: N travels to Bayreuth for eleven days, plays Brahms's *Triumphlied* for Wagner's edification. The maestro is neither edified nor amused.

Mid-August to December: N is in Basel, except for a week-long cure in Rigistaffel and Lucerne in late September.

October: N is teaching in Basel when the third *Untimely* appears in print, published now by Ernst Schmeitzner in Schloßchemnitz.

Christmas and New Year's: N is in Naumburg, returning to Basel by January 7.

1875   *January to mid-July:* N is teaching in Basel. Research in the history of Judaism and Christianity. He considers the possibility of a fourth *Untimely Meditation,* "We Philologists," and begins to sketch it out; it is never realized.

July 16-August 12: N travels to Steinabad bei Bonndorf for a stomach cure. He reads works on political economy and reflects on the possibility of yet another fourth *Untimely,* "Richard Wagner in Bayreuth." His reflections on this and on other projects are far-ranging: some of the notes he sketches during this summer will appear three years later in *Human, All-Too-Human.*

Mid-August to the end of the year: N is teaching in Basel; he continues to work on "Richard Wagner in Bayreuth" until October, interrupting the work until the following spring.

Autumn: N moves to a much larger apartment farther down the Spalentorweg; Elisabeth runs the household for him.

1876   *January-February:* N is teaching in Basel.

First week of March: he visits Chillon and Veytaux, staying in the Pension Printannière.

First week of April: N travels to Geneva, visiting Hugo von Senger; he tours Voltaire's residence at

Ferney. By April 14 he is back in Basel, working on revisions of "Richard Wagner in Bayreuth" and writing its final three sections.

June 17-18: N is in the Hotel Römerbad, Badenweiler, polishing the concluding section of the fourth *Untimely.* "Richard Wagner in Bayreuth" is published early the following month by Ernst Schmeitzner in Schloßchemnitz.

July 23: N's final visit to Bayreuth; desperately ill, he leaves Bayreuth suddenly on August 3 or 4 for Klingenbrunn, in the Bavarian Forest. Here, according to a later account (W *6,* 324; *14,* 490), he writes the first third of *Human, All-Too-Human,* Part One, which still has the title *The Plowshare;* those notes mark a crisis or watershed in his development from philologist to philosopher.

August 12: N returns to Bayreuth for more performances of the *Ring.*

August 27: N returns to Basel, continues work on *The Plowshare.*

October 15: official beginning of N's year-long leave for reasons of ill-health.

October 1–18: N is in Bex, Valais, Switzerland, residing at the Hôtel du Crochet together with Paul Rée, at the beginning of their trip to Sorrento, there to join Malwida von Meysenbug. He works on a projected (but never realized) fifth *Untimely,* "The Free Spirit."

October 19: N continues on to Geneva, where Rée and he are joined by Alfred Brenner; they travel to Genoa via the Mont Cenis Pass in the western Alps; N's first sighting of the sea.

October 23: sea voyage from Genoa to Sorrento, Bay of Naples, with a stop at Livorno (Leghorn) and a visit to Pisa.

October 26: N arrives at Naples, continuing on the following day to Sorrento and the Villa Rubinacci. Further work on the projected fifth *Untimely Meditation,* "The Free Spirit," work that is absorbed instead into *Human, All-Too-Human.*

1877   *January-May:* In Sorrento at the Villa Rubinacci.

Early March: a ten-day visit to Pompei and Herculaneum. Presumably also a trip to Paestum sometime during the spring.

March 23: a brief excursion to Capri.

May 8: N, now pondering the possibility of giving up the Basel professorship permanently, departs from Sorrento, traveling by ship through stormy seas, *"mare molto cattivo,"* to Genoa (on May 11), then on to Milan by rail, continuing via Como to Lugano. Once again he resides at the Hôtel du Parc, May 12–14.

May 15: N begins a "cure" for four weeks at the baths of Bad Ragaz, Switzerland, in the Rhine valley between Chur and Sargans.

June 10: he leaves Ragaz for the remote village of Rosenlaui, high above Meiringen in the Berner Oberland, where he stays until the end of August, working on notes for what will be called *Human, All-Too-Human: A Book for Free Spirits.*

July 10–21: an excursion with Elisabeth to Lake Zug, staying at the Pension Felsenegg.

September 1: N leaves Rosenlauibad for Basel, moving into new quarters, at Gellertstrasse 22.

September-December: intense work in Basel on the many notes and plans for *Human, All-Too-Human.*

October 3–7: N travels from Basel to Frankfurt for a medical examination by Dr. Otto Eiser.

October-December: N is still teaching at the university, but is now released from his secondary-school Greek courses, for reasons of ill-health.

Christmas and New Year's: N remains in Basel.

1878   *January-February:* N is in Basel, teaching at the university; he is seriously ill. Work on the final corrections to the manuscript of *Human, All-Too-Human,* Part One.

March: N is on a "cure" in Baden-Baden in the northern Black Forest.

April 4: he travels to Naumburg, spending several days in Leipzig with Paul Rée and his publisher, Ernst Schmeitzner.

April 24: he returns to Basel.

End of April: Human, All-Too-Human, Part One, appears in print, published by Ernst Schmeitzner in Chemnitz.

July 6–8: N visits Elisabeth in Frohburg, in the Jura mountains. On July 8, she leaves Basel for Naumburg, in order to care for their mother.

July: N surrenders the relatively luxurious apartment on Gellertstrasse and moves to a small furnished flat at Bachlettenstrasse 11, on the outskirts of town, near the zoological gardens.

July 20–21: N escapes from the summer heat of Basel by traveling once again to Frohburg, in the Jura mountains.

July 27: he takes three weeks of summer vacation in the mountaineers' lodge of the "Männlichen," in Grindelwald, Berner Oberland.

End of August-September 17: he is in Interlaken, at the Hotel Unterseen.

September 23: after brief visits in Zürich and Basel, N travels to Naumburg, where he stays until October 17.

October 18 through Christmas and New Year's: N is in Basel, working on "A Miscellany of Opinions and Maxims," appended to *Human, All-Too-Human.* On New Year's Eve, N mails the manuscript of "Miscellany" from Basel to Ernst Schmeitzner in Leipzig.

1879   *January-March:* N is teaching at the university in Basel, in extreme ill-health; this winter semester of 1878–79 will be his last semester of teaching.

March 12: "A Miscellany of Opinions and Maxims" appears as the "appendix" to *Human, All-Too-Human.*

March 21: N travels to Geneva, residing at first in the Hôtel de la Gare, then in the Hotel Richemont, on the lakeshore, staying there until April 21.

April 21: N returns to Basel for further medical examinations. He then goes back to Geneva in the final days of April, returning to Basel in early May in order to close his apartment.

May 2: N officially resigns his university professorship for reasons of ill-health.

May 7: with the help of Elisabeth, who has come down to Basel from Naumburg one last time, he closes up his last apartment in Basel.

May 10: he travels with Elisabeth to Schloß Bremgarten near Bern for a week of cure. He travels alone to Zürich for several days in the third week of May, then, perhaps on May 26, on to Wiesen near Davos, Middle Graubünden (Grisons), residing in the Hotel Bellevue.

June 15: N resolves to leave Wiesen for the Upper Engadine, announcing "Champfèr, Oberengadin, poste restante" as his address. He makes the trip on June 21.

June 23: N writes his first letters from "St. Moritz in Upper Graubünden," several kilometers east of Champfèr, where the Julia Pass opens onto the broad valley of the Inn River. He remains there, residing in a private room somewhere between Champfèr and St. Moritz, until mid-September, writing "The Wanderer and His Shadow," taken up (along with the "Miscellany") into *Human, All-too-Human,* Part Two. "Everything here, with the exception of one or two lines, was conceived while *under way,* and jotted down in pencil in six small notebooks" (B 5, 450).

June 30: the University of Basel grants N's request for early retirement due to ill-health. He receives a pension of 3,000 Swiss francs, limited at first to six years, then extended into the period of his illness.

September 17: N leaves St. Moritz for Naumburg, where he is thinking of becoming his mother's gardener and living in a tower in the Naumburg town wall; he meets his sister at Chur, where they take a four-day walking tour; on September 20, N travels on to Naumburg, remaining there throughout the fall, except for a brief trip to Leipzig on October 18, in order to deliver the manuscript of "The Wanderer and His Shadow."

Christmas and New Year's: N is in Naumburg; once again he is severely ill during the holiday season.

1880   *January:* N remains in Naumburg.

February 10: he travels to the South Tyrol, passing through Bozen to the city of Riva on the north shore of Lake Garda, residing in the Hotel du Lac et du Parc (at that time the "Seevilla," owned by the Austrian family Witzmann) in the company of Heinrich Köselitz (Peter Gast). He works on notes that will eventually be absorbed into *Daybreak: Thoughts Concerning Moral Prejudices.*

March 13: he leaves Riva for Venice, where he stays until June 29, first with Köselitz, at Calle Nuova 5256 (Campo San Canciano, near Cannaregio), then in an apartment of his own (today untraceable) with a view onto San Michele.

June 29: N leaves Venice, traveling through the Tyrol, unable to find a congenial locale that would be sunny yet easy on his eyes; St. Moritz would be too expensive, so N wanders north, by July 5 residing in the "Eremitage" of Marienbad, Bohemia. He remains there until early September, even though it is a rainy and utterly unproductive summer.

September 1 or 2: N leaves Marienbad for Naumburg, where he rests for five weeks.

October 8: N leaves Naumburg for Stresa, on Lago Maggiore, but is ill for several days in Heidelberg and Locarno on his way there; he also interrupts his journey in order to visit the Overbecks in Basel.

October 14: by this date N is in Stresa, enjoying its view upon the Isola Borromeo out in the lake. He picks up the work on *Daybreak,* which still has the working title *The Plowshare,* the same title he had used in the summer of 1876 for the first part of *Human, All-Too-Human.* He plans to spend the winter in Naples, then changes his mind.

November 8: by this date he is in Genoa, changing his lodgings four times in only a few days.

November-December: N remains in Genoa through Christmas and New Year's and on into the spring of the next year.

1881   *January-April:* N is in Genoa, working on the aphorisms of *Daybreak.*

March 13: he mails the printer's manuscript to Ernst Schmeitzner in Leipzig.

May 1: N meets Köselitz in Vicenza, but because N is ill the two travel separately—Köselitz one day earlier—to Recoaro, in the South Tyrol. N remains in the spa town of Recoaro, staying at the Albergo Tre Garofani ("The Three Carnations") until the beginning of July. Work on the proofs of *Daybreak.*

End of June: Daybreak is published, as the fruit of work done in Venice (under the title of "L'Ombra di Venezia"), Marienbad, Naumburg, Riva, Stresa, and Genoa.

July 2: N travels via Lake Como, Chiavenna, and Maloja to St. Moritz, but this time he moves immediately to Sils-Maria, where he stays for three months. He takes a room in a private residence, perhaps already in the tea-and-spice shop of Gian (Hans) Durisch, the "Nietzsche-Haus" of today's Sils-Maria. He works on a sequel to *Daybreak,* the book that will bear the title *The Gay Science.*

Early August: revelation of the thought of eternal recurrence of the same, at Surlej, Silvaplana, as recorded in notebook M III 1 (W *9,* 494).

August 26: in Sils-Maria, the name "Zarathustra," garnered perhaps from Emerson's *Essays* (see the third essay of the Second Series, "Character": a reference there to Zarathustra is heavily marked in N's copy), appears for the first time in N's notes—under the title *Midday and Eternity* (W *9,* 519–20).

October 1: N travels to Genoa for the winter, changing his apartment three times, residing (by the end of October) at Salita delle Battistine 8, interno 6. This steep street, closed to all but pedestrian traffic, bordered by the baroque gardens of the Villetta di Negro, becomes N's preferred street in Genoa.

November 27: in the Teatro Politeana of Genoa, N hears Bizet's *Carmen* for the first time.

1882   *January:* N is in Genoa working on a "continuation" of *Daybreak,* "Books 6–10," which will become *The Gay Science.* However, that book will not yet communicate the thought of eternal recurrence of the same, a communication for which N confesses he is "not yet sufficiently *ripe*" (B *6,* 159).

February 4-March 13: Paul Rée visits N in Genoa.

Early March: the two make an excursion to Monaco.

March 29: N suddenly decides to set sail on a freighter for Messina, Sicily, arriving there by April 1. In the vicinity of the Wagners (at Palermo), N nevertheless does not join them. He works on Book Four of *The Gay Science,* "Sanctus Januarius." (The "Idylls of Messina" were actually written while N was still in Genoa.)

April 23 or 24: N travels to Rome, joining Paul Rée, Malwida von Meysenbug—and Lou von Salomé, whom he meets for the first time in Saint Peter's Basilica.

Early May: excursion of the four to Lake Orta, not far from Stresa, and the outing of N and Lou on their own, the so-called "*mysterium* of Monte Sacro."

May 8: N visits the Overbecks in Basel. Plans for the publication of *The Gay Science.*

May 13: N with Lou in Lucerne at the Lion's Monument. During these days the famous Bonnet Studio photograph of Rée, N, and Lou (not featured in this book) is taken.

May 16: N returns to Naumburg, via Basel. He works on the printer's manuscript of *The Gay Science* until June 16.

June 17: travels to the Grunewald, Berlin, in hopes of meeting Lou, but returns disappointed the next day to Naumburg.

June 25: N travels to the Tautenburg Forest, where he spends the summer, partly in the company of Lou von Salomé and Elisabeth (who are in Tautenburg August 7–26). N misses the premiere of *Parsifal* in July at Bayreuth, remaining in Tautenburg until the end of August, when he returns to Naumburg. Work on the proofs of *The Gay Science,* which is published by Ernst Schmeitzner on August 20.

September 7: N travels to Leipzig, escaping his mother, who is outraged over the N-Rée-Lou affair, as reported to her by her daughter. By the end of September, Lou and Paul Rée have joined him there, although they live at a different address (N resides at Auenstrasse 26, on the third floor of a house owned by a teacher named Janicaud); they remain until November 5, when they depart for Paris—without N.

November 15: N travels to Basel to visit with the Overbecks. Three days later he heads for Genoa, settling at first in Santa Margherita to the south, then back in Genoa, then finally, from early December on, in the Albergo della Posta in Rapallo.

1883   *January-February:* N is in Rapallo, composing the first part of *Thus Spoke Zarathustra.* The printer's manuscript is mailed to Schmeitzner on February 14.

February 13: Richard Wagner dies in Venice.

February 24: N returns to his old apartment building in Genoa: Salita delle Battistine 8 (interno 4). He remains in Genoa until the first week of May.

End of April: the first part of *Thus Spoke Zarathustra* appears, published by Ernst Schmeitzner in Chemnitz.

May 3: N leaves Genoa for Rome, where he stays for five weeks, residing first at Via Polveriera 4, piano II, then on the Piazza Barberini 56 (54?), ultimo piano.

June 14: after a brief visit to Terni-Aquila, he moves north, first to Bellagio, on Lake Como, then on to Sils-Maria. By June 21 he is residing in the house of Gian Durisch. Now and in the many summers to come, Durisch is gracious and helpful to his distinguished guest. N works on Part Two of *Thus Spoke Zarathustra.*

Mid-July: the printer's manuscript of *Thus Spoke Zarathustra,* Part Two, is mailed to Ernst Schmeitzner in Leipzig.

September 5: N leaves Sils for a month-long visit to Naumburg, in spite of his anger over his family's reaction to the Lou affair and Elisabeth's engagement to Bernhard Förster. He remains in Naumburg until October 5.

October 6–8: N recuperates from Naumburg with the Overbecks in Basel.

October 9: he continues on to Genoa; tries in vain to find Malwida von Meysenbug in La Spezia;

returns to Genoa on October 13, residing at his old address, although this time in *interno 5*. He works on the third part of *Thus Spoke Zarathustra*.

November 23: N leaves Genoa for Nice, after spending a week in Villafranca (Villefranche), by way of transition.

December 2: N is in Nice, dwelling on the third floor of 38, rue Cathérine Ségurane, at the foot of the Parc du Château. Visits from Paul Lanzky and Joseph Paneth. Continued work on *Thus Spoke Zarathustra,* Part Three.

1884   *January:* N is in Nice, composing the third part of *Thus Spoke Zarathustra,* which is completed by January 18.

End of March: Thus Spoke Zarathustra, Part Three, is published by Ernst Schmeitzner. N now takes *Zarathustra* to be completed: he works for the rest of the year on sundry theoretical problems, though the notes on these problems are always interspersed with *Zarathustra* sketches.

April 21: N leaves Nice for Venice, remaining until June 12 at the residence of Heinrich Köselitz.

June 15: N visits the Overbecks in Basel for two weeks, then travels to Airolo, on the southern side of the St. Gotthard Pass, residing high over Airolo in the Hotel Piora on Lake Ritom.

July 12: N departs for Zürich, where he meets Meta von Salis-Marschlins.

July 18: he is in Sils-Maria until the end of September; he visits and has conversations with Meta von Salis, Helen Zimmern, Resa von Schirnhofer, and Heinrich von Stein.

September 24: N leaves Sils for Zürich, residing in the Pension Neptun until October 31; Elisabeth visits him there for two weeks, attempting a reconciliation.

October 31 (according to Janz, whereas Colli-Montinari claim that until November 6 N is still in Zürich): departure for Menton, where he remains (in the Pension des Étrangers) for several weeks; he plans to visit Corsica with Paul Lanzky, but does not do so.

First days of December: N returns to his Pension de Genève, on the petite rue St. Etienne, in Nice. He gives up plans for a work entitled *Midday and Eternity;* he works instead on the fourth part of *Thus Spoke Zarathustra*.

1885   *January-April:* N is in Nice; he finishes *Thus Spoke Zarathustra,* Part Four, by mid-February.

April 9: he leaves Nice for Venice, residing in the today untraceable Casa Fumagalli, Calle del Ridotto; work on the proofs of *Thus Spoke Zarathustra,* Part Four.

Mid-April: the final part of *Zarathustra* is published (it is privately printed in only 40 copies, which N distributes to friends) by Constantin Gustav Naumann in Leipzig.

June 6: N leaves Venice for Sils-Maria. He works on plans for a philosophical magnum opus and on notes that will be taken up into *Beyond Good and Evil*. He also prepares a second edition, with new prefaces, of his *Human, All-Too-Human* (Parts One and Two). Finally, he sues Schmeitzner in order to gain control of his "literature," for the purposes of preparing second editions of his works.

September 15: after a work-filled summer, N leaves Sils for Naumburg.

October 5: N leaves Naumburg for Leipzig.

November 1: N leaves Leipzig for the south, heading first to Munich, where he visits Reinhart von Seydlitz. Several days later, he moves on to Florence—which he does not like because of the uneven pavements and the wild traffic.

November 11: after a stay with Paul Lanzky in Vallombrosa, he is back in Nice, at the Pension de Genève. He soon moves to number 26, rue St. François de Paule (2e étage à gauche), across from the Place des Phocéens. He walks through the nearby hills of Cap Ferrat, on the St. Jean Peninsula, near Villefranche, and of Èzé.

December 10: N requests that his mother arrange for a new gravestone to be placed on his father's grave, to be paid for by the money he has won in the suit against Schmeitzner.

1886   *January:* N continues to work in Nice on the new edition of *Human, All-Too Human.*

February: Elisabeth N sets off with her husband, Bernhard Förster, to establish a German colony

("Nueva Germania") in La Plata, Paraguay.

January-March: N begins work on a second edition of or a sequel to *Daybreak,* which will eventually be entitled *Beyond Good and Evil: Prelude to a Philosophy of the Future;* the oldest aphorisms of *Beyond Good and Evil* derive from notes written in the summer and fall of 1881, and much of the material is contemporaneous with the *Zarathustra* period, 1883–85.

April 25: N completes the printer's manuscript of *Beyond Good and Evil;* he prepares to leave Nice for Venice.

April 30: N is in Venice, staying in Köselitz's vacated flat near the Campo San Canciano.

May 11: he is in Munich, trying to arrange a performance of Köselitz's comic opera *The Lion of Venice.*

May 13: he is in Naumburg and Leipzig, visiting Erwin Rohde, now a professor at the University of Leipzig.

End of May: C. G. Naumann, in Leipzig, begins to typeset the manuscript of *Beyond Good and Evil.*

June 5: N takes an apartment in Leipzig at Auenstraße 48, second floor, still working on Köselitz's project.

June 27: he departs Leipzig for Sils-Maria, passing through Rorschach and Chur. He works on the second editions of his books; he continues to work on a magnum opus, under the tentative title of *The Will to Power: Attempt at a Transvaluation of All Values.*

July-August: N in Sils works on the proofs for *Beyond Good and Evil.* This book too, like the fourth part of *Zarathustra,* is privately printed by C. G. Naumann. N receives the first copies on August 4.

July 31: Franz Liszt dies in Bayreuth.

August 5: the publisher Ernst Fritsch buys the rights to N's earlier works, his entire "literature," thus enabling N to plan second editions and to review his entire corpus to date.

September 25: N leaves Sils-Maria for the Gulf of Genoa, settling in Ruta Ligure, near Portofino, Santa Margherita, and Rapallo, where the first part of *Zarathustra* had been composed.

October 10: perhaps because of the "awful cuisine" in his albergo, he resolves to return to the Pension de Genève in Nice. He works on a new preface to the second edition of *Daybreak;* he expands his "Idylls from Messina" to the "Songs of the Outlaw Prince," destined for the second, expanded edition of *The Gay Science,* which now has a Book Five and a new preface.

October 20: N is by now in Nice, working on texts in Greek philosophy; he continues to work on the new editions of his books; he reads the works of Dostoevsky in French translation.

1887   *January 3:* N is finally able to get a room in Nice with a southern exposure, and thus a chance for warmth, on the first floor of number 29, rue des Ponchettes. He calculates that during the seven winters he has spent in Genoa and Nice he has occupied twenty-one different lodgings!

Mid-January: he attends a concert in Monte Carlo, where he hears the orchestral setting of *Parsifal* for the first time—he is enraptured by the *music* of Wagner's last great work. N continues to read Dostoevsky throughout the winter and spring. He continues to write sketches for a proposed philosophical magnum opus.

February 23: severe earthquake in Nice. N's earlier residence, the fourth floor of the Pension de Genève, is seriously damaged.

March: he plans to visit Venice ("the only place on Earth that I love" [B 8, 47]), but then changes his mind.

April 3: N leaves Nice for his summer residence, Sils-Maria, this year by way of the "Villa Badía" in the Val Cannóbio, near the western shore of Lago Maggiore.

April 28: he moves to the Pension Neptun in Zürich.

May 6: after staying for two days in the village of Amden, overlooking the northwest shore of the Walensee, N travels south to Chur, the gateway to Graubünden (Grisons) and the Engadine. He remains for one month in Chur at the Villa Rosenhügel. The spring is quite warm.

June 8: N heads for the high mountains, stopping first in Lenzerheide. He plans to visit his friend

General Simon in Celerina, near St. Moritz, but after receiving the news of Simon's death decides to stay once again in Sils.

June 12: N settles into Sils, again staying in the house of Gian Durisch. During these weeks of spring and early summer, he and Erwin Rohde quarrel by letter. The second editions of his works, which he has been preparing assiduously over many months, now begin to be published, with *Daybreak* and *The Gay Science* appearing first.

July 15: he pays a brief visit to Mrs. Emily Fynn and Fräulein Zina von Mansuroff in the town of Maloja, where they attend a special concert.

July 10–17: N composes the bulk of *On the Genealogy of Morals,* the manuscript of which is mailed to C. G. Naumann on July 17. (The third treatise is revised some weeks later in August.) N is pleased by the news that Johannes Brahms has been avidly reading his *Beyond Good and Evil.* He works on his final musical composition, "Hymn to Life," based on his and Lou Andreas-Salomé's "Hymn to Friendship" of 1873–74; the "Hymn to Life," his only published score, is printed by Fritsch at the end of October. N takes his noonday meal in the Hotel Alpenrose in Sils, where the group surrounding Meta von Salis (including Fräulein Mansuroff and Mrs. Fynn) provides some companionship.

September 2–3: Paul Deussen and his wife come to Sils to visit N, who is overjoyed to see his old school friend. During these weeks in Sils, N once again toys with the idea of returning to the University of Leipzig in order to study the natural sciences.

September 19: N leaves Sils for Venice, stopping over in the hospitable town of Menaggio on Lake Como in order to visit Mrs. Fynn and Fräulein von Mansuroff.

September 21: N arrives in Venice in the evening—it will be his final visit to Köselitz's city. He resides at no. 1263 Calle dei Preti, also near the Piazza San Marco. Here, in the city where Wagner died, N works on notes surrounding Dionysos and Ariadne, including the famous note, "The Perfect Book," which has N's "Satyr-Play at the End" (W *12,* 401–2).

October 22: After a month in the vicinity of Köselitz, a month of music and recuperation, but in the same unfortunate climate, N leaves Venice for what will be his last sojourn in Nice—once again in the Pension de Genève, although presumably not on the fourth floor.

November 10: On the Genealogy of Morals appears in print, published by C. G. Naumann (once again privately printed).

Late November: for the first time, N has a stove in his quarters, to fight off the winter chill, this year extreme in Nice. During these winter months, he works on plans for a second *Genealogy of Morals* and "a systematic magnum opus," at first under the rubric of *The Will to Power.* His letters are full of retrospectives on the last ten years. He labors in vain to have his "Hymn to Life" performed.

1888   Throughout the winter months in Nice, N has the feeling that an "epochal" change is occurring in his life. Intensified estrangement from sister and mother; continued emphasis in the letters on his illness and proximity to death. Correspondence with Georg Brandes (Morris Cohen) at the University of Copenhagen, who is lecturing on N's philosophy to some 300 listeners.

January-February: work on what he hopes will be the magnum opus, now under the title *Transvaluation of All Values.* N believes he now has a "conception of the whole." He works on *The Antichrist,* which is planned as the "first part" of his major work. He reads Baudelaire, fascinated by this most brilliant of *décadents,* but full of doubt.

March: N experiences growing discontent with Bismarck's Germany, especially with the House of Hohenzollern and the Hohenzollern court preacher and leading anti-Semite, Adolf Stoecker.

April 2: N leaves Nice, which is already becoming too warm, for Turin. He arrives on April 5, having gotten lost changing trains at Savona. He is delighted by Turin as a "solution for autumn and spring." He finds a room at Via Carlo Alberto 6, on the northwest corner of the Piazza Carlo Alberto, across from the Palazzo Carignano. He is soon welcomed by a performance of *Carmen.* He works on *The Wagner Case* and on notes concerning art as the countermovement to nihilism and decadence.

June 5: N departs Turin for Sils, via Milan and Chiavenna. The first six weeks of his summer are rainy, and on June 17 N is shocked to find that it is snowing! His health is bad: he complains of "total exhaustion" and lack of "life-force." Once again, for many weeks, N is in the salubrious company of Meta von Salis and her group of friends.

July 17: the manuscript of *The Wagner Case* is mailed to C. G. Naumann. Naumann rejects it as illegible. N rewrites the manuscript, mailing it on August 24.

August 13: N reports that the weather has finally taken a turn for the better. He is now correcting the proofs of his new book. His long-term plan is to spend his summers in Sils, winters in Nice, with the spring and fall seasons in Turin.

September 3: N signs and dates the preface to *The Antichrist*; this is the book that he plans as the first part of his *Transvaluation*. *The Antichrist*, though revised and completed (at least in draft form) between September 30 and October 4, does not appear in print until 1895.

September 7: N mails off to Naumann a manuscript that until the end of the month is entitled *A Psychologist's Leisure*. On September 21, Köselitz, who is correcting the proofs, encourages N to adopt the title *Twilight of the Idols*. The book appears on November 25. N calls it a "general introduction" to his philosophy.

Mid-September: The Wagner Case appears in print.

September 20: N leaves Sils for Turin. Once again he resides with the family of Davide Fino on the Piazza Carlo Alberto. His health during the coming weeks suddenly, inexplicably, improves. A certain euphoria characterizes his letters and notes from this autumn, which he calls his "magnificent *harvest time*" (B *8*, 453). Yet he breaks brusquely with Hans von Bülow and Malwida von Meysenbug, claims never to have admired Bizet, demands a new calendar for the Western world, one not based on the B.C./A.D distinction. He demands that E. W. Fritsch, once his publisher, turn over all the rights to his books to C. G. Naumann of Leipzig.

September 27: N changes the title of his manuscript *A Psychologist's Leisure* to *Twilight of the Idols: How One Philosophizes with the Hammer*. The book is a sibling, even a twin, of *The Antichrist*, as the preface (dated Turin, September 30, 1888) indicates.

October 15: on his 44th birthday N begins to write *Ecce Homo: How One Becomes What One Is*. The first draft is completed by November 4, revisions follow throughout December. N is afraid that the book may be censored or confiscated by the authorities.

November 20: N surrenders his plan to return to Nice. "Turin *will remain* my residence" (B *8*, 483).

November 25: N in Turin receives the first copies of *Twilight of the Idols*, published by C. G. Naumann.

November 26: he no longer conceives of *The Antichrist* as Part One of the *Transvaluation of All Values* (B *8*, 492); his dreams of a magnum opus appear to be in dispersion.

December 7: the corrected manuscript of *Ecce Homo* is mailed to C. G. Naumann.

December 10–11: N's letters to Ferdinand Avenarius and Carl Spitteler tell of his plan to publish a book of excerpts from earlier works, *Nietzsche contra Wagner*. The manuscript of this book, prepared by N himself, is mailed to C. G. Naumann on December 15. Franz Overbeck finds N reading the proofs of this book (apparently without comprehension) on January 8, 1889, when he comes to Turin to rescue his friend.

December 15: N also mails to C. G. Naumann the manuscript of the *Dionysos Dithyrambs*, a collection of poems from the 1880s that he has begun to prepare in mid-November under the title *Zarathustra's Songs*.

December 26 or 27: N writes Overbeck about his plan to incite the powers of Europe, by means of a *Promemoria*, to form an anti-German, anti-Hohenzollern league. In general, an intense concern with "grand politics" marks these days. Correspondence with August Strindberg. Work on a final revision for section three of Part One of *Ecce Homo*, and, into the first three days of January, final revisions of the *Dionysos Dithyrambs*.

1889   *January 3:* breakdown in the Piazza Carlo Alberto, Turin. Letters, postcards, and scraps of paper from this first week of January betray N's madness.

January 5–6: the long letter to Jacob Burckhardt (". . . every name of history I am"), which Burckhardt takes to Overbeck. The two consult with Professor Ludwig Wille, head of the university psychiatric clinic in Basel, "Friedmatt."

Evening, January 7: Overbeck departs for Turin. N once again collapses in the streets of Turin. His landlord, Davide Fino, is distraught, fearing that N may be incarcerated.

January 9: N returns to Basel in the company of Overbeck and a German-Jewish dentist practicing in Turin, Dr. Leopold Bettmann (Baumann?).

January 10: N is taken to the sanitarium "Friedmatt," in Basel. Professor Wille's diagnosis: *paralysis progressiva* induced by syphilitic infection.

January 18: at N's mother's insistence, N is transferred to the psychiatric clinic at Jena, closer to his mother's home. The Jena clinic is directed by Professor Otto Binswanger.

1890   *March 24:* N is released into his mother's custody.

May 13: after a brief stay in Jena, the two return to Weingarten 18 in Naumburg. There they remain, assisted by their servant Alwine, for seven years. By the end of 1891, N is sinking ever deeper into apathy and torpor.

1897   *April 20:* N's mother Franziska dies.

July 20: N is moved to Weimar, where Elisabeth has relocated the "Nietzsche Archive."

1900   *August 25 at noon:* after two strokes and a bout of pneumonia, the bedridden N dies in Weimar. His sister wishes him to be buried on the grounds of her Archive, but this is not legally possible.

August 28 at four o'clock in the afternoon: Nietzsche's remains are interred in Röcken, alongside the common grave of his father, brother, and mother.

1935   Elisabeth dies, having ordered that her grave be inserted at center stage of the family plot, between N and the other three family members.

INDEX

Note: Numbers in *italic type* indicate pages on which photographs or illustrations of the listed item appear. Works by Nietzsche are listed under "Nietzsche, Friedrich Wilhelm, works."